MW00561695

Heaven on the Hudson

HEAVEN ON THE HUDSON

Mansions, Monuments, and Marvels of Riverside Park

Stephanie Azzarone

Photography by Robert F. Rodriguez

AN IMPRINT OF FORDHAM UNIVERSITY PRESS

NEW YORK 2022

Fordham University Press also publishes its books in a variety of electronic formats. Some content that appears in print may not be available in electronic books.

Visit us online at www.fordhampress.com/empire-state-editions.

Library of Congress Cataloging-in-Publication Data available online at https://catalog.loc.gov.

Printed in the United States of America

24 23 22 5 4 3 2 1

First edition

To my family

CONTENTS

The Sights

There is no boulevard in all the world that compares with Riverside Drive in natural beauty.
—*New York Times*, March 10, 1895

Riverside Park is widely regarded as Manhattan's most spectacular waterfront park.
—New York City Department of Parks and Recreation, December 5, 2019

INTRODUCTION

My Riverside

THERE ARE SECRETS in this city—delicious, double-scoop kinds of secrets that, upon discovery, make each of us feel that the city belongs to us alone. I mean those certain sights and sounds, those special moments and memories, that, simply put, make this city—Metropolis, Gotham, the Big Apple, New York—our home.

For me, the city's best-kept secrets are Riverside Drive, Manhattan's westernmost boulevard, and Riverside Park, its lush and verdant front lawn along the Hudson River.

To outsiders or East Siders, Riverside Drive does not have the star status of more celebrated promenades, like Fifth Avenue or our West Side nemesis, Central Park West. But while both Fifth Avenue and Central Park West have a view of Central Park, only Riverside Drive offers the twin blessings of both park and river. Our Riverside Park is a grand yet quirky esplanade, one that snakes and shimmies even farther north than its well-known midland partner. Yet no double-decker tour buses block our swath of green, no "I Love NY" T-shirts are hawked on our corners, no day-trippers bottleneck our streets and sidewalks.

Instead, in summer, the dense and sweet sound of birds awakens us. In spring, the unfolding flowers of crabapple trees soothe the urbanite's senses. Come fall, there is a fireworks display of color so deep and startling it can wrest away one's breath. And in winter, a fog so enveloping above the river that (to my delight) it obliterates all sight of New Jersey.

On Riverside Drive, curves circle street corners and shape buildings, hilly streetscapes rise and fall and rise again to challenge the most dedicated of walkers, and trees arch elegantly toward one another, creating canopies that alternate sun with shade.

In this part of the city, there is so much that has always been the same and little that is new or modern. On the façades of buildings large and small, intricately carved details above doors and windows speak to character formed a century or more ago.

Here, the homes are more grande dame than debutante. It's on Riverside Drive that the Gershwins once lived, Babe Ruth had two homes, William Randolph Hearst ensconced his paramour—and where Amy Schumer owns a 4,500-square-foot penthouse apartment.

Yet different areas within the Drive and Park have their own distinct personalities. To me, the 70s are the most flirtatious, teasing passersby with an irresistible array of row houses bejeweled with ornamentation so alluring it seems designed to seduce. It's here one can find the only complete block of these once-private homes on the entire length of the Drive—along with the first statue in any New York City park to honor an American First Lady.

The 80s once flaunted the Drive's only quintuplex. It's also where Julia Barnett Rice, a nineteenth-century woman who was also a medical doctor, lived in a villa that today serves as a yeshiva. The 80s are where strollers will encounter a rare but striking touch of Art Deco on the Drive and a monument to soldiers and sailors, complete with cannons.

The 90s boast Riverside's beloved People's Garden, every child's favorite Dinosaur Playground, and the setting of the most memorable scene from the hit film *You've Got Mail*.

And the 100s—the 100s are like living in the country, with the Drive's only remaining freestanding, privately owned mansion near one end and its most notable institutions, including the well-nicknamed "God Box," toward the other. It's here that the explorer will discover my favorite of all Riverside monuments, the discreetly situated tomb of the "Amiable Child."

From 72nd to 129th Street alone, there are not one but *six* official Historic Districts encompassing Riverside Drive and a total of fourteen individual landmarks across Drive and Park together.

On Riverside Drive, there are no commercial trucks, no blaring horns; to find a taxi or a subway, we make the trek (often uphill) to nearby Broadway. With rare exceptions,[1] there are no commercial buildings and certainly no stores. There are no crowds. This is New York City, yet on any given day locals can easily wander for blocks on the Drive and have the sidewalks to themselves. There are, however, many dogs and people who walk them.

And they are not the only animal life. From my window, I can spot hawks swooping and diving, and just a few blocks north, two dozen goats—"imported" for the job—were recently hard at work in Riverside Park. In the past year alone, a bald eagle soared high above the park, and a barred owl named Barnard wisely observed local humans from a tree. A family of raccoons famously strolled the park's retaining wall.

Peregrine falcons have made Riverside Drive their nesting place. There was a coyote a few years back along with a wild turkey and possibly a deer, although I missed them.

Then, of course, there's the Riverside Park bird sanctuary.

All this, in the middle of New York City.

Always, on the river lining the park, there are ships—an endless, gorgeous array of barges and tugboats, sailboats and speedboats, and, each summer, a single, tall-masted glory resurrected from a bygone era. There are tour boats, too, an occasional private yacht, and, just once, what looked like a cruise ship that had gotten lost on its way to the ocean.

Within the park, there are fifty sports fields or courts, for basketball and baseball, tennis and volleyball. It's here that I practiced soccer with my young son and later joined a women's team, where I played not well, but energetically. A bike path, meanwhile, rolls alongside the river, assuring those who ride it a serene start and calming end to even the most difficult of days.

Everywhere, there are playgrounds packed with joyous children.

Nature, view, privacy, quiet. These are among our secrets.

But one can only share so many secrets before a person—or in this case, a place—will stop trusting you with them. To give away all that Riverside has to offer would be a betrayal—and an impossibility, since there is so much to tell.

There are miles of mansions, each with its own distinctive story; sculptures that speak silently of history; churches that touch the sky; and museums so discreet that one could, as I did, live here for decades without knowing of them.

Because there is so much—on the Drive above, the river below, the Park between them—this book is dedicated to sharing only the most special of secrets: the ones that, without fail, bring me both pleasure and peace in a city of more than eight million.

Join me for a stroll, down by Riverside.

THE HISTORY

Chapter 1

In the Beginning

Into the Woods

> In the olden time, when this region between the Central Park and Riverside Park was occupied with the villas of the wealthy and luxurious New York merchants, it surpassed anything in the land for the elegance of its buildings and the beauty of its landscaped gardening.
>
> —*West End Avenue, Riverside Park in the City of New York*, 1888

MY FIRST APARTMENT after college was on New York City's Upper East Side, around the corner from Bloomingdale's, the department store du jour. The barely one-bedroom—its width was nearly the same as the bed—was on the fifth floor of a five-floor walkup, a location that had the unplanned but not unwelcome effect of limiting my mother's visits to check on her daughter. The building itself was a "brownstone" painted blue.

To be living on the Upper East Side at the time was exciting, not only because of all the restaurants and bars, ideal havens for the young, restless, and single, but also because a home on the Upper East Side meant you had "made it": This was where the wealthy of New York took off their shoes. Though it was full of tenements the farther east one walked, it was better known for old money, white-gloved doormen, and, from my point of view at least, the importance of applying makeup before appearing in public.

In fact, the Upper East Side was the place to be, even in the New York City of centuries past. While the population long centered near the southern tip, when it came time to move northward, the rich of the nineteenth century opted for the East Side—Central Park and Fifth Avenue—over what was planned to be their West Side counterpart, Riverside Park and Riverside Drive.

One of only eleven officially designated Scenic Landmarks[1] in all of New York City and listed on the National Register of Historic Places, Riverside Park stretches, languorously, along the grand Hudson River, crossing through the neighborhoods of the Upper West Side, Morningside Heights, and West Harlem, also called Manhattanville.

Slender yet sensuous, the park originally lazed its way from West 72nd Street to West 129th Street between the river and what was initially called Riverside Avenue.[2] This earliest stretch of Riverside Park and Riverside Drive will be the focus of our story. And while most of the section from 110th Street to 125th Street is technically part of Morningside Heights, residents of the area from West 59th to 125th Street typically refer to it all as the Upper West Side, and so shall we.

Over time, Riverside Park ambled south from 72nd Street to 59th Street, an expanse named Riverside Park South, and north to 155th Street, blossoming from its original 191 acres to about 370, compared with Central Park's 843 acres.

Five miles long from 59th to 155th Street, Riverside Park is distinctly longer and narrower than the city's most famous green.[3] Yet with its setting on the Hudson and open view of the Palisades, Riverside feels like one of New York's most spacious parks.

Created simultaneously with Riverside Park as part of a single and unique city project, Riverside Drive eventually meandered even farther north. Today it reaches from 72nd Street to Dyckman Street in the Inwood section of the city, weaving and bobbing in and out from the river like some demented wood sprite, splitting itself in two along the way.

While its slightly older and much better-known neighbor, Central Park, calls attention to itself in the center of the endless party that is New York City, Riverside Park keeps to the edge, a wallflower among the guests. Central Park demands that all of Manhattan turn inward to look at it. Riverside Park looks outward, to the river and the cliffs along the far shore.

Unlike its counterpart, Riverside Park exists in multiple tiers, each one leading to the discovery of the next. One doesn't go across the park but rather down *into* it, as it slopes theatrically from a high retaining wall into the steep landscaped grounds below. Broad steps and ramps lead a stroller first to winding paths and rock outcroppings. Below that is a wide tree-lined promenade, once the site of open railroad tracks and where Riverside Park originally ended. Lower still are formal recreation areas, followed by the Henry Hudson Parkway and, finally, the glorious esplanade along the river.

To understand the evolution of Riverside Drive and Riverside Park, it's helpful first to consider the broader Upper West Side story as a whole.

The area was originally the hunting grounds of the Native American Lenape, who once occupied Lenapehoking, roughly the area between New York City and Philadelphia, including all of New Jersey, eastern Pennsylvania, and part of the state of Delaware. The Dutch "purchased" Manahatta from the Native Americans in 1626, and in 1664 the English took over the Dutch-held New Amsterdam, renaming it New York. In the late 1660s, the English began granting leading citizens huge plots of land, 150 or more acres each, along this part of the Hudson. The goal was to create European settlements where there were none. One result was that by the early 1700s, the Lenape were forced out of Manhattan.[4]

One of the earliest land grant recipients was Isaac Bedlow,[5] who in 1667 owned property running from about 89th to 107th Streets, from along the Hudson River to what would be today the middle of Central Park. Two decades later, his widow sold 460 acres to Theunis Ides (or sometimes Idens or Edis), best known for having had the first recorded nervous breakdown in New York City's history (possibly from having to work too much land).

Although a few landowners such as Ides built farms along the river and farther inland, in the seventeenth century much of the land remained forest, appealing only to trappers and traders. To the Knickerbockers, the first Dutch settlers, it was "a wild region, where game abounded, and over whose hills they roamed with dog and gun."[6]

Later, in the eighteenth century and through much of the nineteenth, well before Riverside Park and Drive were imagined, the grander abodes of the Upper West Side typically were country homes, or "country seats,"[7] for wealthy and influential downtown families. These merchants and military officers—De Lanceys, Apthorps, and Livingstons among them—were keen to escape the overwhelming crowds and sweltering heat of the city's center, an impulse familiar to contemporary New Yorkers with their own country homes in the Hamptons or the Hudson Valley or on Fire Island. Back then, these second homes were erected atop the rugged Hudson River cliffs or sometimes farther east.

Figure 1. Strollers don't walk across Riverside Park but rather down into it. Winding paths and steep steps lead the way. *Source*: Robert F. Rodriguez.

Small villages, such as Harsenville, Stryker's Bay, and Bloomingdale, also appeared here and there on the Upper West Side landscape.

In a city where today apartments may measure merely several hundred square feet, some of those early private estates individually occupied land that extended all the way from Central Park to the Hudson.

Here are some of the men and women who lived there.

Oliver De Lancey

Oliver De Lancey built his home in the 1750s on what would much later become 87th Street and Riverside Drive. He was a son of Stephen De Lancey (sometimes spelled DeLancey), a descendant of French nobility who, after arriving in New York, became one of the area's most successful merchants. The De Lanceys were major figures in the city from the time of colonial New York until the American Revolution.

Oliver, unfortunately, was among the less appealing members of that powerful family, at one point fatally stabbing a fellow New Yorker in a drunken brawl. He was also a dedicated Tory, a senior Loyalist officer during the Revolutionary War who commanded De Lancey's Brigade, composed of 1,500 pro-British volunteers.

In retribution for the many battles he led against the Patriots, in November 1777 a rebel band of proindependence Americans invaded the De Lancey home, destroying the building and its contents.[8] At the time, only women and children were there, asleep. *Upper West Side Story,* by Peter Salwen, describes the frightening scene:

> The rebels broke into the house and plundered it (the chronicle continues), abused and insulted the General's lady in a most infamous manner, struck Miss Charlotte DeLancey, a young lady of about sixteen, several times with a musket, set fire to the house, and one of the wretches attempted to wrap up Miss Elizabeth Floyd (an intimate acquaintance of Miss DeLancey's about the same age) in a sheet all in flames, and, as she ran down the stairs to avoid the fire, the brute threw it after her.[9]

In 1742, Oliver De Lancey had secretly married Phila Franks, who belonged to a prominent New York Jewish family. It was not until six months later, in the spring of 1743, that Phila announced the news and left home to live with her husband. Her mother felt betrayed and never spoke to Phila again.

At the time of the raid on the De Lancey home, "Phila De Lancey hid under the stoop until the rebels left; the girls, dressed only in nightgowns and carrying an infant nephew, fled into the swampland that one day would be Central Park. They were found there at eight the next morning and were carried to Apthorpe's House."[10]

Charles Ward Apthorp

The Upper West Side's main thoroughfare in the early days was Bloomingdale Road. Later called the Boulevard and rechristened Broadway in 1899, it connected the Upper

West Side to lower Manhattan. The area surrounding it uptown was known as Bloomingdale or the Bloomingdale District, from the original Dutch *Bloemendaal*, "vale of flowers," named after a town in the tulip region of the Netherlands (and unrelated to the department store, which was named after its founder). Bloomingdale Road also connected the De Lancey estate to that of Charles Ward Apthorp (also spelled Apthorpe).

Between 1762 and 1763, Apthorp, a successful British merchant, had acquired more than two hundred acres of land in Bloomingdale, from Central Park to the Hudson River between about 86th Street and 100th Street, for which he paid roughly $15,000. In 1764, he built a stately mansion, demolished in 1891.

Upon his death in 1797, he bequeathed the land to his ten children. One of those descendants built a home around 1800 on what would become 99th Street to 100th Street between West End Avenue and the Hudson River. It was an elegant white-columned home made of wood, "a substantial and roomy mansion overlooking the Hudson . . . with stately pillared portico on its western front that commands a wide sweep of the river to Castle Point"[11] in Dutchess County, New York. Cool breezes refreshed the deep veranda and all those who chose to visit it.

William Ponsonby Furniss

One William Ponsonby Furniss purchased the Apthorp descendant's home (or built his own on the site, depending on the source) in the 1830s or 1840s, enlarging and embellishing it over time.

An American who made his fortune in the shipping industry, Furniss came to New York from the island of St. Thomas, where he had relocated years earlier. Referred to as a "West Indian merchant prince,"[12] he lived most of the year downtown and each spring moved with his wife and six children to their Riverside address. He also wrote and published poetry about the wonders of Bloomingdale.

The *New York Times* observed, "In those days the lawn sloped to the water's edge . . . here were heard the merry shouts of romping children, who loved the house as their birthplace and played in the lush grass and blossoming groves with the freedom of country life, or bathed or floated, feeling a sense of proprietorship of the river that then was only dotted with occasional sails and formed a gentle boundary to their parental domain."[13]

The adults seem to have had a full life uptown as well, with a long list of notables among their guests. Locals praised the yield from the home's splendid flower garden, which supplied friends, acquaintances, and later the patients in local hospitals with bushel baskets full of lilacs and roses.

When Furniss died in 1871, his Riverside Drive estate was valued at about $1 million—or roughly $23 million in today's dollars.[14] After their parents passed away, the Furniss siblings rented out their childhood home, advertising it in 1871 as "a country house and grounds . . . river view, stable, gardener's lodge, with five rooms, garden and fruit trees; house containing 16 rooms, bathroom, oven and kitchen range,

Figure 2. The Furniss mansion was one of the Drive's best-known old country homes. *Source*: Museum of the City of New York, 36.202.25.

with hot and cold water, stationary tubs, oilcloth &c. Also to let, 6 acres or less, adjoining."

Tom Miller's *Daytonian in Manhattan* tells the story of what happened next: Among the renters was the family of Russell Clarke, who stayed there during the summer for at least two decades. Before the Clarkes were given the key, the Furnisses put double locks on a small room upstairs, indicating in the lease that "this little room—the smallest in the house—must never be touched or meddled with."[15] The Clarke family later rented the fine old wooden house to Alma Walker, whose lease held the same intriguing clause regarding the bolted door. Walker ran the home as something of an artist colony, whose visitors included the writer Gertrude Stein.

After decades of ownership by the Furniss family, the by-then elderly daughters decided to sell the home and its remaining property. Their father's will had decreed that the estate should be sold exclusively for a private residence and never for a public building. In 1909, the *New York Times* wrote, "The sale of the old Furniss mansion with its surrounding plot of twenty-three lots, not only marked the passing of what was perhaps the best known of the historic 'country places,' established in upper Manhattan fifty to seventy-five years ago, but it also emphasized the recent rapid development of the whole Riverside Drive district."[16]

Before the home was demolished around 1910, the little, long-ago locked room on the top floor was opened. "It contained what might be classified as family relics. There was a cradle in which all the last generation of Furnisses were rocked; there were some curious sea shells from foreign shores; there was a small section of a quassia tree with inverted cuplike center, from which all the youngsters had been compelled to quaff a morning draught in the days when a quassia cup was regarded as an aid to health; there were six or seven cases of old wine of different vintages, most of it dating from 1830."[17]

In 1911, the mansion was replaced by the twelve-story Renaissance Revival Wendolyn Apartments at 276 Riverside Drive.

Henry Brockholst Livingston

A "craggy stone pile"[18] known as Oak Villa, the Brockholst Livingston house was built before 1811 near what is now 90th Street and Riverside Drive. The Livingstons were long-standing enemies of the aforementioned De Lanceys.

Henry Brockholst Livingston was a Revolutionary War officer. A defense lawyer alongside Alexander Hamilton and Aaron Burr in New York's first sensational murder trial, he later became associate justice of the US Supreme Court. Known for his "explosive temprement and rambunctious sense of humor," he also survived an assassination attempt and killed a man in a duel. Ironically, one of his first court decisions was to issue a restraining order against dueling.

Figure 3. Henry Brockholst Livingston (l.) and Oliver Delancey (r.) were among Riverside Drive's most prominent early residents. *Source*: Livingston portrait courtesy The New York Public Library; Delancey portrait Library of Congress Prints and Photographs Division.

He was quite fond of his uptown country seat, referring to the "thousand attractions of Bloomingdale" in an 1806 letter he sent to his wife while traveling.

At Princeton, he had been a classmate of James Madison, who later became the country's fourth president. A New York City native, Livingston married three times, was widowed twice, and fathered nine children. He was also a distant forebear of presidents George H. W. Bush and George W. Bush.

Cyrus Clark

While their names may not be as familiar to New Yorkers today as the De Lanceys, Apthorps, and Livingstons, who have city streets and buildings named after them, other notable families also found a room with a view atop the future Riverside Drive.

In 1866, Cyrus Clark purchased the Brockholst Livingston house and its extensive property. By the time he reached his thirties, Clark, born in Erie County, New York, had built a significant personal fortune in the wholesale silk business and later went to Europe to study real estate development.

A key figure in New York's financial community, Clark was known as the "Father of the West Side" for his role as a premier champion of the area, as well as one of its major investors. He lobbied forcibly for neighborhood improvements such as mass transit, street lamps, and sewer and water lines. He also campaigned extensively for the development of Riverside Park and Riverside Drive.

Notably, Clark was for many years president of the West End Association (previously called the West Side Association).[19] It was formed in the 1880s by leading businessmen to promote public improvements north of 59th Street and west of Central Park, thereby bettering both quality of life and the value of their property investments. The association and its members—the true social influencers of their time—were to play a consequential role in the district's development.

In 1889, Clark sold the Brockholst Livingston house to John H. Matthews.[20] After Clark's death, a sculptural bronze-relief memorial was created in his honor and embedded in a rock outcropping near the 83rd Street entrance to Riverside Park, where it may still be seen today.

Edgar Allan Poe

Creative souls also took their place on the Drive along with leaders of industry.

In 1843, three boarders—the writer and poet Edgar Allan Poe; his wife, Virginia; and her mother, Maria Clemm—spent that summer and the next on a 216-acre farm acquired around 1830 by Patrick and Mary Elizabeth Brennan. The wood farmhouse perched on a rocky knoll at 84th Street, between the Hudson River and what is now Broadway.

Poe and Virginia Clemm were first cousins; they married when he was twenty-six and she all of thirteen. In 1842, Mrs. Poe had been diagnosed with tuberculosis. Poe,

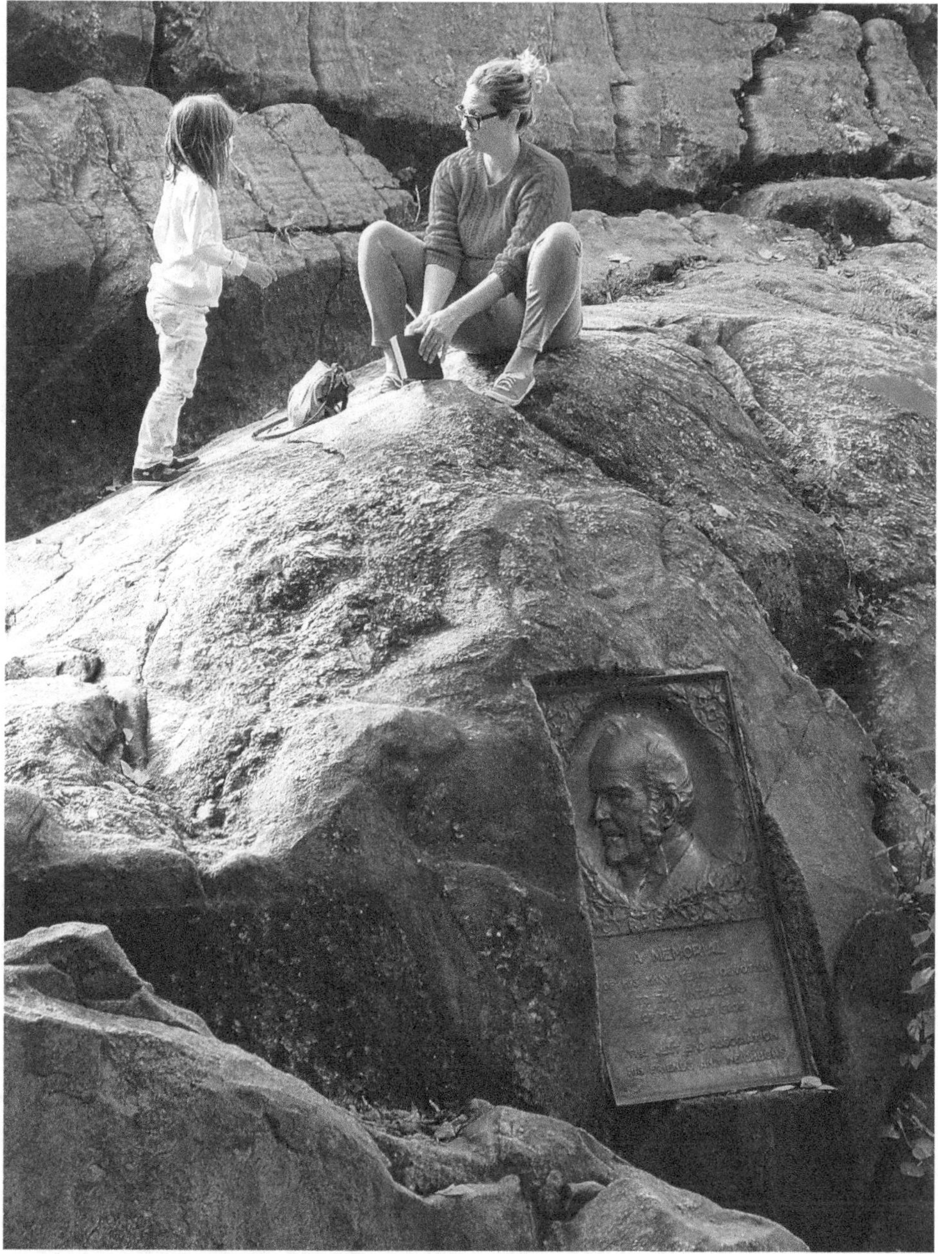

Figure 4. A bronze plaque set into a rock outcropping at 83rd Street memorializes Cyrus Clark, the "Father of the West Side." *Source*: Robert F. Rodriguez.

Figure 5. Edgar Allan Poe (inset) wrote "The Raven" while staying at this farmhouse on 84th Street. *Source*: Poe portrait: Courtesy The New York Public Library; Farmhouse photo: Collection of the New-York Historical Society.

meanwhile, suffered from consumption. Given these health issues, they were advised to seek respite among the farmhouses along the Hudson River.

It was Poe's custom in good weather to gaze out at the river for hours on end from atop "Mount Tom," an immense mound of Manhattan schist between 83rd and 84th Streets that he named after the Brennans' son. Mount Tom remains in full view within Riverside Park today, available for a short climb by other creative types and general passersby. Perhaps it was atop this rock that Poe pondered "weak and weary": It was while living at the Brennan farmhouse that he wrote his famous poem "The Raven."

The Brennan farmhouse was destroyed in 1888.

Andrew Carrigan

Other early residents of the Upper West Side clung to their riverside abodes even after death.

Upon arriving in New York from Ireland at the age of seventeen, Andrew Carrigan began work as a merchant and later in life became president of the Emigrant Savings Bank, now known as Emigrant Bank, the oldest savings bank in New York City. Upon retiring, Carrigan dedicated his time to the welfare of others. This included an early and active role protecting immigrants from the many robberies they suffered at the time. He was president of the Irish Emigrant Society and also helped establish Castle Garden in Battery Park as an immigration center.

Around 1836, Carrigan built an imposing white home at 114th Street and Riverside Drive.[21] With balustrades curving around its roof and stately columns encircling its façade up through a second-story balcony, the Greek Revival Carrigan home reminds me of the White House's South Portico, built earlier. Both buildings had expansive lawns, the Carrigan's long and narrow, setting the residence far back from the avenue. Unlike the White House, however, the Riverside Drive mansion was surrounded by a friendly white picket fence.

The home was sold in 1874 to Janet Lockwood Rudd and came to be known as the "Rudd house" or "Carrigan (and sometimes Carrington) Rudd house." Photos from that era show the opulence of the mansion, with its intricately carved plasterwork ceilings and woodwork, plush chairs and sofas, thick carpets, dark wallpaper, and richly gilded picture frames.

The mansion remained in the Rudd family for thirty-seven years. After Janet Rudd died, her husband, Thomas Edwin Ward, and their daughter, Althea Rudd Ward,

Figure 6. Janet Rudd (inset) and her young daughter, Althea Rudd Ward (seated fourth from r., at her fifth birthday party), lived at the richly furnished Carrigan-Rudd mansion at 114th Street. *Source*: Mansion photo: Milstein Division, The New York Public Library; all others courtesy Althea B. Rudd-Corey Family.

lived in the house until it was sold. In 1909, the court awarded Thomas Edwin Ward $15,000 annually from the income of three-year-old Althea, who had inherited one-half of her grandfather George Rudd's $1 million estate. The decision was in response to Mr. Ward's claim that his own personal income was not enough to maintain the home that his wife had desired for their child or to provide her with a proper education.

On January 5, 1911, headlines announced that "One of Riverside Drive's Oldest Landmarks"[22] had been sold to builders planning a "high class" apartment house that would cost about $1,000,000.

By 1912, the mansion was replaced by the Hamilton, a twelve-story apartment building that offered white-gloved doormen, views of the park, and buzzers on the dining room floor with which to summon, ever so discreetly, the live-in help. A knight in armor, salvaged from the detritus of the building's basement, now stands guard in the high-ceilinged, marble-trimmed lobby.

The Rudd family, it turns out, never entirely abandoned their old home. With its columns and curved-front roof, the Rudd Ward mausoleum in the city's Green-Wood Cemetery bears a striking resemblance to the family's one-time Riverside Drive residence.

Egbert Ludovicus Viele

Like his neighbor Cyrus Clark, the early Riverside Drive resident Egbert Ludovicus Viele played an important role in the development of the Upper West Side. A key member of the West End Association advocacy group, he actively promoted mass transit for the area and was an outspoken proponent of Riverside Park. A true multi-hyphenate, Viele was a West Point graduate, army brigadier general, surveyor, US representative from New York, one of the first sanitary engineers in the country, and engineer-in-chief of Central Park. He also submitted a design for Central Park but lost that competition to Frederick Law Olmsted.

In 1872, Viele built a red brick, ivy-covered villa for his family on Riverside Drive, on the southeast corner of 88th Street. Perfectly rounded windows embellished the tallest of the home's many towers. Later, it would be replaced first by three row houses and in 1911 by a Renaissance Revival twelve-story apartment building, 155 Riverside Drive.

The mansion faced south, with a broad veranda extending around the south, west, and east sides.

Viele was responsible for the "Viele Map," published in the 1860s and celebrated as a great cartographic masterpiece. The map shows New York City's canals, swamps, rivers, ditches, ponds, meadows, and drainage basins superimposed over the street grid. It has been referenced during the construction of some of the city's most famous buildings, including the Empire State Building and World Trade Center.

Viele maintained that, as the city paved over bodies of water and leveled out natural drainage channels on its march uptown, underground waterways would stagnate, leading to yellow fever, malaria, and even plague, among other diseases. As a result,

Figure 7. Major West Side promoter Egbert Ludovicus Viele, inset, and on the steps of his mansion on Riverside Drive and 88th Street, about 1890. *Source*: Collection of the New-York Historical Society; Viele photo: Library of Congress.

he campaigned vigorously for an effective sewer and sanitation system, becoming a key lobbyist for the Metropolitan Health Law of 1866. This was the first New York State legislation for the comprehensive control of sanitary conditions in the cities.

Most importantly for our story, the bill's requirements applied when it came to clearing out the disease-breeding waters of the Upper West Side, contributing greatly to the region's development. Throughout the 1870s, sewers and water mains were built in the area.

Also like Clark, Viele was an enthusiastic believer in the area's worth and future. He wrote, "This entire region combines in its general aspect all that is magnificent in the leading capitals of Europe. . . . In our Riverside Avenue, the equivalent of the Chiaia of Naples and the Corso of Rome."[23] He anticipated that the Upper West Side would become home to "a higher order of domestic architecture than it has been the good fortune of New York heretofore to possess"[24] and maintained that it would evolve into one of Manhattan's most desirable residential districts.

While confident about the area's future, Viele was less so about his own. He harbored a fear of being buried alive, "an unfortunate but surprisingly common problem in the 19th century,"[25] and upon his death in 1902 had a buzzer installed in his pyramid-shaped mausoleum at West Point, "which if pressed by him would alert someone in the cemetery office."[26] There is no record of it having been put into service.

Leopold Eidlitz

Born in Prague, Leopold Eidlitz emigrated in 1843 from Vienna to New York. Called America's first Jewish architect, Eidlitz built a home above the Hudson at 86th Street around 1851. A Swiss chalet in style, it sat on a stone base and was topped by a roof with deep eaves. Multiple balconies overlooked the jagged cliffs.

Figure 8. The architect Leopold Eidlitz's (inset) home overlooked a steep bluff at 86th Street and Riverside Drive, as seen in this c. 1851 photo. *Source*: Collection of the New-York Historical Society.

Eidlitz was a founding member of the American Institute of Architects and a major proponent of the Gothic Revival style. He has been called one of America's leading nineteenth-century architectural theorists. He is best known for his work on the New York State Capitol in Albany; P. T. Barnum's home, Iranistan, in Bridgeport, Connecticut; the original Brooklyn Academy of Music and the 43rd Street and Fifth Avenue location of Temple Emanu-El (both buildings since destroyed); and the completion of the Tweed Courthouse. Eidlitz also built the West-Park Presbyterian Chapel, on Amsterdam Avenue and 86th Street, just east of his home.

A fondness for home design and building ran in the Eidlitz family. His son Cyrus also turned to architecture, and Leopold's brother, Marc, started a construction firm, becoming a major New York builder of hospitals, synagogues, churches, banks, and more.

Michael Hogan/The Claremont

Although most of the earliest mansions had been torn down by the end of the nineteenth century or early in the twentieth, there were memorable exceptions. One of the best known was the Claremont (also spelled Cleremont), built either as early as 1780 or in the first decade of the nineteenth century, depending on the source. It stood on high ground around 125th Street and Riverside Drive, just north of where Grant's Tomb is today, an area known as Strawberry Hill. Originally a private home, it was later transformed into what at the time was the most famous inn in the country.

By most accounts,[27] its story began in 1804 when Michael Hogan purchased all of the land west of Bloomingdale Road from 121st Street to 127th Street for $13,000. Hogan had made a fortune in shipping and either built a home there or had the house moved to that location. Hogan divided his property, calling the southern portion Monte Alta and the upper part Claremont. The name Claremont likely was in honor of County Clare in his native Ireland. However, some claimed the home was named after the residence of the British Prince William, Duke of Clarence, who later became King William IV, Hogan's friend from their time in the Royal Navy.

The rumor was that Hogan lived there with an Indian princess as his wife, causing considerable gossip among the locals.

Hogan lost most of his money during the War of 1812 but managed to maintain possession of Claremont by leasing it over time to an assortment of colorful characters. Among them was the wealthy but eccentric "handsome bachelor" Lord Courtenay, Earl of Devon, who is said to have defied expectations by living alone with only two servants—a manservant and a cook.

In 1815, Hogan rented the house to Joseph Bonaparte, ex-king of Spain and Napoleon's brother, who lived there for two years and may have entertained Lafayette, King Louis Phillipe, and Talleyrand on the site.

Finally, however, Hogan had to liquidate Claremont, which trustees sold in 1820 to Joel Post, who had made his money from the wholesale drug importing business. After Post died, the house was sold again, and in the early 1840s (or "by 1860," according to some historians) it was converted to a roadhouse,[28] known variously as the Claremont Inn or Claremont Cottage. In 1873, the city took over the house and the land bordering the river to serve as the northernmost point of Riverside Park, then rented the building to a series of proprietors who managed it as a restaurant and gathering spot.

The public Claremont was a hit from the very beginning. Travelers heading north by carriage from downtown and, later, visitors to nearby Grant's Tomb would stop at the Claremont for refreshment and a panoramic view of the Hudson. "Statesmen in their frock coats slapped uniformed shoulders and had theirs slapped in return. Art critics admired the collection of Sadler's etchings (popular renderings of domestic scenes of old England) with which the rooms are hung, and collectors of antiques went green with envy at chinas occupying a place on high in the breakfast room."[29]

Claremont was in many ways the Four Seasons or Le Bernadin of its day, a fashionable and pricey destination for the city's elite, but with a better view. "Montreal melons that were shipped in every day in summer cost 75 cents a slice; the planked steak was $5."[30] Guests might enjoy a forty-dollar bottle of wine. Verandas enabled vistas across the lawn and river, and there was dancing and outdoor dining in summer.

Over time, the Claremont hosted a lengthy list of politicians, socialites, and entertainers, including the Astors, Morgans, Vanderbilts, and Whitneys, as well as Lillian Russell, Cole Porter, Admiral George Dewey, and Mayor James J. "Jimmy" Walker. Presidents were feted there so frequently that it's said William Howard Taft had his own chair, specifically designed to accommodate his "portly person." There also was a grand luncheon with four hundred guests in honor of President William McKinley.

A 1907 promotional pamphlet described in part what made the Claremont so appealing: "The gardens of Claremont are the pride of the city. . . . Turn where you will, the picture is never twice alike; . . . beautiful . . . particularly in the late afternoon as the sun sinks behind the Palisades . . . by night [it] is, if possible, more beautiful than by day. The garden is not garishly lighted by electricity . . . [here you will see] well-gowned women, the beauty of whose costumes is further emphasized by the sober black and white evening dress of the men."[31]

Prohibition put a halt to the high life, and it was not until 1934 that the Claremont was rebirthed, not as the most expensive restaurant in town but as a more reasonably priced eatery. Opening night featured a four-course $1.50 dinner menu with choices including crabmeat cocktail, chicken gumbo southern style, roast sirloin of beef with mushroom sauce, and a fresh strawberry tartelette. Cocktails started at 25 cents, and beer sold for 10 cents. A crowd of about one thousand New Yorkers turned out for the evening's victuals and a night of dancing to a full orchestra.

Nothing lasts forever, of course, and in the 1940s the Claremont's popularity plummeted. In 1951, with demolition already begun, a fire started when the coals of a guard's hand-warming barrel set the building afire. What little remained was torn down. Today, a playground sprawls across the inn's former grounds.

Figure 9. The Claremont Inn was once the city's most popular gathering place. *Source*: Milstein Division, The New York Public Library.

Claremont's longevity was an exception, however. More typically, as the lords of these splendid estates so far north of the city met their end, families dispersed, and the buildings decayed. As a result, the land bordering the Hudson became more desolate.

Around the time the Civil War ended, however, a plan was hatched that would mark the beginning of a new era for Riverside Drive and the emergence of a second generation of settlers along the banks of the Hudson.

Chapter 2

Post–Civil War

Veterans and Visionaries

THE POST–CIVIL WAR era was a notable and highly contradictory one in the city's history. Crime was everywhere in New York in the 1860s—violent crimes alone jumped 30 percent in just six years. The city at the time was particularly notorious for pickpockets. The Bowery Boys, one of the most infamous gangs in town, continued their decades-old clash with the Five Points Gang. In 1863, Irish mobs had turned on both the African American community and the police, ransacking sections of the city as part of the Civil War draft riots and leaving one hundred or more dead.

After the Civil War ended in 1865, thousands of war veterans streamed into New York, looking for work. Unfortunately for them, much of the city's economy had centered around the war, and numerous jobs vanished afterward, forcing many former soldiers to beg or live on the streets. The *Soldier's Friend* newspaper urged soldiers not to come to the city, "except in cases where they have friends, situations guaranteed, or means enough to live upon until they can secure a situation."[1]

At the same time, the first great wave of immigration began, primarily from Ireland and Germany, compounding the gap between the amount of work available and the number of people desperate to find it. New York's population reached over 813,000 in 1860 and surpassed 942,000 by 1870. Ten years later, in 1880, there were 1.2 million residents.

Between the droves descending upon an already crowded city and its unfortunate lack of sanitation regulations, the narrow downtown commercial streets at the time were overcrowded, noisy, and filthy. They were filled with "accumulations of manure from the horses that traversed the area, dead dogs, cats and rats, household and vegetable refuse that in winter accumulated to depths of three feet or more." The day's "garbage boxes" were rarely emptied. The water closets, reported the Citizens'

Figure 10. Downtown New York in the 1800s was crowded, noisy, and dirty. *Source*: Mulberry Street photo: Library of Congress Prints and Photographs Division; Street sweepers: George Grantham Bain Collection (Library of Congress).

Association Committee in 1865, were usually "covered and surrounded with filth, so as not to be approachable."[2] The resulting stench at the city's southern end was omnipresent and intolerable.

By midcentury, New York had some of the worst health statistics in the nation. While one out of every forty-four people died in 1863 in Boston and the same number in Philadelphia, New York's rate was one in thirty-six. In 1866, the last major cholera outbreak claimed the lives of 1,137 New Yorkers.

Yet against this exceedingly grim backdrop, New York City was simultaneously emerging as the nation's leader in industry, trade, finance, and communication. New Yorkers were quick to take advantage of these opportunities. It was the confluence of the city's growing population and the emergence of a moneyed class that in the 1860s led to a focus on developing the Upper West Side, including Riverside Park and Riverside Drive. The public health issues that resulted from New York's population increase, along with the minimal space remaining for new housing downtown, prompted the city to adopt a new street plan for above Houston Street (then called North Street) to 155th Street.

Although the Commissioners' Plan of 1811 had created the original street grid for Manhattan, it made minimal allocation for parks, both because land was valuable and because it was assumed New Yorkers would have access to the shoreline for open space and fresh air. The commissioners did not foresee that, as the city grew, burgeoning roadways, docks, wharves, railroads, and commercial sites would in effect block public access to the rivers. Although an 1838 map showed sixteen parks, most of them were small squares.

By the mid-1800s, however, it became clear that some respite from the chaos of urban life was essential. "Cities needed breathing space, places where men and women could walk with their children and contemplate nature in rural serenity—in short, New York needed parks."[3] Parks, it was concluded, were vital for the population's physical and mental health. At that time, there was a movement throughout the country to bring open space and green grass to urban settings, to be enjoyed by all, not just the privileged few.

The motivation in New York, as with many developments in big cities, was not entirely benevolent. It made sense to build homes where the topography was so suited and parks where it was not. Parks would also increase the value of the land surrounding them, benefiting its owners and bringing higher tax revenue to the city.

It was not until long after the creation of the first street grid that the city proposed developing larger public spaces in the northern part of town, where land was cheaper, including the area that would become Riverside Park and Riverside Drive. At the time, there was no New York City parkland along the water except for the Battery all the way downtown.

In 1856, the city created the Central Park Commission, which initially, as its name suggests, was responsible only for Central Park. Over time, however, its duties grew to encompass civic planning uptown. As of 1865, thanks to a new state law, this included implementing the Commissioners' Plan of 1811 street grid within upper Manhattan north and west of Central Park. The grid's straight lines, however, did not take into account uptown's contours, ridges, valleys, and waterways. Streets, avenues, and more would need to be reconfigured.

Enthusiasm abounded for the potential impact of the plan's execution uptown, and when the details of the Upper West Side street system were filed in 1868, a local real estate boom followed. Previously, the only development along the Hudson River on the Upper West Side beyond scattered residences had taken place in 1846. That year, the Hudson River Railroad (later merged with the New York Central Railroad) slashed through dense, virgin woods to lay tracks along the waterfront, allowing freight trains to run between New York City and Albany. Riverside Drive is situated between what would have been Eleventh Avenue[4] and Twelfth Avenue, the latter coinciding with the railroad tracks.

Once the uptown grid was planned, three of the most important visionaries of the city at the time—William R. Martin, Andrew Haswell Green, and Frederick Law Olmsted—combined gale-wind forces to make the dream of a grand Upper West Side, and eventually a glorious Riverside Park and Drive, a reality.

At the time, Martin was a parks commissioner. Like the early Riverside Drive resident Cyrus Clark, he was also a president of the West End Association. In 1865, the same year that implementation of the street grid on the Upper West Side became a requirement, Martin published a pamphlet, "The Growth of New York," that proposed changing Twelfth Avenue into a combined scenic carriage drive and park along the Hudson River. The goal was to encourage development on the West Side by taking advantage of the panoramic views and, naturally, to raise additional funds for the city through taxes.

Riverside Avenue, as Riverside Drive was initially known, was conceived as an elegant and expansive boulevard lined with trees, overlooking the park and the waterfront and bordered by imposing mansions. It was envisioned as forming "the city's preeminent residential street, expected to eclipse Fifth Avenue with ease."[5] In his pamphlet, Martin imagined a time when West Side residents "could come out of a summer afternoon upon the Riverside Park, and, through its drives and walks, among its flowers, under the cool shade of its old trees, in its casinos and refreshment houses, could have in the city all the enjoyment of the millionaire in his one hundred thousand dollar villa at Irvington,"[6] a village on the Hudson River in New York State's Westchester County.

An ambitious dream but also a tantalizing one for enterprising gentlemen of the era, who quickly shared their own romantic visions for the city. "The Eighth Avenue, it was predicted, on the west flank of the park [i.e., Central Park West], would become a street of millionaires' mansions outdoing even Fifth Avenue in spectacle and grandeur. West End Avenue, it was asserted, would one day become a magnificent shopping street, and an even grander future was predicted for Riverside Drive."[7]

The next step toward fulfilling this ecstatic real estate reverie occurred in 1866, when Andrew Haswell Green introduced an act to the New York State Legislature for the development of a park and drive along the Hudson River.

A lawyer, civic leader, and giant of nineteenth-century city planning, Green is considered the "Father of Greater New York" for his leadership role in consolidating the city's boroughs, making New York, at the time, the world's second-largest city (after London). He also served as president of the Board of Education and as the city comptroller. From 1857 to 1870, he was active in or led the Central Park Commission. Green was a key driver behind major New York City sites including Central Park, the New York Public Library, the Bronx Zoo, the American Museum of Natural History, and the Metropolitan Museum of Art. When it came to staunch supporters for his far-reaching proposition for the west coast of Manhattan, Martin could not have found a better partner.

It was not until many years afterward, in 1903, that one Cornelius M. Williams mistook the lifelong bachelor Green for a man of the same last name who was having an affair with Williams's lover. Williams shot Green five times, killing him. At the time, Green was eighty-three years old. In his *Encyclopedia of New York City*, Kenneth T. Jackson called Green "arguably the most important leader in Gotham's long history, more important than Peter Stuyvesant, Alexander Hamilton, Frederick Law Olmsted, Robert Moses and Fiorello La Guardia."[8]

The act Green presented became law on April 24, 1867, empowering the Central Park commissioners to acquire land above 72nd Street between the heights and the railroad tracks for Riverside Park and Riverside Drive. The land was purchased in several stages, with the first portion secured through eminent domain in 1872 for $6 million. Also in 1867, the Park Board was permitted to establish streets and bulkhead lines, condemn waterfront piers and wharves, and otherwise help prevent commerce from encroaching on the park. In 1873, authorization was granted to reestablish the grade of what would become Riverside Avenue.

With the land ready for park and residential development, it was crucial to find a fitting design for what was to be an entirely new community, one meant to attract the city's foremost families. The Park Commissioners, largely influenced by Green, turned to Frederick Law Olmsted to design Riverside Drive and Riverside Park, the upper and lower levels, respectively, of this extensive and exciting new undertaking.

Chapter 3

Olmsted's Plan

Parks for the People

> Nature has done so much; she has here displayed all her charms. Even before the city fathers had conceived the idea of making a park of this region it was known by artists and lovers of beauty . . . on its slopes a forest of trees, a tangle of vines; at its feet a river of surpassing loveliness, with just across the shining current of the stream the tree clad heights of the Palisades.
>
> —*Munsey's Magazine*, October 1898–March 1899

BETWEEN THE IMMEDIATE post–Civil War period and the start of Olmsted's work on Riverside Park, other notable developments were taking place across the country and in the city itself. In 1870, the Fifteenth Amendment to the US Constitution gave black men the right to vote, and Georgia became the last of the Confederate states to rejoin the Union. Two years later, President Grant won a second term in office. On July 4, 1876, the country celebrated its centennial.

In New York in the 1870s, Alexander Graham Bell made the first successful telephone call. St. Patrick's Cathedral formally opened, and from 1876, the hand and torch of the Statue of Liberty were displayed in Madison Square Park to help raise funds to build a base for the statue. Leading cultural institutions, including the Metropolitan Museum of Art, made their debut.

It was against this historical backdrop that Frederick Law Olmsted began his work on Riverside Park and Riverside Drive. Olmsted was the principal landscape architect of his time and a leading pioneer of that profession. Together with the English architect Calvert Vaux,[1] he had designed not only Central Park but also Prospect Park and Fort Greene Park, making him a natural choice to take on this new challenge. Oddly, while descriptions of Olmsted's work nearly always include Central Park and Prospect Park, they often omit Riverside Park.

Figure 11. Calvert Vaux likely designed Riverside Park's first paths. *Source*: Public domain.

As a boy, Olmsted experienced the delights of nature during trips through New England with his family. Later, he was influenced by the writings of English landscape experts and visits to England's parks and countryside.

For many years, Olmsted pursued a most varied career. As a journalist and author, he traveled throughout the American South and Texas for the *New York Daily Times* (now the *New York Times*). In his dispatches to the publication and in subsequent books, Olmsted maintained that slavery was not only immoral but expensive and economically inefficient. He also cofounded the magazine *The Nation*.

Beyond that, he served as executive secretary of the United States Sanitary Commission, a precursor to the Red Cross. He took part in the organization of the Southern Famine Relief Commission after the Civil War and later helped create the New York State Charities Aid Association, where he served as vice president for many years. Olmsted was also active in the founding of the Metropolitan Museum of Art and the American Museum of Natural History. In 1857, he was named Central Park superintendent. As if all of that weren't enough, in 1872 he was nominated for vice president of the United States by a splinter group of liberal Republicans. Although flattered, Olmsted withdrew his name from consideration.

Olmsted had a background in both engineering and farming, as well as a belief that exposure to nature by all classes was important to the health of society. At the time, when "parks" were most likely to be within private estates or, like Gramercy Park, locked behind gates to which only the wealthy held keys, this was a novel concept. He also strongly lamented the common practice in that era of city dwellers visiting graveyards in search of fresh air and rural settings.

Along with being a man of extraordinary achievements, Olmsted was also "of a very kind disposition," according to his obituary, "and it is related of him that he once remodeled his plans for extensive private grounds when it was found that they would interfere with a mother watching her children at play, and changed them entirely so that the mother might not lose the pleasant vista."[2] He also married his brother's widow and adopted their three children. In 1895, when Olmsted was seventy-three, John Singer Sargent painted a portrait of him leaning on his cane against a bucolic scene of flowers and trees.

Olmsted was commissioned for the Riverside project in 1873[3] and submitted a preliminary plan that year and a final plan two years later,[4] designed to develop Riverside Park and Riverside Drive together. Olmsted's proposal for Park and Drive featured a design to fit the area's hilly, rocky topography. A different, less inspired plan presented before his involvement pictured a straight drive one hundred feet wide that followed the city's street grid rather than the shifting contours of the cliffs. Carrying out this first approach would have required extensive leveling and regrading and the construction of a retaining wall far too high to allow practical access to the park. Discontent with this "unimaginative and impractical scheme"[5] led to Olmsted's hiring. The fact that Olmsted's design would also cost less than the original plan, because it required a lower retaining wall and less landfill, likely did not escape the city's notice.

In Olmsted's vision, the park's eastern border would follow the area's undulating pattern of nature. On Riverside Drive, as in life, there are few straight lines.

He wrote in an 1873 report that the location "presented great advantages as a park because the river bank had been for a century occupied as the lawns and ornamental gardens in front of the country seats along its banks. Its foliage was fine, and its views magnificent."[6] He incorporated those gardens and that foliage into his design.

According to the New York City Landmarks Preservation Commission, Olmsted "combined the land purchased for the avenue and that purchased for the park. He considered the existing grades and contours, the existing plantings and views, and designed a winding drive that would be comfortable for horses and pleasure driving, provide shaded walks for pedestrians, and yet would give easy access to real estate bordering it on the east."[7] Olmsted presented a "seemingly simple, but for its time, remarkable design concept, which combined into a single unified design a picturesque park taking advantage of the natural attributes of a dramatic site and an urban parkway providing a landscaped environment for a residential community."[8]

Olmsted considered this location ideal for hosting the city's main promenade for drivers, riders, and walkers alike and designed it to be long and wide enough to accommodate different types of traffic and activities. Plans for Riverside Drive, which would parallel the park and river, included a tree-lined pedestrian walkway, a lane

Figure 12. John Singer Sargent's portrait of Frederick Law Olmsted. *Source*: Used with permission from The Biltmore Company, Asheville, North Carolina.

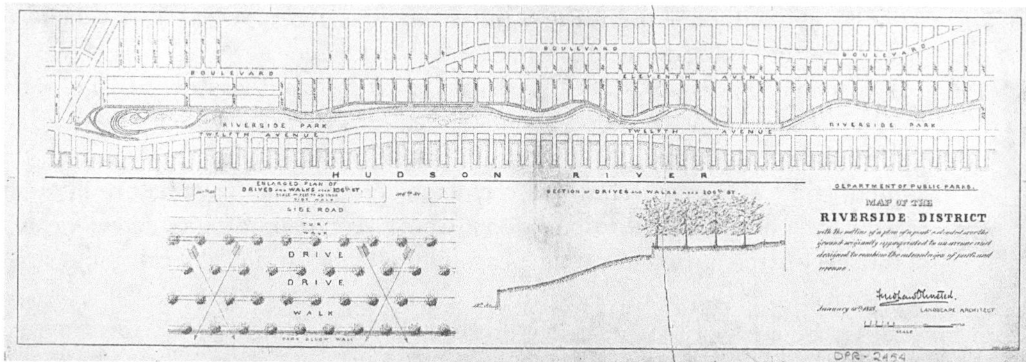

Figure 13. Olmsted's 1875 plan for Riverside Park, signed on the lower right. *Source*: NYC Municipal Archives.

for horseback riding, and two broad lanes for carriages, with a median separating northbound traffic from south. Although the park commissioners had initially suggested such a multiuse promenade in the southern section of Central Park, Olmsted felt that the Riverside location would offer more space.

According to the City Record of February 13, 1874, Olmsted's proposal stated, "Part of the main highway, specifically that portion between 104th and 123rd Streets, was to be arranged as a public promenade to command views over the Hudson and to be shaded in all its parts."[9] The Drive north of 100th Street would be flanked by five rows of elm trees, known for providing excellent shade. To this day, that section of Riverside Drive boasts one of North America's most significant collections of American elms. Linden trees border the Drive to the south. The City Record continued, "North of 123rd Street, in the area of the 'Cleremont,' the park and the drive were to be arranged to allow a resting and turning place for carriages from which the view up the river was to be kept as open as possible."[10]

Like the Park, Riverside Drive varies in width. Where the grade was particularly steep, Olmsted planned a much narrower service or "carriage" road supplemental to the main thoroughfare. Otherwise, it would have been necessary in some areas to cut down through the rock for seventy feet to make Twelfth Avenue level with the intersecting streets.

Those side roads provided even more privacy for the gracious mansions that were expected to border the park. Today the ancillary roads extend from the 90s to just south of 114th Street, separated somewhat haughtily from the main Drive below by sloping islands of green. They often double as front yards for lucky residents or plazas for the avenue's profusion of striking historical monuments.

Although responsible for the sweep and swerve of Riverside Drive, Olmsted's work did not, in the end, extend to the park's interior. He intended it to be, in his words, "plated with shrubs so arranged as to shut out of view the buildings[11] and docks, and allow the eye to range over the expanse of the river beyond."[12] He continued, "Plant materials should thrive, be non-invasive, and require little maintenance. The design should conserve the natural features of the site to the greatest extent possible and provide for the ecological health of the area."[13]

His goal, according to others, was that the park should also not be "obviously designed beauty"[14] or showcase manmade features that demanded attention but instead "create an environment of unconscious influence rather than one that sought admiration."[15] This approach would "heighten certain qualities of nature in order to produce a psychological response that went beyond appreciation of the beauty of the scene, to create a sense of the peacefulness of nature and to sooth and restore the spirit."[16]

In 1878, however, two years before Riverside Park's opening, Olmsted was removed as park superintendent because of Tammany Hall politics. His position was eliminated, although he was retained on a per-project basis as a consultant. Vaux was appointed superintending architect of the Department of Public Parks in 1881 and was likely responsible for laying out the park's first set of paths.

Over the next few decades, there was no comprehensive plan for the design of the park's interior, nor was Olmsted's original concept for it fully followed. Instead, the interior was developed by a series of designers employed by the Parks Department, including Vaux and Samuel Parsons, a founder of the American Society of Landscape Architects and Vaux's business partner from 1887 to 1895. While generally pursuing the rustic English gardening style that Olmsted favored, with informally arranged trees and shrubs and contrasting natural enclosures, his early successors also planted trees that would block expansive views of the river from the Drive, contrary to Olmsted's preference for open vistas. In 1886, Olmsted wrote to the Department of Public Parks that "in many important particulars the design has been mangled."[17]

Olmsted's park halted abruptly at the railroad tracks, a dreary boundary that would remain until the 1930s. As was typical for the era, the vacant land to the west of the tracks would be developed with commercial docks, to serve the shipping companies that plied their trade along the waterfront. The wealthy that Riverside Park and Riverside Drive were intended to attract would have an impressive view of the mighty Hudson but limited access to it—the latter in notable contrast to life along the river here today. The commercial use of land bordering the river would be a major point of contention for years to come.

Once Olmsted's plan had been approved in 1875, local property owners, who already had been assessed $3 million for work preparing the streets, were more than eager for it to start.[18] "The good faith of the city requires it to go on with these improvements or to repay to the owners the money it has taken from them, with the interest," according to a March 1876 *New York Times* letter to the editor.[19]

In the fall of 1876, the city awarded the work on Riverside Park and Riverside Drive to the contractors Decker and Quintard for $516,161.25. Finally, by early 1877, work began on Riverside Park and Riverside Drive, at that time the largest and most ambitious single municipal road-building project ever undertaken in New York.

Unsurprisingly to those familiar with New York City construction efforts, the work on the Park and Drive was not without issue. An 1878 report to the Department of Public Parks observed:

> In building the embankment for the avenue the contractors and superintending engineer have done their work so poorly that the upper surfaces have settled in many places, water has carried the filling through the lower layers of stone, making holes in several instances into which the edging, gutter, and walk areas had fallen. The larger part of the embankment is made, but the committee finds its conditions such that before the walks, drives, &c., are constructed upon it special measures must be taken to prevent their future subsidence.[20]

The report cited multiple additional violations or concerns. The parapet wall differed from specifications, drainage work was done improperly, bluestone "angle stones" were used in place of the required granite ones, gutters were not right, and curbing was of poor quality and "miserable construction."

It concluded that

> the contractors for the construction and improvement of Riverside-avenue have complied with the requirement of the contract in the dimensions of some of the material and in the character of the work thereon, yet they have materially failed in other details and requirements . . . and therefore . . . not only been in disregard of the original design upon which the contract was based, and of its specifications, but it has been in no wise calculated to meet the just expectations of those who are to bear a moiety of its cost, and of the public at large.

Despite a start as rocky as the terrain it applied to, over the next few years problems were addressed, and the Drive was gradually graded, paved, and planted.

By the fall of 1879, Riverside Drive was fully finished between 72nd and 85th Streets. Between 85th and 89th Streets, work was completed except for the driveway, parapet wall, and a side street that required grading. Between 99th and 113th Streets, the roadbed required gravel, and a short piece of wall was incomplete. Extensive work remained to be done between 91st and 95th Streets and north of 120th Street.

The masterpiece that was Riverside Park formally opened to the public on March 1, 1880, but that year the Drive itself still encountered some roadblocks—in one case, literally.

There had been ongoing disputes about money, deadlines, and construction materials with the project's contractors. This came to a head over the gravel used for the last remaining piece of work, sixteen feet of roadway on the upper end of the Drive. In response, the builder barricaded all the existing cross streets with piles of stones, derricks, and heavy timbers and posted guards to arrest any attempted trespassers, effectively cutting off Riverside Drive access to property owners.

Like true New Yorkers, the neighborhood's residents devised their own solution to such vexations. Sometime past midnight on May 7, 1880, a hundred or so determined

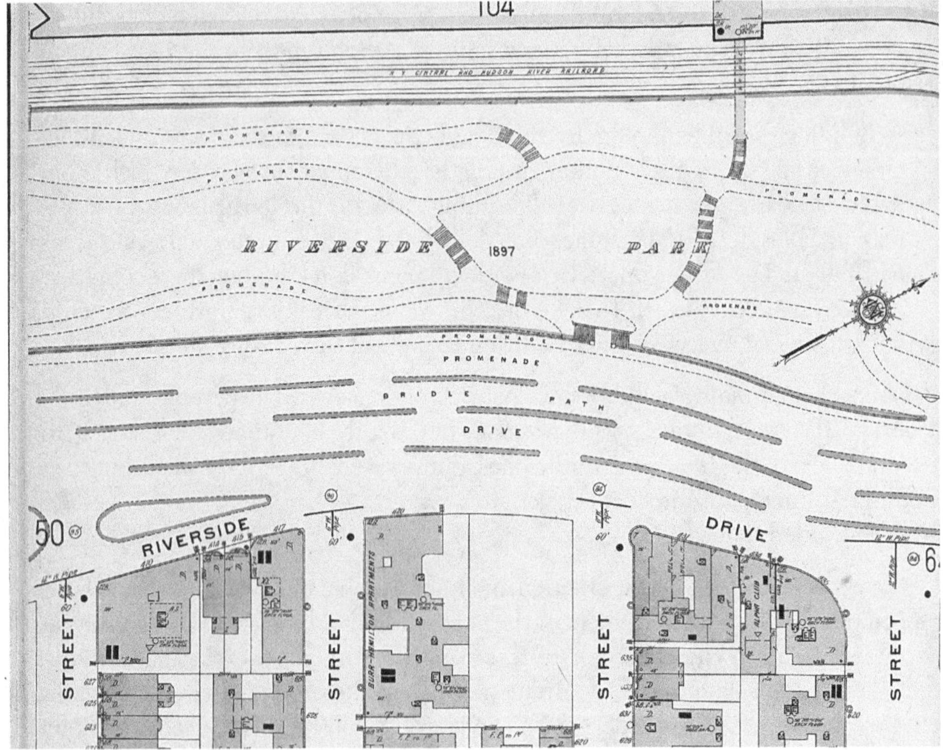

Figure 14. A 1912 map showing the paths in Riverside Park and the bridle path, promenade, and carriage drive on Riverside Drive. *Source*: Courtesy The New York Public Library.

individuals picked up what stood in their way and hurled it over the retaining wall into the park below. As a result, the "sun rose on Riverside-avenue . . . open, for the first time, from one end to the other. The citizens along the avenue were jubilant and all of them conveniently ignorant as to the man under whose orders the barriers had been destroyed."[21]

Photos taken some time after the 1880 obstructions were cleared show the Drive bustling with open carriages and well-bred strollers in nineteenth-century finery. Studebaker, a carriage manufacturer before it began producing automobiles, ran advertisements featuring a well-heeled lady enjoying a carriage ride down the avenue. Alexander Hamilton's great-grandson donated funds to build the Hamilton Fountain at Riverside Drive and 76th Street, to nourish the avenue's hard-working carriage horses. Fine carriages lined the curb along Riverside Drive to watch the annual regatta of the Hudson River Yacht Club.

At the time, several hundred horses were available for rent from stables in the city, at a cost of three dollars for an afternoon. The day's equestrians frequently rode to the north end of Central Park, then up Seventh Avenue (now Adam Clayton Powell Jr. Boulevard north of Central Park), and back down along Riverside Park.

Figure 15. The park retaining wall under construction at 117th Street in 1879. *Source*: Milstein Division, The New York Public Library.

Figure 16. Studebaker ad for a horse-drawn carriage, on Riverside Drive near Grant's Tomb. *Source*: Public domain.

Figure 17. Equestrians enjoying a morning ride on Riverside Drive. *Source*: Courtesy The New York Public Library.

In 1892, they were granted permission to speed their horses on the Riverside bridle paths, going northward only, at a rate not exceeding twenty miles per hour, and only before noon. That same year, an Officer Doolady was commended for stopping a runaway team of horses on Riverside Drive, the latter apparently a fairly common occurrence.

A two-wheeled passion was later to intrude on the Drive's four-legged one. Throughout the mid-to-late 1890s, when cycling in the city drew thousands of riders and spectators alike, the Drive was New York's most popular setting. In 1894, *Harpers Weekly* called it "the paradise of bicyclists." The *New York Times* declared that "the Sunday procession of cyclists has got to be one of the sights of the city."[22]

In 1897, the Riverside Drive bridle path from 104th to 120th Streets was converted into a cycling path.[23] Also that year, bicycle train service on the Ninth Avenue El was briefly available each Sunday from Rector Street to 155th Street. Bicycle racks replaced seats on one side of the cars. The fare was fifteen cents for one passenger and a bike or twenty-five cents for two with a tandem.

On Riverside Drive, dandies of the day took to the streets in high-wheelers—with their laughably large front wheel and tiny rear one—or the more familiar two-wheelers. Women in high collars and sleeves puffed out to fashionable extremes merrily hit the

Figure 18. Riverside Drive was the hot spot for bicycling in the 1890s. *Source*: Ivy Close Images/Alamy Stock Photo

road as well. Suffragists like Susan B. Anthony claimed that bikes had "done more to emancipate women than anything else in the world."[24]

On any given day, carriage drivers, behatted equestrians, and carefully balanced cyclists would compete for space and the opportunity both to enjoy the view and be part of it. Just a few decades later, the automobile would noisily motor into the fray.

In other sports and transportation news, yacht clubs appeared on the Hudson alongside the Park. In 1874, the Hudson River Yacht Club built its first location on the water at West 70th Street. In 1880, it moved to a two-story clubhouse at 74th Street and the Hudson and later relocated to 92nd Street. Columbia University built the three-story Gould Boathouse at 115th Street and the river in 1895. It was famous as the training center for Columbia crews for almost three decades. The building was abandoned by the 1920s, and thousands watched from both sides of the river when it burned down in 1927. The crowds and a fire hose stretched across Riverside Drive brought traffic to a halt.

Yet despite such popularity among those seeking recreation, there was still much to be done in Riverside Park and on Riverside Drive alike long after they opened. In the 1890s and very early 1900s, work was still underway, mostly from 96th Street north, to complete the retaining wall, pave walks and the roadway, and plant the park. The first park paths, from 72nd to 79th Streets, were not fully ready until 1891, and those from 96th to 120th Streets were not designed until 1895.

Figure 19. Circa 1898 view of Riverside Park and the Hudson River. *Source*: Byron Company. Museum of the City of New York, 93.1.1.17156.

All the while, the Parks Commission managed petitions ranging from a yacht club's request for a bridge over the Drive to the river's edge (granted), to a resident's wish to cut and keep the park grass (also granted), to a businessman asking if a pipe could be laid across park and avenue to carry water from the Hudson to his brewery on Ninth Avenue (denied).

Even as late as November 1893, a *New York Times* article said of Riverside Park that "but a small portion of the land thus acquired has been improved so as to be capable of public use."[25]

With Riverside Park opened for enjoyment, Gilded Age investors and West Side champions alike looked forward to the day that New York's upper classes would abandon their Fifth Avenue fortresses and happily cross Central Park and uptown avenues to their palatial new homes on the West End, to enjoy the extraordinary views of the river and the pleasures of the Park. It would be some time before anything remotely like that happened.

Figure 20. Sweeping curves defined Riverside Drive, which splits in two in the 90s. *Source*: Milstein Division, The New York Public Library.

Chapter 4

Expansion

Up and Over

ALTHOUGH OLMSTED'S PLAN terminated Riverside Park at 129th Street, that sparkling emerald swath was to undergo several different types of expansion in the years to come. The first such move took place barely twenty years after the park's opening.

Initially, a significant natural depression at about 125th Street, known first as Manhattan Valley[1] and later as the 125th Street Fault or Manhattanville Fault, blocked any northward movement. The city met this topographical challenge in 1898, when construction commenced on an ornate viaduct carrying Riverside Drive across the deep basin to 135th Street, allowing the Drive to reach farther northward over time. A short section of Twelfth Avenue, its signage intact, still runs beneath the viaduct today.

Designed by F. Stuart Williamson, the Riverside Drive Viaduct comprises twenty-six majestic steel-latticed arches soaring eighty feet above ground level, supported by gargantuan stone walls. Together they call to mind the grandeur of French cathedrals and glory of Roman aqueducts. The combination of steel and stone allows light and shadow to stipple the streets below. At street level, the viaduct created an imposing, broad plaza where much of the Drive's traffic would end, along with a walkway alongside the elevated highway and a clear vista overlooking the Hudson River and New Jersey Palisades.

Opened to traffic in 1903, the viaduct was considered a major feat of engineering and, with its overall design, a prime example of public works that partnered form and function. More recently, the viaduct's underbelly has been the setting for movies and videos. A carwash where a drug deal took place in *American Gangster* stood in the viaduct's shadows. *The Amazing Spider-Man*'s namesake character swung from the viaduct's impressive arches. Lady Gaga chose the setting to play a role in the climax of her "Marry the Night" music video.

Figure 21. Postcard view c. 1905 of the Riverside Drive Viaduct. *Source*: Courtesy The New York Public Library.

The year 1902 marked the opening of a practical but somewhat less glamorous viaduct, crossing a valley at Riverside Drive and 96th Street, where the avenue sloped sharply down to the river and was too steep for safe driving or bicycling. At the base of the hill, commercial vehicles carting heavy building materials, coal, and more to and from nearby docks also impeded safe passage. Today, traffic flows beneath this structure to and from the Henry Hudson Parkway.

In 1908, Riverside Avenue was renamed Riverside Drive. It was not until 1911 when it reached Dyckman Street near the northern tip of Manhattan, however, that Riverside Drive was, finally, completed.

Chapter 5

Getting Ready

Build It and They Will Come . . . Maybe

There seemed to be the promise of a fortune in every breeze which swept over the high plateau west of the [Central] park.

—*New York Times,* 1895

SURELY, WITH THE giddily anticipated 1880 opening of the grand new park along the Hudson and the elegant and scenic drive that ribboned around the green, construction of new homes and an influx of well-to-do residents could not be far behind. The commanding vistas along the river, startling western sunsets, and cool breezes wafting off the water would certainly prove irresistible. This was paradise with a panorama.

Of the Upper West Side, the book *Bricks and Brownstones* noted, "The only assured patterns of development seemed to be . . . fine mansions along Central Park West and newly laid out Riverside Drive."[1] *And yet*—for the first decade or so after Riverside Park and Riverside Drive opened, little followed in terms of real estate development or population. The heralded new community with its boundless aesthetic appeal and matchless open space appeared to be a turn-of-the-century bust.

One of the earliest, and unavoidable, barriers to development was the daunting terrain of the Upper West Side overall. Much rockier than the Upper East Side, it teemed with outcroppings, some of them thirty feet or more in height. Removing them required more blasting, and therefore more expense, to level the streets and allow for building. Understandably, developers were hesitant in even the most prosperous times to undertake the cost. If and when work finally got underway, it could take years to clear, level, grade, and pave a street.

A reminder of that more-than-century-old challenge remains today, tightly squeezed between two aging buildings on what would otherwise be a highly valuable plot of

Figure 22. Huge rock formations slowed the growth of Riverside Drive, like this one between 93rd and 94th Streets. *Source*: Museum of the City of New York, Photo Archives, X2010.11.3102.

land on West 114th Street, less than a block east of Riverside Drive.[2] The two-story high, hundred-foot-long outcropping of Manhattan schist rests on land owned by Columbia University, protected by a tall and uninviting iron fence. The *New York Times* called this remnant of old New York "one of the city's most amazing natural wonders."[3] Neighbors know it as "Rat Rock" for its once frequent tenants. (A "Rat Rock" also exists in Central Park.)

The natural abundance of underground waterways on the Upper West Side—streams, ponds, rivulets, and more—also scared off property developers, as, thanks in part to Edward Ludovicus Viele and his Viele Map, these were flagged as the source of various diseases. Pestilence was never a strong real estate selling point.

It would take a while before the West End Association could boast in its promotional pamphlet that "it is in this West Side region alone that a scientific system of sewerage and surface drainage has been carried out. . . . There is no other region in the city which has received this attention and has secured these sanitary advantages."[4] "For ten years streets were cut through, sewers constructed, water and gas mains laid, and the parks and boulevards beautified." Nonetheless, "the lots remained as bare as the day when Washington's tattered troops marched despairingly in retreat before the conquering Britons. The region looked even more forlorn than in colonial days."[5]

And then there were the squatters. Thousands of squatters blighted the Upper West Side beginning in the 1860s, when the construction of Central Park destroyed

Figure 23. Squatters, such as those near 80th Street in this 1895 photo, were a major deterrent to the area's development. *Source*: Milstein Division, The New York Public Library.

their shacks and shanties, dispersing their occupants—and their many goats—to the streets. The financial crisis known as the Panic of 1873, with its 25 percent unemployment rate in New York City, only intensified the situation.

In the 1880s, the West End Association and the Central Park Board of Commissioners acted to remove the squatters and their eyesore housing. By the mid-1880s, the largest shanty villages were gone, yet enclaves and individual structures, including those in Riverside Park, could still be found—an unlovely blemish on what otherwise was being promoted as a utopian setting. In the early 1900s, a tarpaper shantytown with 125 occupants lined the railroad tracks in Riverside Park.

Like the squatters, certain other residents of the neighborhood were also considered undesirable. The presence of the Bloomingdale Insane Asylum, on what is now the Columbia University campus, also affected the development of the Upper West Side above 110th Street, as few builders were willing to invest in "high-class residences" in the area immediately surrounding it. "While the wonderful transformation of the West Side from a succession of rocky hills into a beautiful residence district has been in progress, this refuge for maniacs has been a barrier and an obstacle to the onward march of population."[6] The asylum's location also meant that streets between 114th

Figure 24. "Maniacs" at the Bloomingdale Insane Asylum frightened off investors. *Source*: Courtesy The New York Public Library.

and 120th could not be cut through to connect with private property to their west, including land alongside Riverside Park. After much pressure from the real estate community, the asylum relocated to White Plains in 1889.

Commercial shipping docks, meanwhile, were slowly taking command of the Hudson River shoreline. It was not until 1894 that the New York State Legislature permitted Riverside Park to encompass all the land west of the tracks. This meant that commercial docks would be restricted to 79th and 96th Streets, with the remaining waterfront devoted to parkland alone.

Meanwhile, the freight trains that regularly chugged through Riverside Park issued nearly ceaseless strikes to the senses, clattering loudly across the tracks while belching copious amounts of smoke up toward the Drive, along with the aromas of the cattle they were carting to downtown butcheries. At times, those freight cars and their passengers' perfume would linger in the park for days. Ugly coal bins and putrid garbage dumps and sewerage ran alongside the railroad bed, coal dust from the trains whirled upward to street level, and railroad storage sheds further eroded the pastoral illusion.

Figure 25. Commercial docks detracted from Riverside Drive's Elysian feel. *Source*: Museum of the City of New York, Photo Archives, X2010.11.3060.

At the same time that the railroads to and from upstate made their presence known in such undesirable ways, local transportation remained minimal, creating another major barrier to settlement. Originally, the Upper West Side was largely accessible only by carriage, horseback, or foot. Before 1870, there was only an unappealing stagecoach on the Bloomingdale Road and the none-too-efficient Eighth Avenue streetcar line.[7] The latter ran a single car on a single set of tracks from 59th Street to 84th Street at long intervals, then turned around and headed back on the same track. There simply was no convenient and affordable way for Upper West Side residents to speed to downtown jobs. "West Siders wailed that without fast transportation their area (as one promoter put it) would remain a 'howling wilderness of vacant lots and rocks and morasses.'"[8]

Upper East Side development, on the other hand, was already well underway. By the 1850s, public transportation on the Upper East Side included omnibus lines on Second and Third Avenues and the New York and Harlem Rail Road on Fourth (now Park) Avenue.

Major fluctuations in land value—both up and down—further complicated and delayed the Upper West Side's advancement. Between 1868 and 1873, the price of land north of 59th Street and west of Central Park inflated by 200 percent or more, making it too expensive for the middle class to purchase, while the wealthy continued to prefer the East Side.

Extensive fraud by the Tweed Ring inflicted its own painful wounds. William M. "Boss" Tweed and the Tammany Hall thugs that he controlled embezzled millions of dollars from the New York City treasury until the ring was exposed and Tweed was arrested in 1871. Tweed held the title of commissioner of the Department of Public

Works, among many other positions, and decided when and where the street grid would be activated.

His modus operandi was to invest in land and then, using city money, pay inflated prices to build water, sewer, and gas pipelines to assure that his land was made habitable and therefore personally profitable. Tweed's East Side investments, however, were triple those on the West Side, which likely contributed to the delay in launching West Side development. Litigation by families whose lands had been taken via eminent domain for Riverside Park and Drive also slowed the process.

Then came another major blow—the Panic of 1873, the original "Great Depression," a description later usurped by the financial crisis of the 1930s. The Panic of 1873 put an end to rampant land speculation and helped push prices below their real value.

With the challenging terrain, "maniacs," squatters, transportation woes, graft and financial crises, Riverside Drive building lots stood empty. It took until 1877 for the economy to recover from the Depression, mortgage rates to decline, and interest in land purchases to renew. Many who had invested in real estate before the Panic of 1873 were suddenly able to sell their holdings at prices nearing, and in some instances exceeding, those immediately before the financial crisis. Landowners kept asking prices high along Riverside Drive, expecting the wealthy to buy property there for their palatial homes.

It was not until after 1879, when the elevated railway line opened along Ninth Avenue above 59th Street to 155th Street, that real estate developers who once had been so wary of the Upper West Side finally began to acknowledge and act on its promise. It was the decisive event in the area's development.

From the early 1880s, the neighborhood saw the start of a great building boom, one that continued nonstop until around 1920. According to an 1886 article in the *New York Times*, "The west side of the city presents just now a scene of building activity such as was never before witnessed in that section and which gives promise of . . . the rapid population of this long neglected part of New York." The article continued, "The huge masses of rock which formerly met the eye . . . are being blasted out of existence. Streets are being graded and thousands of carpenters and masons are engaged in rearing substantial buildings where a year ago nothing was seen but market gardens or barren rocky fields."[9]

The first buildings arose along Ninth Avenue, near the elevated railway stops, then along all of Ninth and Tenth Avenues (renamed Columbus and Amsterdam Avenues, respectively, in 1890). Given the ever troublesome local topography, the Ninth Avenue line veered a sharp ninety degrees east at 110th Street before turning onto Eighth Avenue. At one hundred feet above street level, it was at the time the highest point in the system—and soon became known as "Suicide Curve," the preferred spot for troubled locals to escape what ailed them.

Much of the Upper West Side's building activity in the 1880s and 1890s was the speculative construction of row houses, with those eventually built on Riverside Drive tending to be larger and more imposing than those on the side streets. It was estimated that by 1911, half of all the houses constructed were part of speculative rows. North of 110th Street, in Morningside Heights, private spec homes arose largely in response to the arrival of Columbia University, the Cathedral of St. John the Divine, and other major educational, religious, and cultural institutions. It soon became known as "the center of the city's spiritual and intellectual life" and the "Acropolis of New York."

On March 10, 1895, a *New York Times* article celebrated the area's evolution with this highly enthusiastic headline:

WEST SIDE IS ITSELF A GREAT CITY

Quarter North of Fifty-ninth Street West of Central Park a Model Community.

PURE AIR AND PERFECT SANITARY CONDITIONS

Surrounded by Pleasure Grounds, Crossed by Fine Boulevards and Wide Streets Lined with Artistic Buildings.

ITS RESIDENTS LIVE LONG IN COMFORT AND HAPPINESS

History of a Region of Great Interest—Was the Site of Fine Colonial Mansions and Washington's Headquarters Were There—Buildings Worth $200,000,000 Erected During the Last Twelve Years All Constructed According to Modern Ideas.

While the transformation of the Upper West Side as a whole was well underway, however, little was happening on Riverside Drive.

Because it was several long avenues away, Riverside Drive did not directly benefit from access to transportation via the Ninth Ave El. Development occurred more rapidly on the avenues between Central Park West and Broadway than west of Broadway. With the completion of New York City's first official subway in 1904, however, Riverside's isolation would end. Operated by the Interborough Rapid Transit Company (IRT), the 9.1-mile line cost five cents to ride and originally comprised twenty-eight stations from City Hall to 145th Street and Broadway, adding a 157th Street stop just a few weeks after opening. The line included multiple stops on Broadway only a block from Riverside Drive, or two blocks if West End Avenue separated Broadway from Riverside Drive at that point on the map.

Speedy access to downtown offices, stores, and entertainment boosted land prices in the neighborhoods serviced by the new subway. Buildings arose along with property values. Surely—finally!—the combination of the pastoral delights of the park and the unparalleled views of the Hudson and the New Jersey Palisades would lure the wealthy from Fifth Avenue to Riverside Drive. And, yes, at last, the prosperous did come. They did not, however, come from Fifth Avenue.

Chapter 6

Monumental Change

The City Beautiful Movement

BY THE TIME the subway opened along Broadway, setting the stage for the residential development of Riverside Drive, there was a nascent campaign to further improve—and in the process, change the nature of—Riverside Park.

The City Beautiful movement of the 1890s and early 1900s was an outgrowth of the 1893 World's Columbian Exposition in Chicago. The fair promoted the concept of cities not simply as economic centers but rather as locales for beautiful environments that would contribute to residents' quality of life and to moral and civic virtue. Many American cities responded with public building and art projects, primarily in the Neoclassical style. In New York, Riverside Park and Riverside Drive evolved from being simply a place to enjoy nature to one that also focused on aesthetics, appealing to residents and visitors with beautifully designed monuments.

In 1897, Grant's Tomb was built at 122nd Street, and in 1902, the Soldiers' and Sailors' Monument would arise at 89th Street. The Firemen's Memorial was erected in 1913, and the Joan of Arc Statue was dedicated in 1915. The 1903 Riverside Drive Viaduct was also designed as part of the City Beautiful movement. These monuments offer their own kind of welcome and comfort. Set mostly amid the islands separating the Drive, they promise an intimate, seemingly private perch from which to observe strollers or—in my case—quietly enjoy a solo outdoor lunch or midafternoon cappuccino.

In New York City, Riverside Drive became the favored hot spot for monuments honoring heroes. More than two dozen monuments, plaques, or statues would appear in the Park and along the Drive from the 1900s through the 1920s. While most remain, there is at least one notable exception. In 1909, the Colonial Dames of America placed a monument to Henry Hudson at 72nd Street and Riverside Park to commemorate the three hundredth anniversary of his discovery of the river named

Figure 26. The Henry Hudson monument once occupied the spot where the statue of Eleanor Roosevelt now stands. *Source*: Library of Congress Prints and Photographs Division.

for him. The monument was designed as a street lamp, set on a two-foot-high granite base with a sixteen-foot bronze shaft. It was topped by a milk-glass globe embraced by bronze garlands. Unlike the other City Beautiful monuments mentioned here, that statue is long gone, its whereabouts a matter of speculation. Some believe it may have vanished during a national program created by President Franklin D. Roosevelt to recycle bronze statues into weapons for World War II. According to the New York City Parks Department, however, a truck toppled it in the 1950s. It was replaced in 1996 with a statue of Eleanor Roosevelt.

Chapter 7

Custom of the City

Society Rules

> From the 1890s until after the World War, to be sure, it was popular with the newly rich . . . yet, lacking an old-family tradition, it never rivaled streets like Fifth Avenue in the esteem of fashionable society. In its location, however, with its fine parks, and impressive buildings and monuments, Riverside Drive is unsurpassed by any street in New York.
>
> —*Federal Writers' Project: New York City Guide*, 1939

IN THE 1880S, when Riverside Park and Riverside Drive opened, the Orient Express began running between Paris and Constantinople. President James Garfield was assassinated, the outlaw Jesse James was killed, and Chief Sitting Bull surrendered. Coca-Cola made its debut. In New York City, Thomas Alva Edison's Pearl Street Station began generating electricity to supply four hundred street lamps and eighty-five customers with electrical power. The Great Blizzard of 1888 dumped up to fifty inches of snow on the East Coast and killed two hundred people in the city alone. In 1883, the Brooklyn Bridge opened for traffic.

The 1880s were at the core of the Second Industrial Revolution and the Gilded Age, a period of dramatic transition in the country in general and New York in particular, a time when the city was on its way to becoming the most important in the entire nation. The US economy was rising at the fastest rate in its history, as the country rapidly expanded into areas such as coal mining, steel production, and railroads. Assembly-line production was taking hold, and new technologies made their debut.

In the mid–nineteenth century, fewer than twenty men in the entire country were worth a million dollars. By the 1880s, however, there were several hundred in New York City alone whose assets were valued at a million or sometimes considerably more.

> The Wealth concentrated in the hands of residents of New York is almost inconceivable. Many vast fortunes have been made here; and many enormously

> wealthy Americans have come here to live and enjoy the fortunes accumulated elsewhere. A recent table of the wealth of New-York's millionaires estimates that at least two New-Yorkers are worth more than $100,000,000 each; six more have above $50,000,000 each; more than thirty are classed as worth between $20,000,000 and $40,000,000 and 325 other citizens are rated at from $2,000,000 to $12,000,000 each.[1]

Keep in mind, these are nineteenth-century dollars.

The period was also known as one of excessive greed and corruption, the era of the "robber barons" who amassed their wealth by exploiting the working class, ignoring standard business practices, and sometimes even the law. Some of the wealthiest men in history made their fortunes during the Gilded Age, among them J. P. Morgan, William Vanderbilt, Andrew Carnegie, and John D. Rockefeller. The rich dwelled in opulence, enjoying large homes with luxurious amenities, while the poor were relegated to small, dark tenements.

It was the age of the Four Hundred, the "official" registry of members of New York society. Caroline Schermerhorn Astor, known far and wide as *the* Mrs. Astor, created the infamous list, said to be based on the number of people she could fit into the ballroom of her Fifth Avenue mansion. It was, largely, a compendium of old New York families, the heads of which had inherited money rather than working for it (or earned it through "respectable" means, such as profiting from real estate). An invitation to Mrs. Astor's would formalize one's place in the American aristocracy—and those who were "in trade" were not likely to receive one.

As it happened, Mrs. Astor lived directly across from Alexander Turney Stewart, an entrepreneur who made his multimillion-dollar fortune as a purveyor of dry goods and founded the A. T. Stewart & Co. department store. That Stewart made enough money to live on Fifth Avenue, so near, no less, to the doyenne of society, did not forgive the fact that he worked for a living. Mrs. Astor once remarked, "Just because I buy my carpets from Mr. Stewart's store doesn't mean he should expect to walk on them."[2]

If an enormous residence on Fifth Avenue couldn't assure that a family made society's "cut," living on the Upper West Side clearly swelled the resistance. "Society would never place its sacred imprimatur on that part of town."[3] This was, after all, the era of Henry James, Edith Wharton, and customs that rarely allowed for breach. Even characters in those authors' books who had the misfortune of living on the Upper West Side—such as the insatiable social climber Undine Spragg in Wharton's *The Custom of the Country*—bemoaned their fate.

In 1860, most New Yorkers on the west side of town still lived below 23rd Street. In 1880, 42nd Street was considered the "northernmost limit of fashionability."[4] By the 1890s, some society trendsetters decamped north to the 50s and 60s but typically no farther west than Fifth Avenue itself.

When Edward Cabot Clark was building the city's first luxury apartment building, the Dakota, on 72nd Street and Central Park West in the early 1880s, it was referred

Figure 27. Caroline Webster Schermerhorn Astor, *the* Mrs. Astor. *Source*: From the collection of the Metropolitan Museum of Art (public domain).

to as "Clark's Folly" because of its location in a sparsely inhabited area far from the center of the city. A friend of Clark, evaluating the developer's prospects, observed, "You may attract a few purse-proud nabobs from the world of trade. You are building for them, sir, but not for the gentry."[5]

It was no secret that West Side land was less expensive than on the East Side. "Instead of expending from $30,000 to $50,000 for a corner on Fifth avenue, from four to six lots can be here now purchased for that sum."[6] Indeed, in 1880, bids for lots on Riverside Drive and 101st Street ranged from $6,850 to $12,300. Who among the wealthy would dare risk the perception that they could better afford to live in the less expensive part of town when, in theory, they could afford to live anywhere?

And, of course, it was far easier for the ladies of the day to shop at their favorite stores and leave their calling cards on one side of Central Park than to journey all the way to the city's opposite shore. Besides that, the established elite whose summer homes faced the sea in Newport and other locales had no need of river views in New York City.

The demographics of the Upper West Side caused the elite to hesitate for other reasons as well. Thousands of Eastern European Jews had immigrated to the city. Unwelcome among society on the Upper East Side, these upwardly mobile new arrivals headed west. East Siders were not inclined to follow.

In the last decades of the nineteenth century, it seemed to many that there were only two classes in New York City: filthy rich and desperately poor. In 1880, the average wage for industrial workers was about $380—annually. Although that leaped to about $564 by 1890, that same year only 45 percent of American workers earned yearly wages above the poverty line. In contrast, one of the richest men in America at the time, Andrew Carnegie, *gave away* $350 million in Gilded Age dollars, or roughly $10 billion today.

According to James D. McCabe's 1868 book *The Secrets of the Great City: A Work Descriptive of the Virtues and the Vices, the Mysteries, Miseries and Crimes of New York City*, "The middle class, which is so numerous in other cities, hardly exists at all here."[7] However, in *Gotham*, the Pulitzer Prize–winning history of New York City by Edwin G. Burrows and Mike Wallace, the authors state that this perception was understandable but wrong, noting that somewhere between a quarter and a third of the population was middle class.

Although most people at the time worked for low wages, in factories or sweatshops, the requirements of the era's industrialization created new types of positions, which fostered the growth of a middle class, which then developed its own social strata. At the top end of this new middle class were professionals and managers—doctors, lawyers, professors, retailers, and entrepreneurs among them. Shopkeepers, schoolteachers, clerks, and salespeople—those more in the category of employee than boss—made up the lower end of the middle spectrum. The boundaries between classes were "fuzzy," *Gotham* continues. "At the top, the Gilded Age middle class bled imperceptibly into the haute bourgeoisie, with the border peopled by independently wealthy professionals descended from mercantile and landholding families."[8]

Although they were the residents that Riverside Drive's eager promoters envisioned, it was not the old-name members of the Four Hundred, the denizens of Fifth Avenue, who ventured uptown and across town for the panoramic views of Riverside Drive and the bucolic delights of Riverside Park. No Astors, Vanderbilts, or Whitneys ventured near. They remained on the East Side, along with the rest of the ultrarich, the Morgans, Fricks, and Carnegies among them, who did not necessarily come from old money but profited extravagantly from railroads and steel.

Instead, it was the members of that "fuzzy" but clearly financially comfortable mix of businessmen and professionals—presidents and vice presidents of banks and manufacturing companies most frequently among them—who would pioneer their own opulent abodes atop the rugged cliffs above Riverside Park and create an entirely new community on the city's western edge.

Chapter 8

The Pioneers

Marvelous Mansions and Ravishing Row Houses

RIVERSIDE DRIVE AND Riverside Park officially opened in 1880. Yet the new Gold Coast rush was slow in coming. In the mid-1880s, several noteworthy mansions newly graced the landscape along Riverside Drive, especially in the low 100s. There, particularly high elevation and a relatively wide Park and Drive better protected residents from the clamor and odors of the tracks and commercial waterfront below. Still, by late 1888, there had been "scarcely more than a dozen houses built fronting the Drive since the Drive was constructed."[1]

By the turn of the century, however, the city's west coast garden was in bloom. In 1899, there were fifty homes under construction on Riverside Drive and its cross streets between 104th Street and 108th Street. That same year, at least five of the families noted within the chapters of this book appeared in *Notable New Yorkers of 1896–1899*, an indication of the prestige of Riverside Drive families. Just a few years later, eighty Riverside Drive families would be listed in the 1904 New York *Social Register.*

In an era when most single private residences were worth $25,000 to $50,000 each in New York City, Riverside attracted families able and willing to spend considerably more. "Above $50,000 in value come the houses of the millionaires, occupying several city lots, splendid examples of architecture, and decorated and furnished at lavish expense."[2] These freestanding homes were often referred to as "villas." As of 1888, according to the *Real Estate Record and Builders' Guide*, the houses on the Drive were all such villas, almost assuring that "the border of the Drive will not be converted into a city street by rows of attached houses and in this one part of the city, the speculative builder will find no opportunity."[3] That scenario, it turns out, was more aspirational than practical.

Figure 28. The rambling Noakes mansion, between 113th and 114th Streets. *Source*: Collection of the New-York Historical Society

Noakes Mansion

Among Riverside Drive's early residents was the family of George Noakes, a native New Yorker and wealthy restaurateur, who lived in a distinctive Romanesque Revival mansion between 113th and 114th Streets, just south of where the old Carrigan-Rudd mansion stood. Designed by Arthur B. Jennings, the rambling, three-story abode was built of textured granite and trimmed with stone. Completed in 1884, it was a sight to behold.

Regally situated on a terraced lawn atop three flights of stairs, the home exuded eccentricity. An open terrace, recessed portico, loggia, and prominent bay windows joined forces with a sharply angled roof and pointy-topped corner turret fit for a fairy-tale princess. Still, the design was "admirable; it combines both elegance and convenience, and has many pleasing features."[4]

The interior was as striking as the home's public face. There was an eighteen-foot-high conservatory with white marble floors, a vestibule with unglazed tiles, halls with mahogany trim, and ceilings striped with mahogany beams. Stained-glass windows shone down on an elaborate staircase with carved newel posts. The first floor had eleven-foot ceilings. A fireplace featured a tiled hearth and mahogany mantel; the parlor, music room, and dining room were trimmed, respectively, in ebony, maple, and oak. The home held ten bedrooms, four on the second floor, six on the third, as well as a dressing room, billiard room, and two wainscoted bathrooms.

Though it looked sufficiently hunkered down to last forever, the Noakes house met its demise just twenty-two years later, in 1906, to be replaced in 1910 by the thirteen-story Chateauesque-style Riverside Mansions apartment building at 410 Riverside Drive.

Kittel and Gibbons Mansions

In 1885, a year after designing the Noakes home, the same architect, Jennings, also built a house just south of 122nd Street on the Drive for Joseph J. Kittel. One of the country's leading dealers in china and glassware, he was known as the "Napoleon of china." After retiring from that business, he became president of a bank. In 1887, Jennings did the same for John J. Gibbons, a partner in the famous glass and china emporium of Gilman, Collamore & Co., who made frequent trips to Europe to scout potential purchases for his company. Kittel was born in Brooklyn of German heritage; Gibbons hailed from Ireland.

Figure 29. The Kittel and Gibbons mansions, just south of 122nd Street, dwarfed by new construction and Grant's Tomb in this c. 1926 photo. The entire block down to 120th Street was later razed to make way for Riverside Church. *Source*: Courtesy of Rockefeller Archive Center.

With glass and china as the unifying theme here, it's easy to envision what a glorious dinner table these families set, to welcome guests that, at the time, might have included ladies clad in silks or satins, velvet or lace, and equally well-tailored gentlemen. "Nowhere in the world are seen such splendidly dressed, such gorgeously bejeweled women as in New York," noted one observer, adding, "The elite do not wear the same dress twice."[5] In New York in the 1870s and again in the early 1880s, the back bustle was at the forefront of fashion for women.

Books of manners at the time advised that a good dinner host ought to "help ladies with a due appreciation of their delicacy, moderation, and fastidiousness of their appetites"[6] and, further, should "never pour gravy on a plate without permission."[7]

At the Kittel and Gibbons homes, china vases and crystal pitchers surely adorned splendid sideboards in the well-appointed dining rooms. Fireplaces likely warmed spaces laid with parquetry floors. Polished woods burnished walls, and heavy draperies cosseted windows. Gaslight gently threw flattering shadows on evening festivities—unless those families were among the first to have electricity. A bountiful array of fresh flowers greeted guests. On Riverside Drive near the turn of the century, bay or bow windows, deeply coffered ceilings, and finely carved wainscoting and staircase railings often set the scene for an evening's entertainment.

Furniture belonging to the affluent at the time typically was upholstered with luxurious fabrics such as velvet or damask. There might be galleries to show off fine art, their paintings stacked in rows one above the other, and an ample store of sculpture. Lavish decorative pieces such as pottery and porcelain, along with fine tapestries, throw rugs, and tall columns, often confirmed a homeowner's wealth. Judging by photos of the time, potted plants—typically ferns or palms—were everywhere. A 1903 auction notice for the contents of a home at 74 Riverside Drive included Sevres vases, Aubusson tapestries, tiger and polar bear rugs, and a rock-crystal table service.

Located where the landmarked Riverside Church stands today, the Kittel and Gibbons homes were somewhat smaller than the Noakes house but, with their picturesque gables, towers, and chimneys, just as appealing.

Doelger Mansion

In 1885, the same year that the Kittel mansion was built, Peter Doelger purchased a large lot on the northeast corner of 100th Street, part of the original Furniss estate. An immigrant from Bavaria who arrived in the United States in 1850 at the age of eighteen, Doelger established a brewery that became one of the largest in the country.

In a way, Doelger was ahead of his time: He produced a product that today might be called "craft" beer, because it focused on serving its home market, New York, rather than a broader audience. Ads referred to his product as "healthful liquid food" or described it as "a nerve, body and strength builder." The company remained in business until 1947 and is perhaps best remembered today for the vast array of promotional giveaways, such as branded beer trays, it offered before Prohibition.

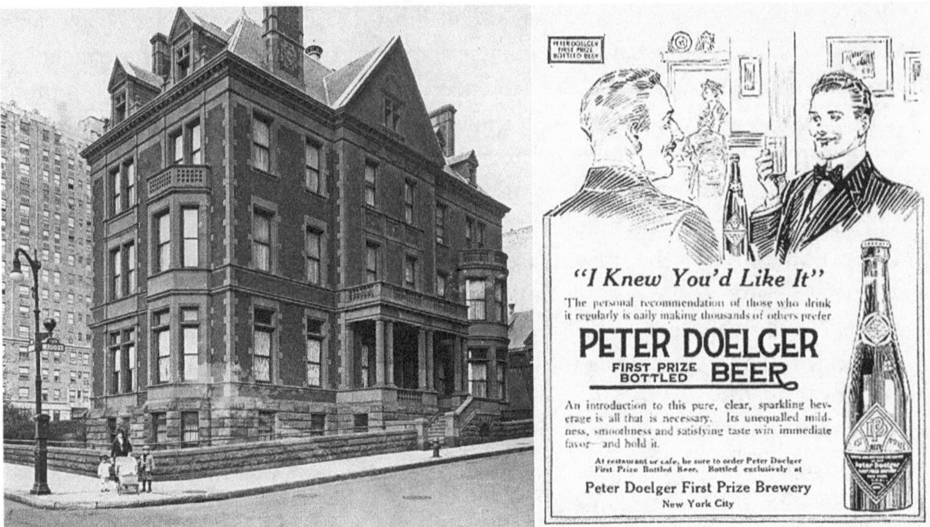

Figure 30. The Doelger residence on the northeast corner of 100th Street and an ad for Doelger beer. *Source*: Milstein Division, The New York Public Library.

Doelger selected William Schickel, also Bavarian, to design a residence and carriage house. A devout Catholic and the father of ten, Doelger was in need of a spacious home, to which he added an adjoining chapel. The anticipated price of the residence, as reported at the time, was $100,000.

Completed in 1889, the Queen Anne four-story mansion of red brick trimmed with brownstone included a balustraded balcony on the second floor and two more balconies above two-story bay windows. Stone columns shored up the portico, while pedimented dormers of various sizes erupted on the rooftop. Gardens surrounded the home on three sides, and a stone wall shielded it all.

In 1906, the guidebook *Seeing New York* observed, "Peter Doelger's large red-brick house . . . is one of the landmarks from the river. A small herd of white deer is usually to be seen in a netted enclosure."[8] *Munsey's Magazine* added, "A score of white pigeons flutter around the stables, and quacking ducks and cackling hens do their utmost to persuade Mr. Doelger—to say nothing of his neighbors—that he is in the midst of a country farm."[9]

In 1894, Doelger also bought 2641 Broadway on the northwest corner of 100th Street, a three-story wooden building built in 1871 (now home to the Metro Diner), located around the bend from his mansion. He turned what was first a grocery and later a roadhouse into a bar in front and a restaurant in back.

Just the year before, in 1893, Doelger's daughter Matilda married a boxer named John Patrick West. Their daughter was Mary Jane West—also known as the Hollywood icon Mae West.

Just like their successors today, wealthy businessmen of the era were expected to support worthy causes. In 1899, there was a successful campaign to expand the Central

Park Menagerie. One gentleman gave a monkey and a peccary, another provided two alligators, and still another, an eagle. Doelger gave an opossum.

The Doelger family lived on Riverside Drive until Mrs. Doelger's death in 1925, when the house was sold for $900,000. A year later, the fifteen-story Colonial Revival 280 Riverside Drive apartment building stood in its place.

Foster Mansion

In 1888, William F. Foster purchased a large mansion on the northeast corner of 102nd Street and Riverside Drive—as a teardown. Foster was born in England and

Figure 31. The flamboyant Foster mansion, on the northeast corner of 102nd Street. *Source*: Milstein Division, The New York Public Library.

made his fortune in the kid-glove business, inventing and patenting a fastener. Because he felt the existing mansion was too old-fashioned for his taste, he had it razed and replaced that same year with a three-story brick and stone mansion, designed by the architect Halstead Fowler and set far back from the corner. At the eastern end of the plot on 102nd Street were a two-story garage and a one-story brick building.

The resulting home was considerably more flamboyant than its predecessor. A deep cast-iron frieze banded the residence just below the roofline, a design choice not to the taste of certain critics of the day. The mansion's most notable feature, a large, mostly glass room on the second floor, extended over the entrance and served as the "principal sitting room of the house by its inmates, who never tire of the views up and down the Hudson, the long range of heights beyond the wide river, the glorious winter sunsets, and the ever passing human stream."[10]

Foster lived in his new home with his wife, Bertha, until his death in 1895. In 1922, the buildings were sold for $2.5 million and demolished to make way for a fourteen-story apartment building at 300 Riverside Drive and a nine-story apartment house adjoining it on 102nd Street.

Bayne Mansion

Construction of imposing freestanding villas on Riverside Drive continued in the 1890s. Like Noakes, Kittel, Gibbons, Doelger, and Foster, the Irish-born Samuel Gable Bayne and his family also took up residence on Riverside Drive in the 100s, where "no part of the Drive affords a more picturesque view of the Hudson and Palisades than does the crescent-shaped section lying between One Hundredth and One Hundred and Ninth Streets, and which holds many of the best residences on the Drive today."[11]

Bayne came to the United States in 1869 at the age of twenty-five. He began his career manufacturing linens, moved on to the oil business, and then to banking, eventually heading the Seaboard Bank.

The neighborhood proved to be quite the draw by century's end for those in the banking business. The Drive from 104th Street to 108th Street, in particular, became known as the "Bankers' Colony." Bayne was the first banker to buy and build there. He was also president of the Riverside Drive Property Association and somehow found the time to write at least a half-dozen books, on subjects ranging from astronomy to travel.

Over time, he built *two* grand residences, both designed by Frank Freeman and both Romanesque Revival in style. The first house, of yellow brick trimmed in red sandstone, was built in 1887 on the northeast corner of 108th Street. In 1889, Bayne began buying up all the lots between 107th and 108th Streets, from Riverside Drive to West End Avenue. He sold his first home in 1890 and in 1891 built a larger, more dazzling place on the southeast corner of 108th Street, directly across from his earlier residence.

The new home joined brick with stone. A towering four-story corner pavilion distinguished the house, along with a tantalizing array of dormers, bays, and balconies and rows of windows grouped tightly together. At the entrance, a massive arch offered an outsize welcome to visitors. The curves above the door and numerous windows contrasted the multiple peaks at the expansive and visually entertaining red-tiled roofline. In 1891, the architecture critic Montgomery Schuyler observed:

> The building thus far done along Riverside Drive has sufficed to commit that boulevard to a suburban rather than a strictly urban character. It is especially fortunate since among the villas already erected, which are for the most part decorous and dull, with one or two exceptions which are highly undecorous and even duller, it has given opportunity to Mr. Freeman to put up two villas . . . which are not only by far the most artistic examples of the Richardsonian Romanesque in our domestic architecture, but are among the most artistic of our dwellings in any style. Without being grouped each enhanced the effect of the other.[12]

When Bayne resold the remaining lots in 1899, he restricted future construction on them to no more than two detached homes and required that there be at least thirty feet between the houses in the middle of the block and those on either corner, thus assuring appropriately upper-crust residences. As a result, on an avenue where

Figure 32. The two Bayne homes, on the corner of 108th Street. Bayne (inset) moved from the one on the left (northeast corner) to the one on the right (southeast corner). *Source*: Wallach Division Picture Collection, The New York Public Library.

most buildings today are packed tightly together, there are airy openings between 355 and 353 Riverside Drive and between 352 and 351 Riverside Drive.

Bayne remained in his (second) home until 1921, when he sold it to make way for 355 Riverside Drive, a fourteen-story dark-brick Renaissance Revival apartment house designed by his son-in-law Alfred C. Bossom, on the southeast corner of 108th Street. Bayne planned to occupy the full-floor penthouse apartment.

In 1896, Henry S. F. Davis bought Bayne's original home on the northeast corner. After Davis's death, his widow, Cora, and her new husband, John A. Rutherfurd, were living there when the Bonavista apartment building arose next door at 362 Riverside Drive, between 108th and 109th Streets. Mrs. Rutherfurd did not stop by with a welcome basket. Instead, she erected a thirty-six-foot-high, seventy-five-foot-long brick "spite wall," blocking many of the residents' views not only of her garden but also of the river to the south.

In 1915, her home would become the thirteen-story Renaissance Revival apartment building named the Rutherfurd at 360 Riverside Drive.

It appears her neighbors made no comment.

Cyrus Clark Mansion (Again)

Villas appeared elsewhere on the Drive in the 1880s and 1890s as well. In 1866, Cyrus Clark,[13] the "Father of the West Side," had purchased the Brockholst Livingston house and its extensive property at 90th Street and Riverside Drive. In 1888, he commissioned a fanciful turreted house from Henry F. Kilburn for the southern corner of 90th Street at a cost of $90,000.

The new three-story home united French Renaissance and Romanesque Revival styles. Faced with rough-cut granite, it flaunted a red-tile-covered hip roof set apart by chimneys, winsome dormers, and two hard-to-miss towers. It was surrounded by porches that were the ideal setting for the area's stunning views of the river and beyond.

What did the Clarks see from those ivy-covered porches? Tugboats, to this day a constant, sturdy presence on the Hudson as they maneuver barges many times their size upstream and down. Steamships and sailboats, ferries and small fishing boats, too. Even now, the parade of ships on the river is a form of entertainment, the Hudson a great stage beyond twenty-first-century curtains.

While the *Real Estate Record and Builders' Guide* did not find the Kilburn design to be particularly distinguished, it contended that it at least had "the advantage of being unmistakably a villa and not a city house and in this respect set a good example for succeeding builders."[14]

Eventually, with two of their children married, the Clarks decided to downsize from their villa and move to a new row house on West 76th Street. In October 1897, Clark sold part of his property. Mary Llewellyn Swayne Parsons, a widow who had inherited a substantial fortune, purchased the southern half of the block, about ten building lots, for $200,000.

New Yorkers have never been shy about battling what they consider to be an injustice or, at the very least, a personal inconvenience. In 1900, Parsons sued various city officials to block plans for construction of the Soldiers' and Sailors' Monument at Riverside Drive and 89th Street. She maintained that the monument would interfere with her view and obstruct the flow of light and air, to boot. The lawsuit failed, and the memorial was built in 1902.

In 1897, restrictive covenants had been placed on the 90th Street property, barring for thirty-five years the construction or use of any buildings except for private dwellings intended for single families. This, according to Tom Miller's *Daytonian in Manhattan*, led to some local legal drama.

After Parsons died, her brother leased the house to Florence B. de G. Shaw, who moved her Hamilton School for Girls into the mansion. Just as they are today, exclusive private girls' schools in New York City were typically located within upscale residential areas, and Riverside Drive proved a popular choice. In 1900, the Ely sisters relocated their finishing school for girls to Riverside Drive between West 85th and 86th Streets. Forty-Two Riverside Drive, between 76th and 77th Streets, was the location for the Graham School, founded in 1816 and New York City's oldest private school for girls, whose students came from the wealthiest families in the East.

Mrs. Shaw's neighbor William Barnard was not happy with the new arrivals. Barnard, president of the International Salt Company, had purchased the Scriven Clark/Bishop Potter residence and later the entire Cyrus Clark property. Barnard sued the Graham School, maintaining that it was a business and therefore in violation of the restrictive covenant. Mrs. Shaw, in turn, asserted that Barnard had already broken the covenant by leasing his mansion to a motion picture company, to film scenes of a silent movie starring Billie Burke (perhaps most famous today for playing the good witch Glinda in *The Wizard of Oz*). Barnard won his case, but Mrs. Shaw appealed to the State Supreme Court. The ruling was overturned and Barnard's suit dismissed. The court decided that the restrictions applied to future buildings rather than existing ones.

In 1925, the Barnard and Shaw mansions, both built on the original Brockholst Livingston property owned by Clark, were demolished. They were replaced with 173–175 Riverside Drive, a Neo-Renaissance apartment building that fills the entire block between 89th and 90th Streets.

John H. Matthews Mansion

Meanwhile, back in 1889 Clark had sold the original Brockholst Livingston house at 90th Street and Riverside to John H. Matthews, the "soda water king." Matthews had moved to the United States from England in 1832 to take advantage of Americans' new-found passion for mineral water and its perceived healing and medicinal properties, including its ability to "cure" obesity. Spas were bubbling up at Saratoga Springs and elsewhere, where visitors could drink and bathe in the waters. Matthews, who had been trained in the art of carbonation, recognized the potential in manufacturing

Figure 33. The Matthews residence (l.) and the Cyrus Clark home (r.), both with head-turning towers, on opposite corners of 90th Street. *Source*: Museum of the City of New York, 36.202.29.

that drink artificially and invented a machine to produce fizzy soda water—also known today as sparkling water or seltzer.

New Yorkers are endlessly swapping out what is for what could be, and their nineteenth-century predecessors were no different. Matthews demolished the old Brockholst Livingston mansion and replaced it in the early 1890s with a rambling shingle-style cottage by Lamb & Rich, on the northeast corner of 90th Street. Rough-cut stone, brick, and terracotta completed the exterior, along with a conical cap that jauntily topped the corner tower. Sumptuous caryatids—an adventurous ornamentation—supported a second-floor bay, and numerous stained-glass windows let in light. Multiple balconies adorned the façade, and a welcoming porch filled the width of the side facing Riverside Drive. "The home of Mr. John H. Matthews . . . is easily the most striking bit of architecture on the river front, its ample porches and picturesque tile roofs distinguishing it from its more conventional neighbors."[15] A cast-iron fence, with a decorative vine-like pattern, surrounded the house, which cost over $200,000.

The mansion adjoined a private stable, although stables belonging to the wealthy were usually located several blocks away or at least spaced far from the main house. In the winter of 1896, fire broke out in the stable's hayloft. While the horses and a few carriages were saved, four other carriages, all of the hay, and part of the interior woodwork burned. The blaze itself caused about $5,000 in damage, but the chaos of the event also provided sufficient distraction for turn-of-the-century ne'er-do-wells to abscond with many of the family's possessions.

Unlike other millionaires who might prefer to spend their free time sailing yachts or racing horses, Matthews liked to breed bulldogs, and he served as president of the Bulldog Club. Media of the period abound in notices of the various competitions won by his show dogs.

Matthews died in 1870 and, like Andrew Carrigan,[16] was buried in Brooklyn's Green-Wood Cemetery. Matthews's monument, one of the tallest there at thirty-five feet high, is festooned with gargoyles, animal heads, the faces of loved ones, and other notable ornamentation. A marble effigy of Matthews gazes up at carved scenes depicting moments of his life—among them, experimenting with the production of carbonic gas and inventing devices for the making of soda water. The elaborate structure was so exceptional that in 1873 it was voted mortuary monument of the year.

In January 1905, the Matthews family sold the mansion to John B. Russell, president of the Russell Contracting Company, who spent nearly $100,000 renovating it. Five years later, Russell sold the house to the real estate operator Franklin Pettit, who, just a week later, resold it to Mary Bogert Pell for slightly over $500,000.

Apparently, house flipping is not solely a twentieth- or twenty-first-century phenomenon—nor is a somewhat different version of urban NIMBY (Not In My Back Yard). Mrs. Pell, it seems, bought the Matthews place, adjacent to her own home, to prevent construction of an apartment house next door—a move that might have inspired envy in the spite-wall-building Mrs. Rutherfurd.

Mrs. Pell died in her Riverside Drive residence in 1913, but the two properties she owned survived until late in 1921. A thirteen-story Neo-Georgian red-brick apartment building, 180 Riverside Drive, rose on the site in 1922.

Elizabeth Scriven Clark Mansion/Bishop Potter Residence

Elizabeth Scriven Clark was the daughter-in-law of Edward Cabot Clark, creator of the Dakota, the city's first luxury apartment house. Unlike him, she preferred the delights of Riverside Drive to those of Central Park West. In 1897, she purchased roughly a half-block of property on the northeast corner of 89th Street from Cyrus Clark for about $215,000.

Three years later, in 1900, she built an imposing, four-story white marble and red-brick Georgian-style mansion designed by Ernest Flagg, who also designed the Singer Building, once the world's tallest. A conservatory and bowling alley in an attached wing were among the home's more unusual features, and it was surrounded by formal gardens and a wrought-iron fence.

Unfortunately for Mrs. Clark, her husband, Alfred Corning Clark, Edward's son, is said to have led something of a double life, one with her, the other with a Norwegian tenor named Lorentz Severin Skougaard. In 1869, the same year he married Elizabeth Scriven, Clark began making annual summer visits to Norway with Skougaard, and at one point he built a house not far from Skougaard's family home. When in New

Figure 34. The elegant Scriven Clark/Potter mansion on the northeast corner of 89th Street, with Bishop Potter (inset). *Source*: Milstein Division, The New York Public Library; Potter portrait: Library of Congress.

York City, Skougaard lived in an apartment Clark owned downtown. It's said that their relationship lasted for nineteen years. On Valentine's Day, 1885, Skougaard died of typhoid fever in New York City. In his memory, Clark created a $64,000 endowment for Manhattan's Norwegian Hospital. He also gave his eldest son, Edward, the middle name Severin.

After Alfred's death in 1896, Mrs. Clark came into her own, becoming prominent in society and developing a reputation as a philanthropist. Her son Stephen Carlton Clark started the famous Cooperstown Baseball Hall of Fame, and her son Robert Sterling Clark created the Clark Art Institute in Williamstown, Massachusetts.

The imposing Clark house on Riverside Drive was also referred to as Bishop Potter's residence. The Right Reverend Henry Codman Potter, a bishop of the Protestant Episcopal Diocese of New York, was known for continuing his uncle Rt. Rev. Horatio Potter's work in establishing the Cathedral of St. John the Divine. The world's largest cathedral,[17] the mother church of the Episcopal Diocese of New York and the seat of its bishop, St. John's is located two blocks east of Riverside Drive at 112th Street. Potter's first wife was Elizabeth Rogers Jacob, who died in 1901. In 1903, at the age of sixty-seven, Rev. Potter married Elizabeth Scriven Clark, by then a widow for six years.

It was in the cathedral's Chapel of St. James, first named the Potter Chapel, that I married my husband many decades later. The ceremony took place, memorably, steps away from the tomb and recumbent effigy of Bishop Potter himself, who died in 1908. The chapel was the gift of Elizabeth Scriven Potter in memory of her husband.

The Scriven Clark mansion (later the William Barnard home) was eventually demolished. In 1927, it was replaced by the block-long, sixteen-story 173–175 Riverside Drive apartment building, the same building that rose in place of the Shaw mansion.

Charles Schwab Mansion

Charles Schwab was president of the Carnegie Steel Company; then of US Steel, where he earned $2,000,000 annually; and later founder of the Bethlehem Steel Company. He was also one of the richest men in the country. Schwab built his Riverside Drive home after leaving Bethlehem, Pennsylvania, for New York City. Called Riverside, it stood on the former site of the Orphan Asylum, the first private orphanage in New York, founded by Alexander Hamilton's widow, Eliza Hamilton.

In 1901, Schwab began construction on an exceedingly lavish French Renaissance chateau. Upon completion in 1905, the estate filled the entire block bordered by Riverside Drive and West End Avenue, 73rd Street to 74th Street, a plot of land that cost about $800,000. Before that, no one in Manhattan had ever acquired an entire block for his or her own occupancy. With seventy-five rooms and fifty thousand square feet of space, the Schwab home was among the grandest houses ever built on the island of Manhattan. Construction itself cost $2.5–3 million in turn-of-the-century money. The house featured a 166-foot tower with panoramic views, as well as a chapel, bowling alley, gymnasium, pool, music room, a room for playing cards, and multiple elevators. An art gallery filled the entire northeast wing, while a conservatory stretched across the southern length of the house.

There was also a self-contained power plant and the era's version of air conditioning, along with a four-car garage and a receiving lodge for incoming goods. A service tunnel ran beneath the garden, which surrounded the house and was "the size of a small park."

The Schwab home required the talents of more than one hundred artists, designers, modelers, architects, and engineers. Designed by Maurice Hebert, Schwab's personal four-story castle was an eclectic stone extravaganza that combined details from three French chateaux: Chenonceau, Azay-le-Rideau, and Blois. "It was the apotheosis of French renaissance architecture in New York—just as the style was going out of fashion."[18] A wanderer who had tippled too many manhattans, a popular cocktail of the day among high society, would easily think himself lost in time and the Loire Valley. Schwab spent several million dollars more creating an interior reflecting the styles of various dead French kings and filling it with fine furnishings, art, and antiques, including tapestries for the dining room and a $65,000 custom-made pipe organ. The total cost of the home, including construction, landscaping, and furnishings, was estimated to be between $6 and $8 million.

Figure 35. The castle-like Schwab mansion, interior and exterior, with owner Charles Schwab (inset). *Source*: Exterior and portrait: Library of Congress; Interior: Irving Underhill, Museum of the City of New York, X2010.18.317.

Apparently, opulent homes were de rigueur among New York's steel magnates at the time. Two other well-known residences were built on Fifth Avenue: Henry Clay Frick's at 70th Street and Andrew Carnegie's at 91st Street. Carnegie is said to have once remarked, referring to the Schwab mansion, "Have you seen that place of Charlie's? It makes mine look like a shack."

Schwab's wife, Eurana, had opposed moving to Riverside Drive, for fear she would never again see her Fifth Avenue friends. Interestingly, the financier Jacob Schiff had bought the land on which the Schwab mansion was later built, but unlike Mrs. Schwab, Mrs. Schiff successfully blocked moving to the "wrong" side of Central Park.

Schwab went bankrupt in the Wall Street crash of 1929. He died ten years later, bequeathing Riverside to the city as a suitably ostentatious residence for New York's mayors. Fiorello La Guardia, mayor at the time, turned it down as his official residence—supposedly responding, "What, *me* in *that*?"—and opted instead for Gracie Mansion.

The exuberant Schwab mansion stood empty from 1939 to 1948, when it was torn down. During World War II, its grounds hosted victory gardens—vegetable, fruit, and herb gardens that helped reduce pressure on the public food supply during wartime. In 1950, the site became home to the full-block, sixteen-story Schwab House, featuring a straightforward red-brick exterior in staggering contrast to its palatial predecessor. The Frick and Carnegie houses, however—the East Side companions to Schwab—survive until this day, both as art museums, the Frick Collection and the Cooper Hewitt.

The Clarence True and C. P. H. Gilbert Row Houses

Freestanding villas such as the homes described in this chapter were the most arresting residences along Riverside Drive at the end of the nineteenth century; about thirty of them reigned over the landscape. Yet around one hundred chic row houses could also be found at that time, in large part thanks to one man, Clarence True.

By one estimate, True built as many as 270 houses on the Upper West Side alone, mostly in groups, between 1890 and 1901. Acting both as developer and architect, he purchased all available lots along Riverside Drive south of 84th Street. As of early 1898, "about 30 handsome dwellings"[19] were planned for the Drive itself, and more were built adjacent to it. Among True's Riverside Drive residences were homes between 76th and 77th Streets and 80th and 81st Streets, as well as on the southeast corner of 83rd Street. True was in large part responsible for promoting the growth and establishing the character of lower Riverside Drive.

True objected to what he considered the sameness and monotony of Upper East Side row houses, including the uniformity of brownstone fronts, and focused on individuality for the Upper West Side. While his residences were not quite as large or dramatic as the existing standalone mansions, they were undeniably distinctive, uniquely combining several different styles, including French and English Renaissance along with Flemish inspiration, into his version of Elizabethan Revival.

This eclectic approach meant that his designs were more ornate and captivating than the typical row house of the time, with flourishes such as elaborate cornices, whimsical balconies, and round corner bays, along with dormers, turrets, and gables. Steeply pitched roofs, often with curved or stepped gables, crenellation, parapets, and chimneys, further enlivened the scene, as did decorative ironwork. Light-colored limestone and brick predominated over brownstone.

He also popularized the American basement plan, which lowered the typical high stoop, replacing it with a ground-floor entrance that held a reception room up front and a kitchen in the back. This approach elevated the parlor and dining room to the second floor, offering more privacy and elegance for entertaining. The *New-York Tribune* said of him, "Mr. True is noted for boldness and originality in his building enterprises, and has probably done more toward the introduction of new styles and plans in our local domestic architecture than any other architect."[20]

Most of True's homes were built on speculation. Once it was clear that old money was making a stand on the East Side, West Side developers targeted businessmen or professionals making $25,000 to $100,000 per year, a considerable sum around the turn of the century.

Many of True's Riverside Drive houses later became apartments and schools, and a *New York Times* article shares the history of one of their more colorful residents. In 1926, "Gladys Cooper, an actress living in an apartment at 74 Riverside Drive, walked into a police station and opened her fur coat to reveal nothing but her underwear. She said she wanted to prove to the police that she had been bruised in an accident at the Princetonian Club. Of no connection to the college, the Princetonian was a gambling operation that had been raided by the police more than once."[21]

The area along Riverside Drive and its side streets from 75th to 85th Streets boasts the city's greatest concentration of True houses still in existence. While some still hold apartments today, others have been converted back to private residences. His designs between 76th and 77th Streets comprise the only complete street of row houses extant on Riverside Drive today—and the only remaining nineteenth-century buildings of those noted in this chapter.

The architect Charles Pierrepont H. Gilbert, known as C. P. H. Gilbert, was also highly active in row houses on Riverside Drive and in fact designed more than one hundred residences in New York City, including Fifth Avenue mansions for the likes of Frank W. Woolworth, Felix Warburg, and Otto Kahn. While the Woolworth home was demolished, the latter two are better known today as, respectively, the Jewish Museum and the Convent of the Sacred Heart. Gilbert was also responsible for the Fletcher-Sinclair Mansion at Fifth Avenue and 79th Street, now the Ukrainian Institute of America.[22]

Gilbert, who lived at a (since demolished) row house at 33 Riverside Drive, was talented in other ways as well, able to shoot at a gallop from underneath a horse's saddle, an impressive accomplishment in any era. His son, Dudley, made headlines in 1912 when, at the age of thirteen, he sold his overcoat to buy a steamship ticket to Europe, intending to see the world. He made it as far as Washington, DC, before being returned to his family.

In the late nineteenth century, however, there remained those who felt that free-standing villas versus row houses were the way to go for Riverside Drive:

> Some examples of the "city" house have crept in already, and on one corner, where such a villa as the parklike character of the location demands might be erected, the owner advertises that he will build three "city" houses, two of which will be for rent. But detached houses of considerable architectural merit, surrounded by grounds of sufficient area to set them off to advantage, have been built at the southeast corner of Ninetieth Street and at One Hundred and Eighth, and other corners, and the promise of an attractive vista on the east, as well as the west side of the drive is encouraging.[23]

Notably, even among the residents, there were efforts to restrict the number and type of homes that could be built on the Drive. In 1887, owners along Riverside Drive between 116th and 120th Streets tried to limit development to no more than three houses per block, to assure that only large homes for the affluent would result. They were unsuccessful.

The abundant advantages of life along the Hudson increasingly appealed to adventurous and free-spending families who erected standalone villas on Riverside Drive or took up residence in its pleasing row houses. Yet by the end of the nineteenth century, the curvaceous and leafy boulevard with its panoramic vistas had yet to achieve its anticipated status in the world of New York society. Its residents, while undeniably affluent, were not "old money." Riverside would, instead, become popular with the newly wealthy or what one source referred to as "only the moderately rich."

It would take until the first decades of the 1900s for Riverside Drive to gain its present-day concentration of upscale homes. By that time, instead of grand villas and gracious row houses, the area became better known for their antithesis, the "modern" apartment building.

Chapter 9

Movin' On Up

The Rise of the Apartment House

The building façades parallel the drive, following its curves and creating a serpentine wall which can be seen from a great distance.

—Landmarks Preservation Commission Designation Report, 1980

OUR FIRST UPPER West Side apartment filled the parlor floor of a worn but gracious nineteenth-century brownstone on 88th Street between Columbus and Amsterdam Avenues. We painted the kitchen a deep yellow and tiled the floor with alternating squares of black and white linoleum, creating, unintentionally, our personal culinary Checker cab. The working space between appliances on one side and cabinets on the other was about as wide as that taxi, at most four feet across. My husband, the family chef, could easily scoot from stove to fridge and back again on a rolling desk chair during the months a broken ankle and thigh-high cast kept him at home.

The apartment itself charmed with fourteen-foot-high ceilings, a carved oak mantel over a no-longer-working fireplace, and the brightest of Crayola-red shutters across a Palladian front window. The small building stood, with a certain Old World dignity, across the street from an offensively gray tenement whose tenants liked to drink beer on our stoop and adjacent to a boarded-up building whose insides had been ravaged by squatters.

When our rent doubled—from all of $800 per month to $1,600—we decided it was time to buy instead and warily followed a real estate agent across what was then, in the crime-ridden 1980s, the "safety" divider line at 96th Street in search of a place to call home. There, on the corner of 110th Street, we found our first Riverside Drive apartment, in a twelve-story, fully staffed apartment building, where during our time in residence the doorman was fired for stealing elderly residents' social security checks. Our apartment, in the back of the building, faced away from the park and toward other people's windows. Still, we loved it for its herringbone floors, picture-frame-trim walls, proximity to the park, and the subway stop on the corner.

Although our home was built in 1922, it was primarily the years from 1900 to about 1920 that marked the dramatic influx of apartment houses to Riverside Drive and thus the flowering of this long-planned and much anticipated community. Until late in the nineteenth century, the idea of apartment house living was foreign to New Yorkers—literally, given its European origins—and more than a little scandalous. The city's elite were, at first, aghast at the idea of being limited to a single floor or at having other families—complete strangers!—sharing the building's entranceways and stacked above and below them like layers of a cake.

Most shocking was having bedrooms on the same floor as public rooms—an invitation to immorality, according to some. There were customs and courtesies to be observed—how would ladies properly leave their calling cards?—and architectural requirements within which to observe them. In those days, "failure to own your own home was a confession of shabby antecedents or disreputable habits."[1] Plainly put, respectable people lived in a home of their own, whether a freestanding mansion or a row house intended for one family's exclusive use.

Multiple-family dwellings were associated with tenements, the standard mode of housing for the poor. These five- or six-story dwellings were known for cramped quarters, little light, limited ventilation, and poor drainage. As of 1867, 52 percent of Manhattan's tenements were considered to be in a condition detrimental to the health and dangerous to the lives of their occupants.

That same year, New York State passed its first tenement-house law, requiring a window or "ventilator" in every sleeping room, a fire escape, and one water closet for every twenty residents (versus the usual one per hundred). The law forbade connecting cesspools to tenement houses, requiring instead that buildings be graded, drained, and joined to a sewer. It also limited the number of people allowed to reside in a given amount of space.

While this law was a notable step toward tenement reform, it was seldom enforced and in reality did little at the time to improve unsanitary living conditions. It was not until much later that legislation had any real effect. The 1901 Tenement House Act,[2] the 1916 zoning ordinance, and the 1929 Dwelling Law regulated light, ventilation, fireproofing, and height and lot-coverage size for new buildings, resulting in significant upgrades to building quality. Advancements in the design and construction of multiple dwellings also contributed to their eventual popularity.

New Yorkers' attitude toward shared dwellings for the middle and upper classes began to change when the city's first version of an apartment house appeared in 1870. The Stuyvesant Apartments at 142 East 18th Street was built by Rutherfurd Stuyvesant and designed by the prominent Beaux Arts–trained architect Richard Morris Hunt, whose work also includes the Great Hall of the Metropolitan Museum of Art, the pedestal of the Statue of Liberty, and the 250-room Biltmore estate in Asheville, North Carolina. Hunt remodeled a series of row houses already on the site. Because the result was inspired by a popular Parisian housing style, the Stuyvesant and other early apartments were referred to as "French flats." While it praised the private home as ideal, an 1869 *New York Times* editorial begrudgingly noted that with postwar real estate values spiraling, the only realistic response was "the house built on the French apartment plan."[3]

The Stuyvesant was the first apartment building in New York City planned specifically to attract the middle class. A five-story walkup with two apartments per floor, it featured eight-room living spaces complete with high ceilings, wood-burning fireplaces, and private bathrooms. Sizeable courtyards guaranteed light and air in every room. A service stairway separated residents and their guests from servants and deliveries. The Stuyvesant was an instant success, fully rented even before completion at a not-too-shabby $120 per month. It demonstrated that apartment living could appeal "if not to the rich-rich, at least to the respectably well-to-do."[4]

Despite the positive response to the Stuyvesant, construction in New York City overall slowed as a result of the Panic of 1873. Starting in the late 1870s, however, other builders cautiously began to follow Stuyvesant's example. New middle-class apartment layouts reflected nearby row houses, using similar materials and architectural elements. Unlike tenements, flats typically included a parlor, separate dining room, and a small room for a servant. (Respectable families had at least one.) Unlike in the tenements, indoor plumbing was *not* shared with any other families.

As of 1892, according to that year's *King's Handbook*, there were notable differences in the quality and price of apartments. "You can get one as low as $300 a year, or you can pay as high as $7,000 or even more annually." Moderately priced flats—those renting for roughly $25 to $50 per month— typically offered five or six small rooms with a private hall, bathroom, kitchen range, gas chandeliers, "very fair woodwork" and wallpaper, along with steam heat and a janitor. "Above $50 a month the apartment may be of seven, eight or nine rooms, handsomely finished, and with much luxurious show in the way of tiled floors, marble wainscot in the public halls, carved over-mantels, stained glass and other fine appointments."[5]

At this point, a contemporary New Yorker might be drooling. Apartments that rented for above $50 per month stationed uniformed "hall-boys" at the entranceway, and those charging $1,000 a year included a passenger elevator among other conveniences. The West Side offered the majority of medium-priced apartments, those renting from $30 to $75 a month, as well as "several of the highest class houses of the kind."[6] When it came to private homes, meanwhile, renting a "tolerably decent" house in the heart of the city ranged from $1,000 to $2,000 annually; that increased to $3,000 and upward "if something desirable is sought."[7]

It was not until the 1880s that apartment buildings were designed to attract the wealthy, who could easily afford their own single-family homes. The Dakota led the way. Developed on Central Park West and 72nd Street at a time when the Upper West Side was still sparsely settled, the Dakota was built by Edward Cabot Clark, who pioneered apartment living in the neighborhood. It was designed by Henry J. Hardenbergh, who was also commissioned to build the Waldorf and adjoining Astoria hotels, later combined as the Waldorf-Astoria.

Clark famously named his building the Dakota after a western territory. It's generally believed that he chose to do so because, like the Dakotas, his building was so far north and west of the rest of the city. Completed in 1884, the Dakota was New York's original luxury apartment building. With its exceptional design and profusion of amenities, it was the first to showcase what apartment living could be like for those of means. Its success helped change the attitudes of the affluent toward apartment living.

Still, those with the greatest means were slower than others to abandon their private homes. That all began to change noticeably in the first decade of the twentieth century for a simple reason known to anyone who has rented an apartment or bought real estate in the city: money. With the opening of the elevated railroad and later the subway, Upper West Side land and building costs rose to a point where new single-family home construction became prohibitively expensive for speculators and potential homeowners alike. Multiple-family dwellings rather than homes for individual families promised more profit for developers and a better deal for residents.

By that point, only the mega-rich could afford to build and maintain a single-family home on Riverside Drive, and just a few continued to do so. Apartment living enabled families to maintain as high or a higher level of living for a lower cost than owning and managing their own home. For one thing, apartment dwelling as a way of life meant employing fewer servants. Building staff, for example, might manage laundry. Personal cooks also became less essential, as "residents of the finer addresses took their meals in vast and elegant central dining rooms. . . . Those who preferred to eat at home but lacked a cook could have their cleverly boxed lukewarm meals prepared by the building staff and sent up by dumbwaiter"[8]—the early version of takeout and delivery, so essential to today's New Yorkers. Luxury for less—an offer hard for New Yorkers of any era to turn down.

All of this directly affected the Riverside Drive skyline. As of 1902, more than half of the available building sites along Riverside Drive were still vacant. Yet even before those empty lots had been filled, existing mansions, built at most a decade or two before, were being demolished to make way for the more profitable multiple-residence buildings.

There was a clear hierarchy among Upper West Side avenues. Land for buildings on wide, light-filled streets offering views or near subway stations—all of which applied to Riverside Drive—was more costly than other types of property. This meant builders would have to charge higher rents to recoup their investment. To make that rent palatable, they would target the upper classes and provide them with the opportunity to live in the style they had been accustomed to in their own homes. Economics and the likely class of residents would then determine various construction and design elements, such as a building's height, number of apartments, and the size and number of rooms. They would also affect the look of lobbies and vestibules, along with exterior details and the degree of amenities.

By the first decade of the twentieth century, construction was well underway on impressive apartment houses on Riverside Drive. The first apartment building appeared

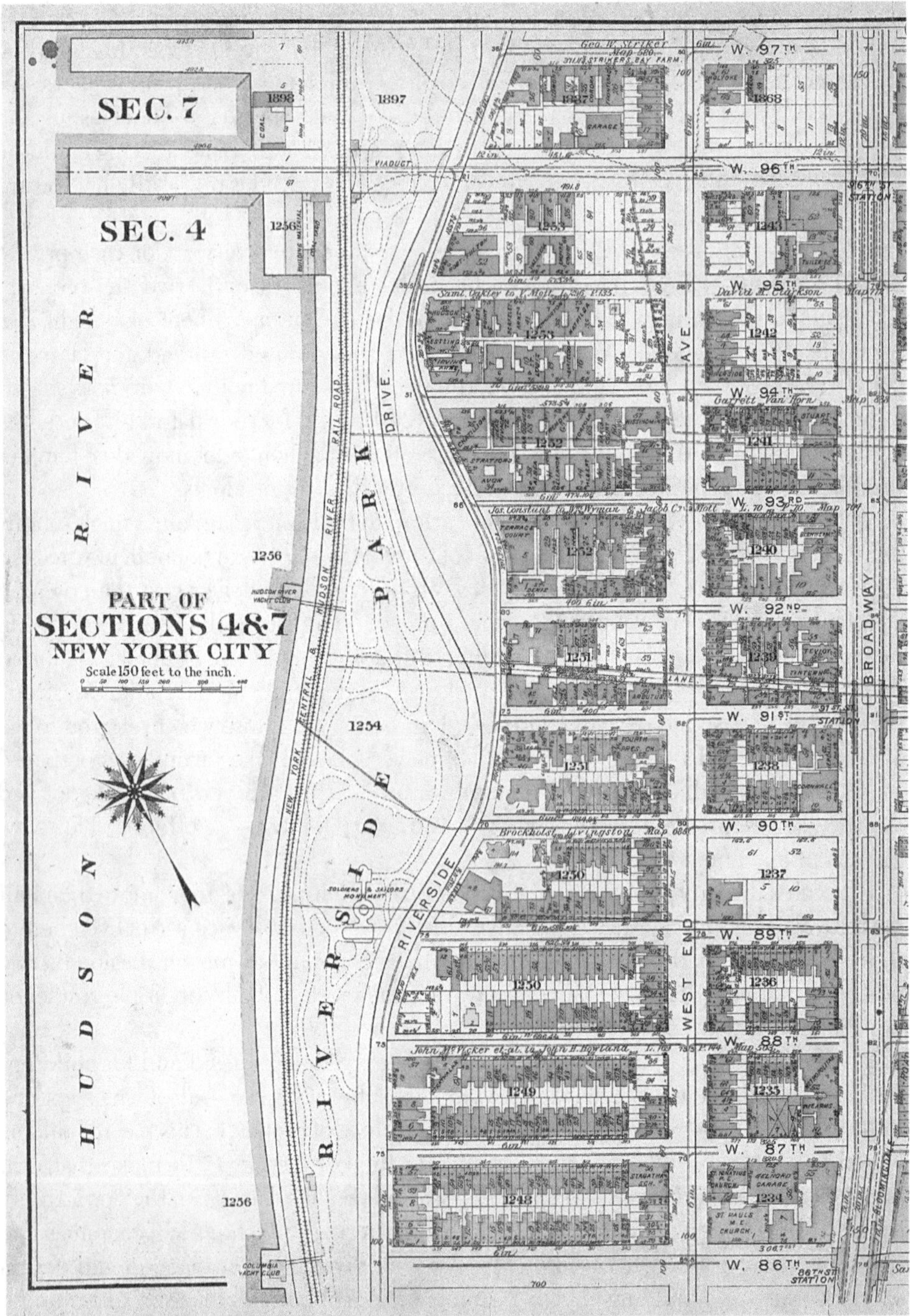

Figure 36. A 1911 map showing Riverside Drive with row houses, freestanding villas, and the earliest apartment buildings, including the long-gone Robert Fulton on the northeast corner of 95th Street. *Source*: Courtesy The New York Public Library.

on Riverside Drive and 83rd Street in 1895, since replaced by the full-block 110 Riverside Drive. The 80s and 90s were popular locations for the earliest apartment houses. One-Twenty-Seven Riverside Drive was built in 1896 on the southeast corner of 85th Street. One block south, on the northeast corner of 84th Street, 120 Riverside Drive opened in 1900.[9]

One-Ninety-Four Riverside Drive arose in 1902 on the southeast corner of 92nd Street, and the Chatillion, 214 Riverside, appeared that same year on the southeast corner of 94th Street. Midway between 94th and 95th Streets was the Estling, at 224 Riverside Drive, built in 1901. Avalon Hall, formerly the Hudson, was located next door at 227 Riverside Drive, on the southeast corner of 95th Street. It was completed in 1898, with a slight curve to conform to the Drive. By 1900, nineteen families were in residence. All of these buildings remain on the Drive today. Farther uptown, the Columbia Court, 431 Riverside Drive on the northeast corner of 115th Street, was built in 1902. It is now Columbia University's Woodbridge Hall dorm.

The earliest apartment buildings on Riverside Drive—those built in the very late 1800s or the first years of the twentieth century—were typically seven to nine stories. From then until about 1917, new buildings generally ran seven to twelve stories high. Afterward until the late 1920s, twelve-, fifteen-, or sixteen-story buildings most often arose across from the park. It was not until the end of the 1920s and into the 1930s that residences grew even taller.

By the end of 1910, Riverside Drive had twenty-seven apartment buildings. A year later, apartment houses on the Drive north of 95th Street alone included the Robert Fulton, Rhineland Court, Victoria, Peter Stuyvesant, Chesterfield, Clifden, Glencairn, and Gwendolyn. All remain today except the Robert Fulton, once on the northeast corner of 95th Street and replaced in 1931 by 230 Riverside Drive. The nine- to twelve-story residences between 116th and 119th Streets were all erected in just five years, from 1907 to 1911. They span a single block, without cross streets, on Riverside Drive.

Around World War I, apartment hotels also began to appear. Considered commercial buildings, their height and lot coverage were not regulated, and because individual kitchens were not allowed, fireproofing requirements were less stringent. Both factors made them an attractive option to developers. Some buildings provided amenities such as sinks, refrigerators, and outlets for hot plates and burners. Suites of rooms were typically offered for long-term leases and came with complete hotel services.

After the war, Upper West Side developers more aggressively acquired existing row houses and smaller apartment buildings to assemble sites for more lucrative apartment house construction. Riverside Drive was particularly vulnerable to this trend.

Unlike apartments for the middle class, twentieth-century spaces for the affluent offered more, and more spacious, rooms, with the amenities of private home ownership—and often, innumerable other advantages. For upper-class buildings, the appearance of the vestibule and lobby were important. Classical, Renaissance, or Gothic styles inspired much of the detail. Lobbies might include glossy marble floors or tiles in intricate patterns, marble or marble and plaster walls, and ceilings embellished with

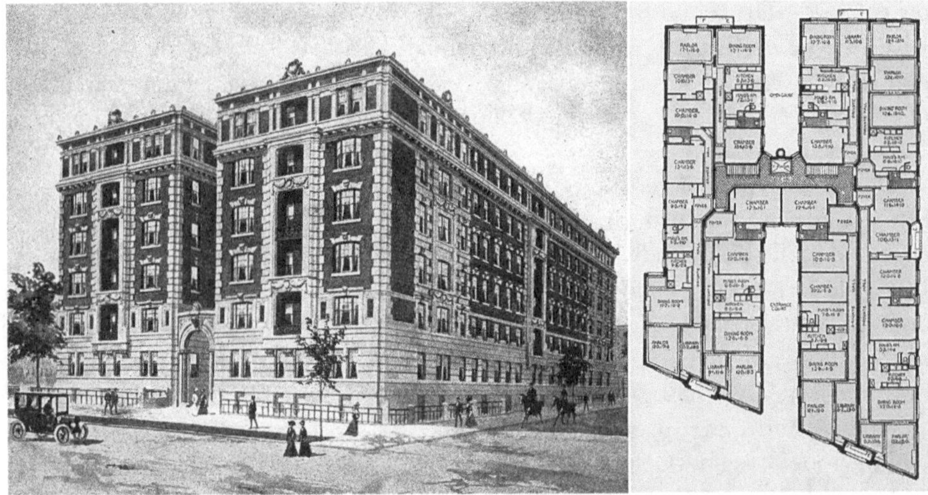

Figure 37. The Robert Fulton, shown with floor plan, was replaced by 230 Riverside Drive. *Source*: Courtesy The New York Public Library.

ornate plasterwork. Stained-glass windows, skylights, and fireplaces, along with furniture and rugs, often enhanced the public areas.

Individual apartments for the affluent could have up to twenty rooms, although eight to twelve rooms were the norm for larger families; smaller apartments were also available. Some of the larger homes were duplexes or filled entire floors. Public rooms such as the living room, parlor, dining room, or library would be the largest and best situated, with windows overlooking the street. The public rooms typically would be separated from bedrooms, bathrooms, and the service spaces, such as the kitchen, pantry, and servants' rooms. Interiors often featured a full forest of woods—hardwood and parquet floors, dining rooms with mahogany-beamed ceilings and wainscoting, parlors and libraries bedecked in quartered oak.

Select Riverside Drive luxury buildings might feature billiard rooms, barbershops, hair salons, and wine cellars, along with water-filtration systems, central vacuum cleaning, and central refrigeration. Others appealed with long-distance telephone service in each apartment, mail chutes, gas ranges, wall safes, laundry facilities, basements with private storage, and separate elevators for residents and staff. Dumbwaiters, "porcelain lined refrigerators,"[10] and linen closets were also popular offerings on Riverside Drive in the first decades of the twentieth century. Staff in apartment buildings for the wealthy might include switchboard operators, uniformed doormen, elevator operators, and hall attendants.

Typical rentals for this bounty of amenities? In 1908, 125 Riverside Drive, on the corner of 84th Street, required an expenditure of $2,000–$3,600—*per year.* The St. Denis, 200 Riverside Drive at 92nd Street, offered apartments with nine or ten rooms and three baths for an annual rent of $1,600–$2,800. At 155 Riverside Drive on the corner of 88th Street, nine rooms with three baths and thirteen closets were going for $4,500. Meanwhile, at the Stratford Avon, 210 Riverside Drive on the corner of 93rd Street, ten rooms were available for the comparatively exorbitant rent of up to $5,000 per annum.

Early ads for apartments on the avenue frequently announced that they were "absolutely fireproof"[11]—apparently a big selling point in that era—while also highlighting views of park, river, and Palisades; proximity to subway stations; and "freedom from noise and traffic."[12] Most of those features would be just as alluring today. Later ads, such as one for 370 Riverside Drive, pointed out that their buildings offered "fine type tenants."[13]

As if this scope of design and amenities weren't persuasive enough, developers took to naming upscale buildings to make them even more appealing to potential residents. Tenements and middle-class apartment buildings had no names, only addresses. Many apartment buildings built for those with higher incomes bore British, French, Spanish, Italian, German, or Scottish names. Some preferred naming their buildings after Native American tribes. State names were also popular.

Once the benefits of apartment living became apparent, the city's elite traded in their lovely but time- and money-gobbling private homes and moved up to the day's version of the high-rise. By the early 1890s, apartment living had become "popular and to a certain extent fashionable. Even society countenances it, and a brownstone front is no longer indispensable to at least moderate social standing. And as for wealthy folk who are not in society, they are taking more and more to apartments."[14] In fact, "By the turn of the century, the mansion had become an albatross, not just expensive but primitive" compared with the "technological wonderland" of its apartment house successors.[15] "The West Side, it suddenly seemed, was becoming a mecca for those who revered apartment living and were choosing a social life independent of the rules and rituals of the Four Hundred. . . . West Side apartment living might not be really fashionable, but was becoming, to use a term that was then coming into use, 'smart.'"[16]

Styles along the Drive in the early decades of the twentieth century ranged from Renaissance Revival to Beaux Arts to Arts and Crafts. Some of the most prominent architects of the day were responsible for sculpting the avenue's face, among them Schwartz & Gross, Rouse & Goldstone, Neville & Bagge, George F. Pelham, and Gaetan Ajello. Following Olmsted's lead in creating a park that followed a serpentine progression of cliffs, several apartment buildings curved or angled to accommodate the landscape, most notably the Paterno and Colosseum, on opposite corners of 116th Street.

In the first two decades of the twentieth century, a panorama of the Riverside Drive skyline traveled from the valleys of row houses and a few death-defying villas to the peaks of apartment buildings, and back down again, until by the 1920s the apartment building had become the norm across Manhattan and on Riverside Drive itself. In 1922 alone, there was a flurry of apartment house activity within a few short blocks in the 100s. This included nine-story and fourteen-story apartment buildings that replaced the old Foster mansion and its related structures at 102nd Street. Another fourteen-story apartment building rose where the Bayne mansion once stood at 108th

Figure 38. Aerial view (date unknown) of the Schwab mansion surrounded by new and much taller apartment buildings. *Source*: George Grantham Bain Collection, Library of Congress.

Street, and two more of that size appeared on the southeast corner of 110th Street (including our first home on the Drive) and the adjoining corner of 109th Street, respectively.

In the 1920s and 1930s, the Drive's luxury apartment houses continued to attract the prosperous, many of them East European Jewish merchants who began moving into the Upper West Side once the subway expansion connected the area to the city's Garment District, where many worked. For years, Riverside Drive was the place to be for the upper middle class, an attractive and peaceful oasis far from Midtown. Unfortunately, time, legislation, and the economy eventually began to drag the forward movement of the Drive's luxurious apartment housing.

In 1919, the Tenement House Act was amended to permit the conversion of single-family row houses into multiple-family residences. Beginning in the 1920s, escalating by the 1930s, and continuing into the 1940s, landlords subdivided many of the neighborhood's most spacious apartments into smaller and more affordable units, significantly increasing the number of apartments per floor. In 1939, the twelve-story Wendolyn at 276 Riverside Drive, on the southern corner of 100th Street, divided thirty-six large apartments into ninety-five apartments of two to four rooms.

Some apartment buildings became single-room-occupancy residences (SROs), where individuals of modest means could rent private rooms with shared baths and communal cooking facilities. Many of the charming row houses were remodeled into apartments or operated as boarding houses. As a result, "a twenty-dollar-a-week clerk may rent a small room and write the folks back home that he is living on the Drive."[17] In the years following World War II, many of the middle class in New York City left for the suburbs. A number of buildings, including several on Riverside Drive, were converted into inexpensive hotels.

Any new construction in those middle decades was simpler in style than it had been in the past, with fewer rooms, lower ceilings, and distinctly less drama in detail and design. In part because most Riverside Drive blocks south of 129th Street are now protected through historic districts, postwar buildings are relatively rare.

My current Riverside Drive apartment, a few blocks north of where we first lived on the Drive, had been split in two during the 1950s—a timeline revealed when we discovered a newspaper page from that decade crammed behind a living room wall sconce. In the process, a former bedroom had been turned into a kitchen, tall double doors had been removed, and wainscoting had been completely stripped from the dining room walls. Before being able to put the two halves of the apartment back together, we spent months traversing a hole we slammed in the wall so that we could access the original kitchen without going out into the hallway. Also by the 1950s, the striped awnings that had protected many of our building's windows were missing, as were its sizeable four-globe entrance lamps. Various interior architectural features had been torn out and trashed. Balconies that still existed on some of the building's fifth-floor apartments were later removed.

Nevertheless, legislation in the 1950s set the stage for improvement. The twelve-year exemption from real estate taxes offered by the 1955 J-51 tax exemption and abatement law prompted some owners of properties such as boarding houses and SROs to begin converting them into "Class A" apartments, attracting young professionals.

In 1979, tragedy struck when masonry falling from a building at 601 West 115th Street on the corner of Broadway, just one block east of Riverside Drive, killed a Barnard College student. As a result, Local Law 10 was passed the following year (strengthened in 1998 with Local Law 11), requiring façade inspections every four years. This produced a frenzy of façade stripping, especially cornice removal, that affected many prewar buildings.[18] Our own cornice was pulled down in the late 1980s when the building became a cooperative.

With all of these changes, and despite the prewar palaces that still graced its curves, in the twentieth century Riverside Drive and its once paradisiacal front lawn, Riverside Park, saw a steep and sad decline, one that would last for decades.

Chapter 10

Downhill Racing

Moses to the Rescue

EVEN AS LUXURY apartment houses enjoyed a sudden and swift rise on Riverside Drive during the first few decades of the twentieth century, Riverside Park—that once sublime urban oasis—was in a disheartening state of decline. The main causes? The railroad's ever increasing dominance of the park and a general neglect of what made this western greensward special.

From the early days of Riverside Park and Riverside Drive, the railroad had affronted the senses of those who lived on the avenue and those who, as a result, determined never to do so. Today, a passing train's low whistle from within the tunnel, followed by a deep, guttural chug, is a soothing sound. But back then, the endless clattering of wheels over open-air tracks grated on the nerves. All the while, passing steam engines spewed smoke upward to the Drive and its residents, accompanied by the scents of the livestock being transported and the garbage dumps lining the tracks. Summer, when windows were thrown open for cool breezes from the river, presented a particular challenge to residents' olfactory glands.

During the Depression of the 1930s, the dispossessed had once again set up living quarters alongside the tracks and river. As of April 1934, there were fifty-two "veterans' shacks"[1] within the seven blocks between 72nd and 79th Streets and eighty-three other shacks along Riverside Drive on the Hudson River.

At the same time, the railroad continued to block access to the waterfront except for commercial purposes, separating the citizenry from the river with barbed-wire fences. Despite its vital role in commerce, the railroad increasingly came to be viewed as a nuisance rather than an essential and inevitable part of the park.

South of the park, where train cars were at the same level as pedestrians and carriages, there was a different issue. To prevent accidents, the New York Central Railroad hired "West Side cowboys," men who rode horses and waved flags in front of the freight trains on Eleventh Avenue to alert the public. But because New Yorkers have never been known for their patience, Eleventh Avenue was also unfortunately known as Death Avenue, from the high number of collisions there. In 1910, one organization estimated that there had been 548 deaths and 1,574 injuries over the years along that road.

There were multiple efforts from the 1870s on, by community organizations and the city alike, to force the railroad to clean up its act. Finally, to the delight of many, in 1913 the New York State Legislature pressured the railroad into developing a plan to enclose the tracks in a tunnel that could support a park or an esplanade from West 72nd Street to West 123rd Street.

Still, it was not until more than a decade later, in 1924, that change began to happen. That year saw the passage of the Kaufman Act, mandating that all trains in New York City run on electric power rather than steam. Electric-powered trains were not possible at grade level, primarily for safety reasons.

Around that time, meanwhile, the automobile began to dominate as a form of transportation. One-third of New York City residents had cars. Traffic choked the city's streets, and there was interest among officials in creating a highway along the western end of Manhattan to decrease congestion and provide a rapid route to and from the city, as well as an opportunity for scenic pleasure driving.

Also in 1924, Charles L. Craig, the city's comptroller, proposed a plan for a parkway near the Hudson to alleviate traffic on local streets. The idea was to use landfill to extend the park past the railroad tracks and include an esplanade along the waterfront as well as a roadway on top of an enclosed railway. The project also would involve landscaping the new land, restoring the existing park, and providing playgrounds and athletic facilities.

Craig's plan was the first of four recommendations for Riverside Park's reconstruction proposed in the 1920s alone—not a single one of which was implemented that decade. One problem was that while there was overall support for a parkway, there was little consensus on where exactly it should go. Some, like Craig, suggested building the parkway above the proposed railroad tunnel, which would have brought the sounds of passing cars much closer to the residents of Riverside Drive than they are now. Others preferred converting the top of the tunnel into parkland and building a waterfront parkway instead.

Various civic organizations weighed in over time. The City Club endorsed building the parkway on the waterfront, to give more space to recreational uses. At the time, however, the waterfront parkway proposal had little support, and the Board of Estimate voted it down. The Women's League for the Protection of Riverside Park opposed building the parkway within the park. Leaflets announcing a meeting organized by the league encouraged New Yorkers to "Save Riverside Park! It Belongs to All" and "Parents! Save Riverside Park for Your Children."

Finally, by 1927, the city and New York Central agreed to share the cost of covering the tracks and building what would become the original, elevated West Side Highway to 72nd Street.[2] In June 1929, the city approved a plan that would build the parkway

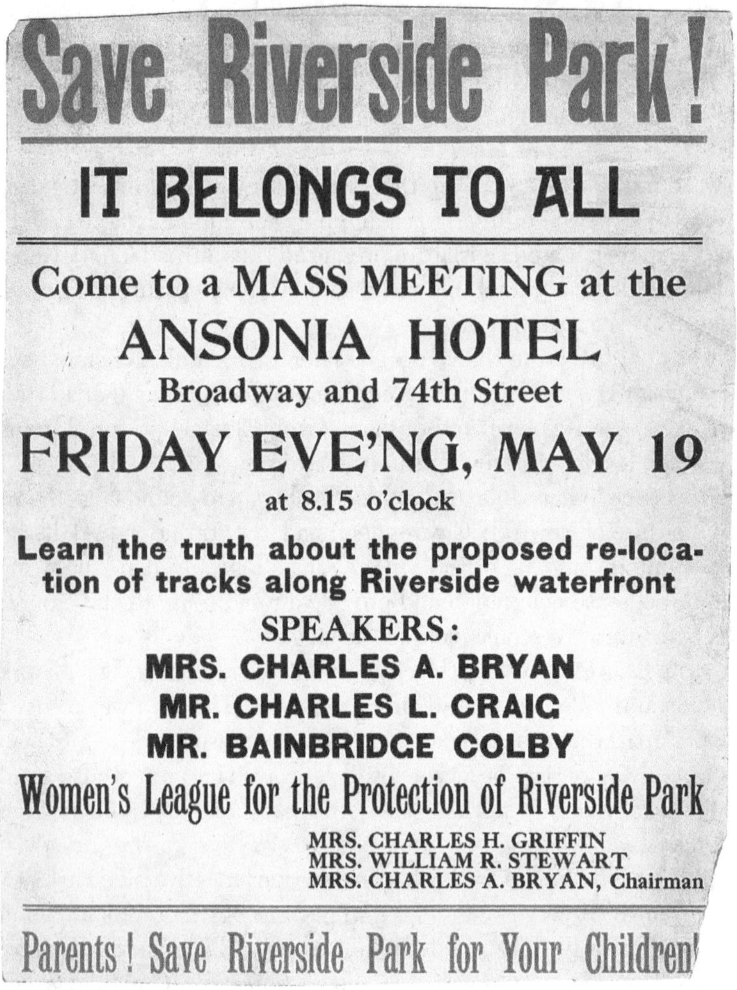

Save Riverside Park!

IT BELONGS TO ALL

Come to a MASS MEETING at the

ANSONIA HOTEL

Broadway and 74th Street

FRIDAY EVE'NG, MAY 19

at 8.15 o'clock

Learn the truth about the proposed re-location of tracks along Riverside waterfront

SPEAKERS:

MRS. CHARLES A. BRYAN

MR. CHARLES L. CRAIG

MR. BAINBRIDGE COLBY

Women's League for the Protection of Riverside Park

MRS. CHARLES H. GRIFFIN
MRS. WILLIAM R. STEWART
MRS. CHARLES A. BRYAN, Chairman

Parents! Save Riverside Park for Your Children!

Figure 39. A broadside published by the Women's League for the Protection of Riverside Park. *Source*: Collection of the New-York Historical Society.

above the tracks, not on the waterfront. All was, at last, good to go. Just four months later, in October of that year, the stock market crashed, and plans for railroad tunnel and highway alike were stopped in their tracks.

While all of this was happening—or rather, not happening—Riverside Park itself was suffering from neglect. Water had destroyed some of the existing landfill, forming massive puddles in various spots where it had seeped through.[3] Mud was everywhere, sucking at the heels of those in search of a stroll. Between the railroads and the rain, Riverside Park was a mess.

Then came Robert Moses. Brilliant. Impatient. Ruthless. Arrogant. Powerful and politically savvy. A believer that his way was the only way. Moses was a man who knew what changes he wanted to make in New York City and made sure that no one and nothing—from mayors to money—stood in his way. Riverside Park was among the long list of projects for which, over time, Moses was to receive a surfeit of both credit and blame as the city's master builder.

As a child, I knew of Robert Moses from Jones Beach, the go-to escape of friends and family and, it turns out, Moses's first successful experience creating a public park. He was also responsible for Astoria Pool in Queens, where my protective mother had a habit of testing the cleanliness of the water with a plastic kit before she would allow me to swim.

Moses was born in 1888, eight years after Frederick Law Olmsted's version of Riverside Park opened, and he lived on the Upper West Side much of his life. As a young man, he often visited Riverside Drive, looking out over the park from the high bluffs. In his book *The Power Broker*, Robert Caro writes that what Moses saw in Riverside Park then was "a wasteland . . . nothing but a vast low-lying mass of dirt and mud."[4] Caro shares a memorable tale about Moses and Riverside Park:

> One Sunday in 1914, he was crossing the Hudson by ferry to picnic in New Jersey. With him were some college friends and their dates, one of whom was Frances Perkins, later to be United States Secretary of Labor. As the ferry pulled out into the river, Moses leaned on the rail, watching Manhattan spread out behind the boat. Miss Perkins happened to be standing beside him and suddenly she heard Moses exclaim, "Isn't this a temptation to you? Couldn't this waterfront be the most beautiful thing in the world?"[5]

He described his vision of what it could be like: "The ugly tracks hidden by the great highway, cars traveling slowly along it, their occupants enjoying the view and along the highway, stretching green parks filled with strollers, tennis players and families on bicycles. There would be sailboats on the river and motor yachts tied up at gracefully curving basins." As Moses continued, Perkins realized, according to Caro, that "the young Bureau staffer beside her was talking about a public improvement on a scale almost without precedent in turn of the century urban America, an improvement that would solve a problem that had baffled successive city administrations for years." At the age of twenty-five and years away from a position of power and influence, when it came to Riverside Park, she added, "he had it all figured out."[6]

By the early 1930s, however, Moses had the position and power to realize his vision—and it took him just three years to do so in full. In 1934, two decades after sharing his concept for Riverside Park on the ferry ride across the Hudson, Moses, then park commissioner, introduced his West Side Improvement Plan. This enormous undertaking involved covering over the New York Central railroad tracks and transforming Riverside Park.

And that wasn't all. It also included completing the West Side Elevated Highway, begun in 1927 but then abandoned, constructing the new Henry Hudson Parkway, which would run for 11.2 miles from West 72nd Street to the city limits in the Bronx, and then connecting the highway to the parkway at 72nd Street. According to Moses, if the Henry Hudson Parkway was built properly and a great park created alongside it, New Yorkers would not have to leave town to find beauty. "They would be able to drive along the water, the river stretching to one side of them, the green of the park to the other, above the park the spires of Manhattan. It would be a public improvement unequaled in the world!"[7]

The projected cost of the West Side Improvement Plan as submitted to the New York City Board of Estimate was $11 million. Six million of that would go toward the railroad tunnel alone. Accumulating the required city, state, and federal funds in the midst of the Depression—an unholy time, when skyscrapers had been left unfinished and men lined up at soup kitchens—required exceptional skill, along with, often enough, a strenuous bending or even breaking of the rules. Moses marshaled millions of dollars by patching together appeals to an extraordinarily diverse array of organizations. Financial support also came from New York Central and an assessment on property owners.

One source of money was the Grade Crossing Elimination Fund, intended to support infrastructure improvement, including the elimination of places where train tracks crossed roads. It traditionally had been used to lift a highway over tracks at a single point. Moses presented the fund with plans for his "Seventy-Ninth Street Grade Elimination Structure." In reality, however, there was no intent to raise a highway over the tracks around 79th Street; the money was actually for Riverside Park's new boat basin, which stood more than two hundred feet away from the rail line. Moses got the money.

Before Moses's involvement, the celebrated architectural firm of McKim, Mead & White had been asked to prepare plans for covering the railroad. A section of this design from 72nd to 79th Streets was already under construction when Moses became park commissioner and quickly discarded the architects' plans. Instead, he commissioned the landscape architects Gilmore D. Clarke and Michael Rapuano and the architectural engineer Clifton Lloyd to develop the West Side Improvement Plan.

To accommodate Riverside Park's new design, nearly four million cubic yards of landfill, much of it from subway excavations, extended the shoreline an average of 250 feet along the entire expanse of the park to 125th Street. Five hundred truckloads of dirt and rock fill were delivered to the area daily. Six thousand WPA workers took part in the West Side improvement effort. It was on this landfill that Moses built the Henry Hudson Parkway, along the waterfront. Here, "access and exit ramps descend into the landscape behind berms that damp road noise. The road crosses gently arched, stone-faced overpasses that look as if they had grown out of the park contours."[8] The road provided views to the river and into the park for travelers.

The architectural focal point of the Moses expansion was the multipurpose Rotunda at 79th Street, which featured a traffic circle providing an easy entrance to and exit from the Henry Hudson Parkway. Most importantly, thanks to the sunken circular plaza that led to the water, it granted New Yorkers their long-awaited access to the river—beyond the few existing narrow footbridges that led to the yacht clubs along the shore—with no need to risk life and limb crossing traffic. In fact, "By extending

Figure 40. Robert Moses (inset) with a view of the Rotunda and Henry Hudson Parkway, under construction. *Source*: Moses photo: Library of Congress, Prints & Photographs Division; Construction photo: NYC Parks Photo Archive.

the park outward from the line of the railroad to the river, Manhattan will have opened one of the few places along its thirty-mile river-girt rim where the waterfront is accessible to the public."[9] The structure's lower levels hosted a fountain and a restaurant with an arcaded terrace overlooking a marina that was designed to be "the City's front door for visiting yachts and marine dignitaries."[10] There, in 1938, small boats could dock for a monthly rate of $25.

As for the railroad, Moses encased it in a tunnel under the park from 72nd to 123rd Streets, eliminating street-level railroad crossings. The structure was later called the Freedom Tunnel, not because it served any grand and noble democratic purpose but rather after Chris "Freedom" Pape, a graffiti artist who decorated the tunnel walls during the 1980s and 1990s. The tunnel was used for freight trains until 1980, then closed until 1991, when Amtrak took ownership. It now serves to transport Amtrak passengers in and out of Penn Station.

The top of the tunnel was then allocated to parkland. It's here where landscape architect Rapuano's background came into play. At the time, he was in charge of landscape design in Gilmore Clarke's office at the Westchester County Park Commission, designing parks and parkways. Rapuano had studied the design of estates with European garden and villa inspirations and toured the villas and gardens of Italy, Spain, and France. Under his guidance, changes included filling in the park to the east of the train tunnel to raise the grades to the height of the new railroad roof; flattening sharp slopes; and removing many of the original stairways, paths, and plantings. The new paths were designed with a "French curve" template on paper in the architects' offices rather than laid out on site with existing natural features and views in mind.

Figure 41. Graffiti in the Freedom Tunnel. *Source*: Robert F. Rodriguez.

Figure 42. The Riverside Park promenade covers part of the railroad tunnel. *Source*: Robert F. Rodriguez.

Masses and allées of trees, including *Robinia* and London plane, highlighted the new plantings. Fast-growing shrubs and groundcovers were gathered together in large sections of two to four different types rather than in the more diverse groupings the park's originators preferred. Wooded areas, meanwhile, were planted with a broad variety of trees and shrubs in irregular masses, the indistinct woodland edges showing "much more variety in shade, shadow and texture than would have been natural."[11] These areas also included the oldest trees in the park, some dating from before the park itself. Overall, the park shifted from a pastoral landscape to a more "sculpted" one. The difference is particularly apparent in the park between West 72nd and West 79th Streets.

Because of the promethean changes made during the Moses era to accommodate tunnel and parkway, the interior of the park, for the most part, was no longer the vision of Olmsted or the work of the landscape architects that immediately followed him. It is the topography nearest the retaining wall—with its winding paths, rock outcroppings, and naturalistic appearance—that was least affected by 1930s developments and today best reflects the park as it once was.

Yet, for park goers, the most significant difference between Olmsted's Riverside Park and the one we know in the twenty-first century is not how it was planted but rather where this nineteenth-century plot of Paradise ended—at the railroad tracks. Furthermore, the Moses park focused on recreation, while the original did not. The 1930s design created a profusion of playgrounds and sports facilities, including basketball, tennis, handball and volleyball courts, ball fields, and more. They lie on the roof of the tunnel or, more often, on the landfill between the tunnel and the parkway. Thanks to Rapuano, they are fully integrated into the new topography "with terraces and structures reminiscent of Renaissance villas,"[12] including grand arched openings.

Given all these changes, it is the master design of Park and Drive together for which Olmsted deserves the greatest recognition today. The sinuous Drive adapted to the topography's shifting contours, the islands separating the main and ancillary roadways, and the retaining wall best represent Olmsted's lasting impact on Riverside Park and Riverside Drive, when compared to developments in the Moses era.

Under Moses, it took just three years, from 1934 to 1937, for the entire West Side Improvement Plan to be implemented. Landfill added 132 acres to Riverside Park along the Hudson's shores, nearly doubling its size. About 140,000 linear feet of footpaths were introduced. There was a manmade promenade within the park for the first time, over the tracks enclosed by the tunnel. All of this—covered tracks, playgrounds and recreational facilities, additional park space—was in addition to the marina, Rotunda, and, of course, the completed West Side Highway and new Henry Hudson Parkway. On Riverside Drive itself, the project added thousands of new trees and shrubs, restored lawns and installed hundreds of new benches.

"When work was finished," noted one observer, "Riverside Park was once again one of the most elegant parks in the city"[13] and Riverside Drive, noted another, "one of the most beautiful metropolitan parkways in the world."[14] The "new" Riverside

Figure 43. A 1937 view of Moses's just-completed Riverside Park, showing the railroad yard to the south of 72nd Street. *Source*: NYC Parks Photo Archive.

Park, along with most of the plan's other improvements, officially opened to the public on October 12, 1937.

Commenting on the West Side Improvement Plan's results, Moses sounded in some ways like the park's early proponents who spoke of its future in grandiose terms. "Dozens of cars zoom or crawl through Riverside Park and down the West Side Highway and view the matchless, unspoiled Palisades. By comparison, the castled Rhine is a mere trickle between vine-clad slopes."[15]

Moses maintained power in New York for over four decades, through five mayors and six governors. Before Moses, New York State had a limited amount of parkland; afterward, under Moses, it had 2,567,256 acres. He was responsible for 658 playgrounds in New York City, 416 miles of parkways, and thirteen bridges.

Still, there were those who were not entirely impressed by Moses's achievements. The bulk of his Riverside Park improvements occurred below 129th Street, where landfill expanded the park and a tunnel topped the tracks. Between there and the park's terminus on 155th Street, a neighborhood that over time housed a largely African American and Hispanic community, things were different. No acreage was added, the tracks remained visible in an open cut, and the highway was supported on an elevated platform rather than on landfill along the water. There was little in the way of playgrounds or recreational facilities. Access to the park by foot was limited.

Furthermore, despite Moses's early love of and vision for Riverside Park and his promotion of parks throughout his career, there are those who say his real interest was in the parkway: that the "new" Riverside Park was not built for the people as a whole but rather for the drivers who would speed their way through it. With the parkway situated along the river, it was drivers and passengers—rather than pedestrians—who enjoyed the full benefit of the panoramic view.

For better or worse—and I'll venture that for the children and parents along Riverside Drive, for better—Moses expanded Olmsted's vision of a park dedicated to the enjoyment of nature and charming views to one that also became a center of recreation, the Riverside Park, for the most part, that we know today.

Certain other Moses projects may raise more questions. On the Upper West Side alone, Moses evicted seven thousand low-income, African American and Puerto Rican families from the San Juan Hill community (where the original *West Side Story* was filmed) in the West 60s to build Lincoln Center. He substituted those seven thousand apartments with 4,400 new ones, all except four hundred of them luxury apartments. Also on the Upper West Side, Moses replaced the housing of more than three thousand other low-income families, predominantly people of color, with Park West Village, between 98th and 99th Streets, from Columbus Avenue to Central Park West. Caro estimates that Moses displaced tens of thousands of people in all, most of them poor minorities, for urban renewal and various other endeavors—and 250,000 for highway construction alone.

In the process of rebuilding Riverside Park, Moses dispensed—summarily—with one of its more long-standing shoreline residents: the old Columbia Yacht Club. Moses declared that the club was in the way of his improvement plan and had no rightful claim to the location it had occupied at the foot of 86th Street since 1874. In March 1934, he announced that it would be torn down, immediately—despite the fact that the improvement plan was in its early stages and there was no urgent need for that small parcel of land.

Understanding that the Park belonged to the city, the club members simply asked to remain in the clubhouse until September, given the club's prior commitments. Moses said he would allow the club to do so only if it donated its clubhouse and marina to the Park Department. The club commodore agreed in mid-April, indicating that he wanted only enough time to submit the proposition to the entire membership, which he expected would approve it.

The very next day, however, Moses ordered the club to vacate its site by May 1—a mere twelve days hence, positioning the issue to the media as one of private interests versus the public. A judge issued a temporary injunction against ousting the club so quickly, but before he could do so, steam shovels began destroying the area around the clubhouse, and its electricity was suddenly shut off. The club officials, under attack, agreed to leave as soon as they could remove their property. By summer, the clubhouse was gone.

It's not clear what the West Side Improvement Plan actually cost. Moses chopped his own estimate of as high as $109 million down to an official $24 million in the press releases he issued at the project's completion. The *New York Times* estimated it at more than $150 million. *The Power Broker* contends that the real amount has never been revealed and calculated it to be as much as $218 million in 1930s dollars. By comparison, the Hoover Dam, completed in 1935, cost a mere $49 million.

The West Side Improvement "constitutes one of the greatest public projects ever undertaken in any city. Riverside Drive, now that through traffic passes along the parkway at the river's edge, is an elongated park and drive surpassed by few similar developments anywhere."[16] Riverside Park "remains a model of thoughtful urban planning."[17] For many years, Riverside Park upheld Moses's vision, neither needing nor seeing further improvement. It was not until some decades later that Riverside Park and Riverside Drive would undergo yet another major change, this time not for the better.

Chapter 11

Decline and Fall

Gritty City

Ford to City: Drop Dead

—*New York Daily News* headline, 1975

FOR NEARLY HALF a century after the West Side Improvement Plan was completed in 1937, few changes were made to Riverside Park. Over the next several years, locals delighted in the reborn, fresh-faced park space and the opportunity to add the pleasures of recreation to leisurely strolls and impressive monuments. Combined with the ever-inspiring views, there was no other park like Riverside Park and no other residential location as fortunate as Riverside Drive anywhere in New York City. The euphoria would be short lived.

Understandably, the only upgrade to the park in the wartime 1940s was a memorial grove planted in 1946 near Grant's Tomb. Starting in the 1940s and lasting until the 1980s, the Upper West Side and New York City as a whole saw a number of changes that influenced every aspect of life, including the continued development of Riverside Park and Riverside Drive.

The population of the West Side began a major shift. Previously, the area had been primarily a white middle- and upper-middle-class stronghold, a mix of largely Protestant native-born residents and European immigrants, especially Italians, Irish Catholics, and Eastern European Jews. In the 1940s and 1950s the area saw an influx of African Americans, Russians, Dominicans, Puerto Ricans, Haitians, and Ukrainians, and in the 1950s and 1960s, Cubans, Dominicans, and Puerto Ricans, along with new waves of Eastern European Jews.

In the 1950s, landlords across the Upper West Side expanded the use of an earlier law intended to alleviate a housing shortage by making it profitable to break up large apartments and turn row houses into rooming houses. It was also in the 1950s that the city began its policy of major urban renewal, implementing "slum clearance" to make way for developments such as Moses's Lincoln Center, considered by many to be the first step in the revival of the Upper West Side.

Developers responsible for demolishing the worst housing as part of urban renewal,[1] and then rebuilding, instead often continued to demand rent from current residents, while not providing maintenance or basic services. When those residents moved out as a result, the city began filling furnished rooms and deteriorating hotels with people in need of social services—petty criminals and the mentally ill among them—without providing those services. "High crime rates, poor schools, indifferent bureaucrats, corruption and graft—all of the classic characteristics of urban disaster—were visiting the Upper West Side in the '50s,"[2] according to a 1969 *New York Magazine* article.

Other news stories from the era tell of beer cans thrown into Riverside Park playgrounds, "vagrants," and a mother and child nearly hit by a boulder pushed from the heights above the park. In June 1955, two hundred teen gang members descended on Riverside Drive for a turf battle over the Park, armed with bayonets and iron pipes along with dozens of other weapons. The only positive change to Riverside Park in the 1950s was the installation of a new playground at 76th Street. Riverside Park's own New York City Police Department precinct was abolished in 1954.

The 1960s saw a rise in low- and middle-income housing developments. Buildings that had served as rooming houses were renovated to appeal to middle-class tenants. Writers and artists, among others, found a place here, along with young families. According to *New York* magazine, "The same kind of young, successful and relatively affluent middle-class families that moved to the suburbs 20 years ago and to the East Side 10 years ago are moving to the West Side today."[3] This was partly thanks to better housing values but also to a good transportation system and an abundance of park space. At the time, families could rent an apartment on Riverside Drive with three bedrooms, a dining room, and maid's room for $300 per month.

In the Swinging Sixties, Riverside Park's 103rd Street playground was cleaned up, its smashed windows replaced and restrooms repaired. Storage space for toys was increased and playground equipment added. A "recreation leader" was assigned for older children, a Health Department representative was available to counsel mothers, and the Parks Department staff was greatly reinforced. A comfort station and recreation building supplemented the playground at 91st Street, and tennis courts and a comfort station were built at 119th Street and tennis courts at 97th Street. Unfortunately, "none of these additions besides the tennis court at West 97th Street attempted to advance the 1937 plan for the Park through the use of the established palette of materials or landscaping concepts. They were built of brick and concrete block, in areas designed for scenic enjoyment."[4]

Meanwhile, New York hosted the 1964–1965 World's Fair and completed the world's longest suspension bridge, the Verrazano-Narrows (yet another Moses project).[5] New Yorkers met the Mets for the first time, and half a million strong celebrated at the

Woodstock Music and Arts Festival upstate. John V. Lindsay became mayor. New Yorkers began renovating brownstones around the city.

But all was not rosy. During that same decade, New York was pummeled by a transit strike that shut down the city, a seven-month teacher strike, a sanitation strike, racial tension, the Stonewall riots, and a mammoth blizzard. Nationally, the Vietnam War raged on. Life in the metropolis plunged to its nadir in the 1970s, a dark and dangerous decade best remembered among locals for the city's fiscal crisis and the crime that accompanied it. From 1960 to 1970, New York's homicide rate more than doubled. Car thefts, burglaries, robberies, and rapes also increased from the 1960s to the 1970s. A blackout led to widespread looting. On the Upper West Side, drug addicts hung out on corners, prostitutes walked the streets, car windows were regularly smashed, and children carried "mugging money."

In just five years from 1969 to 1974, the city lost over five hundred thousand manufacturing jobs, and the unemployment rate topped 10 percent. More than one million New York City households depended on welfare by 1975. As homelessness grew in the 1970s and 1980s, the Upper West Side in particular became home to SROs, along with an extensive array of mental health facilities, welfare hotels, homeless shelters, halfway houses, and methadone clinics.

In the 1970s and 1980s, riding the graffiti-scarred subway meant taking your life in your hands. John Lennon was murdered on the Upper West Side. The serial killer Son of Sam was on the loose in New York City. People were murdered in Riverside Park. Among them was Eleanor Clark, a seventy-eight-year-old widow, stabbed to death in 1970 while walking her two small poodles.

We all felt vulnerable. Gritty city. The middle class fled.

The citywide descent into the abyss continued in the 1980s. AIDS reared its poisonous head, and crack cocaine vials pocked the streets. In 1982, two men killed my building superintendent's son in a holdup attempt one block east of our current home.

Riverside Park itself remained perilous. Underfunded and with minimal maintenance, its many structures and statues in various states of disrepair, the park became a bedroom for the homeless (many of whom took up residence in the Freedom Tunnel) and a recreation room for drug users. Vandalism abounded; monuments were disrespected and disfigured with graffiti; and playgrounds, many with broken swings and otherwise in shabby condition, became dumping grounds for garbage. Broken streetlights in and alongside the park remained broken. Benches deteriorated, and stairs and pathways alike crumbled.

Riverside Park had no full-time security personnel, no recreation workers in its playgrounds, and no park rangers. People were afraid to wander past the retaining wall that separates Park from Drive. Dog owners did not walk their pets very far at night.

At that point—the end of the 1970s and the early 1980s—Upper West Siders had had enough.

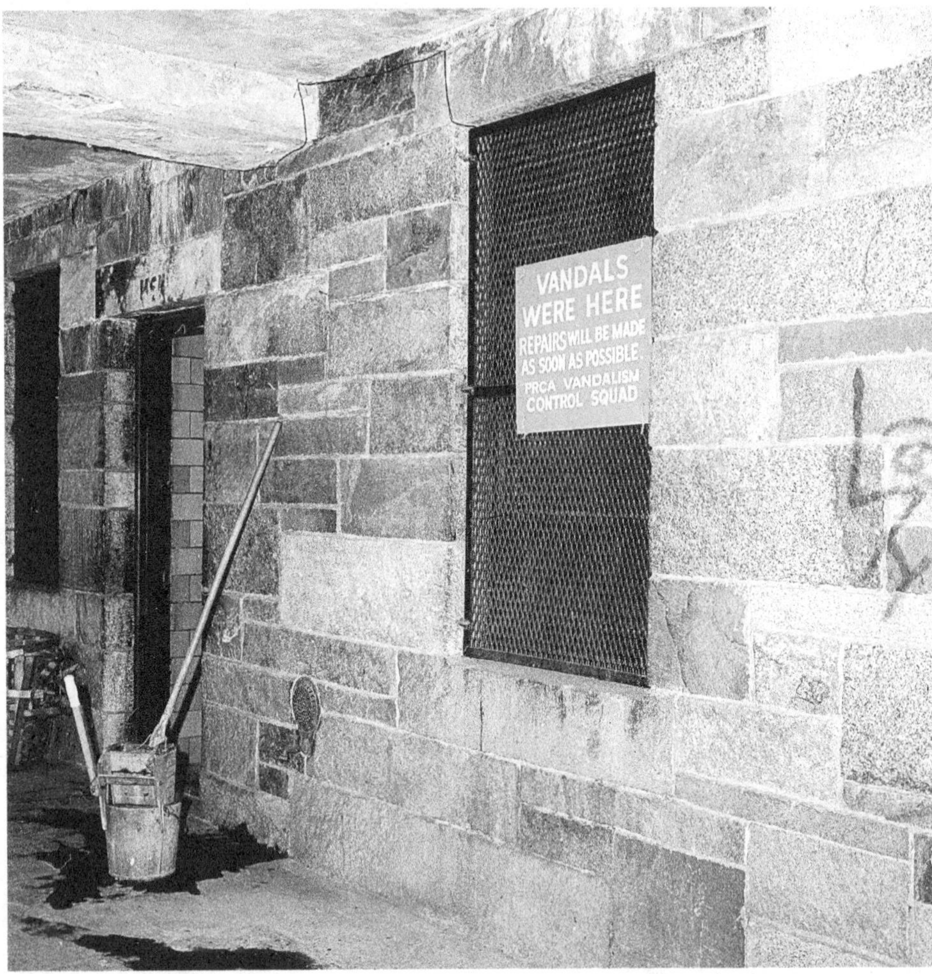

Figure 44. Vandalism plagued Riverside Park in the 1970s and 1980s. *Source*: NYC Parks Photo Archive.

Chapter 12

Getting Better

The 1980s until Today

AS NEW YORK City finally lumbered back into shape in the 1980s (and to some degree, the late 1970s), the Upper West Side regained its appeal. For decades, property values on the West Side trailed far behind those of the East Side, but suddenly the margin narrowed considerably.[1] Rents rose and, along with them, so did the income brackets of the residents who chose to live here—affluent young professionals attracted by more space for less money. Landlords began to renovate the grand old buildings of an earlier era, along with the row houses that had been divided into warrens.

In the late 1970s and 1980s on Riverside Drive and throughout the city, rental buildings were converting to cooperatives in droves. The transformation enabled property owners to pass many of the maintenance costs along to the new co-op owners and make higher profits as a result. Landlords began upgrading lobbies, hallways, and elevators. The properties became more valuable to them but also appealed to current and future residents flush enough to buy those apartments. Baby Boomers whose parents had fled the big bad city were moving back and choosing to own.

It was not until then that Riverside Park and Drive once again experienced an upward swing. After efforts by advocates, in 1980 Riverside Park and Riverside Drive were together designated a New York City Scenic Landmark. Having landmark status precluded any major construction, such as a future version of Westway, that could take away parkland. Three years later, Riverside Park and Riverside Drive were listed on the National Register of Historic Places.

In 1981, the New York City Department of Parks & Recreation was charged with developing a comprehensive plan for Riverside Park's restoration. In 1984, it presented its findings, which addressed immediate needs as well as future goals. The master plan included "guidelines for the park's restoration, a conceptual master plan and a capital plan intended to save important landscapes, remove hazardous conditions, satisfy community recreational needs and reduce maintenance expenses."[2]

The Parks Department plan acknowledged that many problems were severe and rapidly growing worse and that the need for a continuous program of maintenance, erosion control, horticultural care, and incremental restoration was obvious. They assigned the highest priorities to deteriorated infrastructure, hazardous conditions, strategic improvements, and the more popular recreational facilities.

It was also in the 1980s that the local community sprang into action, in a way that would have an equally lasting impact on the future of Riverside Park. In 1986, residents banded together to create the Riverside Park Fund, whose goal was to raise money and work in partnership with the Parks Department to restore and maintain the park. Fourteen Riverside Drive co-ops provided seed money. In November 2012, the fund was renamed the Riverside Park Conservancy, in recognition of its role in protecting and maintaining Riverside Park.

Funded entirely by private contributions, the organization typically provides half of the money for operating Riverside Park. The conservancy's operating budget, recently about $7 million, is much more limited than that of its neighbor, the Central Park Conservancy. The latter raises nearly $100 million annually and since 1980 has overseen the investment of nearly $1 billion in Central Park.

At the Riverside Park Conservancy's core is a dedicated force of neighborhood volunteers, whose work includes restoring landscapes, playing fields, and park structures. This dedication was evident even in the organization's earliest days, when there was no running water in Riverside Park. Some volunteers hauled buckets of water from home, while others dragged garden hoses across Riverside Drive.

In fact, the organization manages one of the largest park volunteer programs in the city. When Hurricane Sandy hit in 2012, submerging part of the park under four feet of water and depositing tons of debris, the conservancy staff coordinated over 1,300 volunteers to clean it up. It also has a full-time paid staff, many of them responsible for maintaining a particular area of the park. Over time, the conservancy has supported activities ranging from cleaning up and landscaping the park to renovating and constructing new playgrounds and restoring monuments. It has contributed to dog runs and tennis courts and supplied and maintained equipment and vehicles.

Sustainability is a key focus, and the Riverside Park Conservancy has invested heavily in horticultural care and Dutch elm disease prevention. Beyond all that, it also runs a summer sports program serving more than one thousand children and a summer activities program for adults and children that ranges from Shakespeare performances to art exhibits to yoga in the park.

The Parks Department, meanwhile, is responsible for park maintenance, long-range planning, capital improvements, and management of park personnel and budget. It provides lawn maintenance and trash pickup.

Many problems remained in the Upper West Side and the city as a whole in the 1990s—a few hundred homeless were living in Riverside Park at the time, and, hitting close to home, my middle-school-age son was mugged nearby. Nonetheless, Riverside

Park and Riverside Drive improvements were well underway. During that decade, park projects included restoring the retaining wall between 98th and 120th Streets and renovating the popular Hippo Playground.

Real change began to happen, however, in the first two decades of the twenty-first century. Within the first ten years, much of the park south of 129th Street had been restored. Artificial turf was added to ball fields, deteriorated concrete on the promenade was replaced with asphalt, and new benches were installed.

In 2010, Riverwalk welcomed park goers to the shorefront between 83rd and 91st Streets. Here a platform extending over the river and running parallel with the Henry Hudson Parkway replaced what had once been an extremely narrow and dangerous piece of shoreline and the resulting detour away from that part of the Hudson. Riverwalk linked to the park esplanade along the river, marking the final phase of the Riverside Park waterfront connection. It created Hudson River access for the entire length of Riverside Park, except for a small gap in West Harlem, and allowed an otherwise uninterrupted paved path for bikers, joggers, and strollers from 72nd Street to the George Washington Bridge.

Riverside Park developments also positively affected Riverside Drive. A 2011 Corcoran Group report stated that the "Riverside Drive Market has come into its own in terms of pricing. It is beginning to compete with the more storied Avenues such as Central Park West, Park and Fifth Avenues."[3]

In 2016, the Parks Department issued an ambitious second master plan for Riverside Park, developed with intensive community input. It called for major projects, including restoration of the 79th Street Rotunda, the Soldiers' and Sailors' Monument, and Cherry Walk. It also cited the need for improved pedestrian walkways and a modernized marina, as well as for new bike paths, a new ADA-compliant 111th Street entrance, and new play areas north of 105th Street. Riverside Drive's retaining walls, stairs, granite, and river bulkheads were to be inspected and the stone reset and repointed.

Since then, the shoreline has been reconstructed and the bike path repaved at several points along the Cherry Walk from 100th to 125th Streets, where they were badly damaged during Hurricane Sandy. Further repairs are planned where tree roots have caused bumps and cracks. Separately, to reduce congestion and collisions between bicyclists and pedestrians, the bike path along the shoreline was detoured, much to the chagrin of bikers, who, instead of following a flat path, must now pump up and down two hills.

In other recent developments, several step ramps were updated between 97th Street and 116th Street, there was new paving installed between 112th and 115th Streets, and the skate park at 108th Street was completely revamped. The deteriorated sidewalk between 95th and 97th Streets on Riverside Drive was repaved. The Parks Department finished reconfiguring and improving several bus stops along Riverside Drive between 100th and 123rd Streets to provide easier access to buses for people with disabilities and safer street crossings. The Riverside Park Field House was repaired and its basketball courts completed.

Pathway reconstruction was scheduled for areas of the 80s, 90s, and low 100s. In April 2021, plans to improve the park lawns on Riverside Drive between 108th Street and 112th Streets were announced. In the fall of that year, thanks to a $50,000 gift from a private donor, structural cracks and other damage were addressed at the Firemen's Memorial at 100th Street.

Significant work was scheduled for the 79th Street Rotunda infrastructure, for which $200 million has been allocated. The project will include complete reconstruction of the traffic lanes, restaurant level, and operations garage and restoration of the central fountain. The first rehabilitation of the Rotunda since its completion in the 1930s, it was projected to take four years. Work on the marina across from the Rotunda will include major structural upgrades and dredging the basin. A budget of $89.2 million has been earmarked for the marina effort.

One of the biggest problems yet to be fully resolved at this time is the park's aging drainage system and the issues that result from it, including erosion and damage to staircases and other access points. Flooding occurs after every rainstorm. It's at its worst between 105th and 119th Streets, where sharply sloped streets funnel copious amounts of rainwater into a natural basin, forming long stretches of muddy ponds. Not long ago, this included one along the lawn at 115th Street, where passersby could spy a pair of mallard ducks at play. In December 2019, the city allocated $11.5 million to address the park's chronic drainage issues.

In May 2021, New York City announced plans to provide $348 million in funding to Riverside Park to halt the deterioration of the tunnel roof between 72nd and 123rd

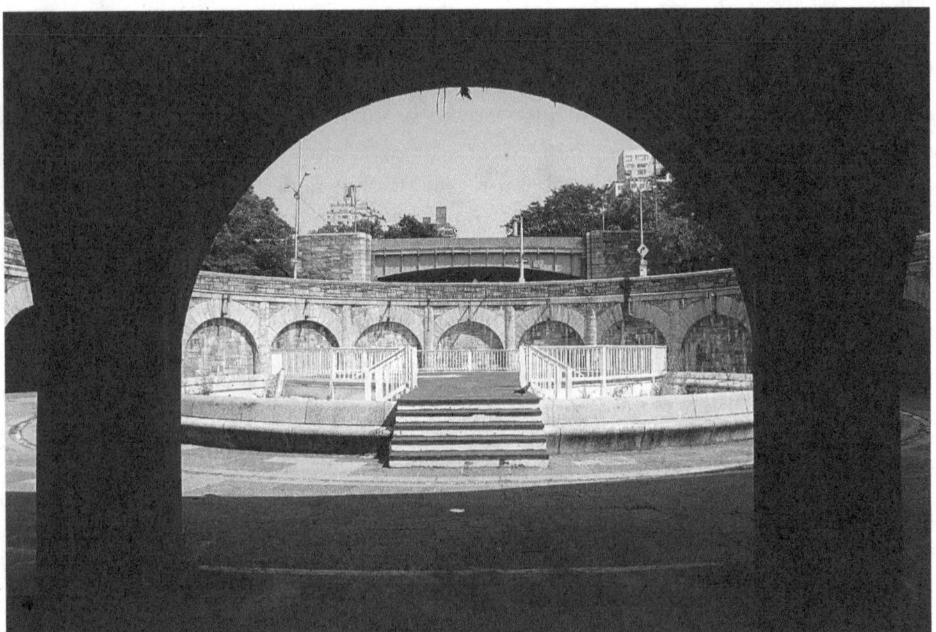

Figure 45. 79th Street Rotunda, scheduled for repairs. *Source*: Robert F. Rodriguez.

Figure 46. Major funding has been allocated to address damage caused by deterioration of the train tunnel "overbuild." *Source*: Robert F. Rodriguez.

Streets—also called the "overbuild"—which has "damaged pathways, limited access for vehicles and created a condition of disrepair in the Park—and the problems have gotten much worse in recent years."[4] Project details and timeline are currently to be determined.

The overbuild budget, together with the more than $300 million allocated for upgrades to the Rotunda, boat basin, pathways, staircases, and drainage system, totals well over half a billion dollars, marking the largest investment in Riverside Park since the West Side Improvement Plan of the 1930s.

Figure 47. Today, locals enjoy Riverside Park year round. *Source*: Robert F. Rodriguez.

THE SIGHTS

Chapter 13

The Seductive Seventies

WHATEVER THE FUTURE may bring, Riverside Park and Riverside Drive continue to celebrate a smorgasbord of mouth-watering delights from the past, with each section from 72nd Street to 129th Street serving up its own tasty morsels.

The 70s host the only remaining complete street of row houses on the entire Drive, picturesquely embellished in the most charming of ways. As elsewhere on the avenue, front-facing rooms and secret spaces—rooftop gardens, balconets, terraces, and more—gift residents with spectacular park and river views. Here, too, may be found the only statue in New York to honor an American First Lady, the site of what was once the city's most extraordinary private home, a marina designed to grandly and proudly welcome the world's finest yachts—and the location of at least one nineteenth-century suicide.

Many of its buildings fall within the West End–Collegiate Historic District, which includes Riverside Drive from 74th Street to 77th Street.[1] Brown street-name signs visible along much of Riverside Drive indicate when a street has been designated as part of a historic district by the New York City Landmarks Preservation Commission.

Riverside Park/72nd Street: The Eleanor Roosevelt Memorial

Despite a recent movement to address the situation, there remain relatively few statues of women in New York City's parks—or anywhere in town, for that matter. One of the loveliest is the eight-foot bronze statue of former First Lady Anna Eleanor Roosevelt, warmly greeting visitors at the very entrance to Riverside Park. Hers is also the first public statue in the nation devoted to a president's wife.

Mrs. Roosevelt was born, spent much of her life, and died in New York City. She is presented here not in the cold, formal pose of so many statues but rather in

Figure 48. The Eleanor Roosevelt Memorial at the entrance to Riverside Park is the country's first public statue devoted to a president's wife. *Source*: Robert F. Rodriguez.

contemplative mode, leaning against a rock as she might in real life in the park itself, chin resting on her hand. Live oak trees circle around her. Though she is pictured alone, it's easy to envision her surrounded by a small crowd eager to hear her considered response to an important question.

Born in 1884 to a socially prominent family, she was a niece of President Theodore Roosevelt and was orphaned at age eleven. Her interests differed from those of many other well-brought-up young women of the era: After finishing school in England, she volunteered as a social worker in the slums of the Lower East Side. She married her distant cousin and the future president, Franklin Delano Roosevelt, in 1905.

Mrs. Roosevelt tirelessly used the influence resulting from her husband's political success to promote social causes. She lobbied for civil rights, spearheaded women's rights, and fought both Lower East Side sweatshops and Tammany Hall. She was also a delegate to the United Nations. The statue is said to be near the spot in Riverside Park where she took her son Franklin D. Roosevelt Jr. to see the shantytowns people lived in during the Depression.

The American sculptor Penelope Jencks won a national competition to choose a design for the memorial. Jencks used Mrs. Roosevelt's great-granddaughter Phoebe Roosevelt as the model for the statue's torso. Phoebe later said she was chosen because she has the Roosevelt "slouch."[2]

The city carved space for the monument out of a demolished entrance ramp to the Henry Hudson Parkway. A plaque on the sidewalk quotes from Mrs. Roosevelt's 1958 speech to the United Nations Commission on Human Rights: "Where, after all, do universal human rights begin? In small places, close to home. Such are the places where every man, woman and child seeks equal justice, equal opportunity, equal dignity." In 1996, the Roosevelt memorial was unveiled, with remarks by then First Lady Hillary Clinton.

Notably, the first statue of a real-life woman rather than say, Mother Goose or Alice in Wonderland, did not appear in Central Park until 2020.

1 Riverside Drive/72nd Street: The Prentiss Residence/Islamic Cultural Center

Directly across from the Eleanor Roosevelt Memorial, on the northeast corner of 72nd Street, 1 Riverside Drive marks the entrance to the Drive from the south and is the first of its many view-worthy buildings.

Near the end of the nineteenth century, that corner plot, which gently curves northward, was owned by John S. Sutphen. Sutphen planned a home on the 72nd Street side of the space, while Lydia S. F. Prentiss was to build on Riverside Drive itself. The original deeds for the property imposed a number of restrictions, including a ban on erecting a slaughterhouse, brewery, livery stable, carpenter shop, nail factory, sugar refinery, menagerie, "or any other manufactory, trade business, or calling which may be in anywise dangerous, noxious, or offensive to the neighboring inhabitants."[3]

Sutphen added further requirements for the Prentisses. Their residence was to be a "first class building adapted for and which shall be used only as a private residence for one family," and it must "conform to the plan thereof made by C. P. H. Gilbert, Architect,"[4] who would become responsible for numerous residences on Riverside Drive. By stipulating that all his buyers work with the same highly respected architect, Sutphen assured the quality and harmony of the homes in his neighborhood.

Completed in 1901, the five-story, limestone, Beaux Arts 1 Riverside Drive was designed to complement but not duplicate the Sutphen mansion. A striking bowed façade demurely traces the curve of the Drive and hosts a balustraded balconet (or Juliet balcony) at the second story. A portico flanked by a pair of Ionic columns adorns the building's entrance while also supporting a second-story balcony. Most of the visual drama plays out at the upper stories. On the fourth floor, more columns round the corner, outlining windows crowned by a leaf-patterned copper cornice. One flight above, gabled dormers, tall chimneys, and a marvelous turret with a conical top like a squat birthday hat vie for attention from a mansard roof.

Gilbert created a triangular courtyard between the two homes, enabling a full sidewall of light and air for both, an advantage normally found only in standalone or corner structures. The families also shared a garden and a common wall toward the rear of the houses. Inside, an entrance-hall stairway led to the second floor, built for entertaining. A large drawing room at the front of the house was followed by an expansive dining room at the back and a music room in between. Seven bedrooms (including two guest rooms), multiple bathrooms, a library, and a billiard room completed the space, along with the kitchen, servants' rooms, and a storage area.

The Prentiss family remained in their home until 1956, when they sold it to the Nippon Club, an exclusive gentlemen's social club for wealthy Japanese Americans. The following year, the organization sold the house to the New York Mosque Foundation. The building is now a satellite location for the Islamic Cultural Center of New York and houses a mosque. Arabic lettering appears at the main entry transom. A line of taxis can often be found parked outside, as the city's many Muslim cab drivers take time out for prayer services. The building was designated a New York City Individual Landmark in 1991.

3 Riverside Drive/72nd–73rd Streets: The Kleeberg Mansion

The delicious eye candy that is 3 Riverside Drive was once the Kleeberg mansion. Like its neighbor on the corner, it was built on land owned by John S. Sutphen. Philip Kleeberg's deed included restrictions resembling the Prentisses' when it came to the use of the property and the preferred choice of C. P. H. Gilbert as architect. The Kleebergs paid $145,000 for the land alone, with an additional $55,000 projected for construction costs.

The Kleebergs' fortune resulted from a variety of enterprises. After starting in the wholesale lace business, Kleeberg became an executive of ore and oil companies and of the William Radam Microbe Killer Company.[5] He also invented a calculator, was

Figure 49. Once a private home, 1 Riverside Drive is now a mosque. *Source*: Robert F. Rodriguez.

president of the National Calculator Company, and earned the distinction of having crossed the Atlantic more than 150 times.

Built in 1898, the five-story, thirty-seven-foot wide, 11,000-square-foot limestone and brick mansion exudes charm with a twinkle. The *AIA Guide to New York City* calls it "freely interpreted Dutch Renaissance,"[6] while the *New York Times* describes it as highlighting a "delirium of French Renaissance Revival details."[7]

Gargoyles guard it at street level, and a chubby stone cherub perches at its peak, perhaps smiling down at the exuberant display below. On the red-tiled roof, spiky finials reach skyward alongside S-shaped brackets. An elaborate gabled dormer with curved sides "protrudes from the copper-trimmed roof like the top tier of a Gothic wedding cake."[8] There are shields and scrolls, wreaths and ribbons. It is, for the passerby, a hallucinatory feast.

A four-sided projecting bay graces the Riverside façade for three floors, creating a terrace at the fourth floor whose carvings are so lacy and fine they recall filigree. Carved vine moldings define four windows as well as the home's elaborate entrance, which is flanked by stylized pilasters. A loggia enhances the home's profile on the southern side. Unlike its neighbors, its entrance is situated on the left rather than in the middle of the building, creating additional parlor space. Original interior details

Figure 50. 3 Riverside Drive is known for its architectural details. *Source*: Robert F. Rodriguez.

included a large paneled entrance hall, wide marble stairway, solid cherrywood floors, and bronze-grille entrance doors.

Despite the beauty of the original Kleeberg home, all was not always well within its walls. Under the headline "Rich Woman Ends Life," the *New York Times* told the tale: In the summer of 1903, the Kleebergs hosted a dinner party. Around 10:30 that evening, Maria Kleeberg, the lady of the house, stepped away. When she did not return, her sister, Mrs. Sands, became concerned and followed her to the bathroom, surprising Mrs. Kleeberg as she was downing a bottle of carbolic acid. Mrs. Sands knocked the bottle to the floor, but it was too late. When the ambulance arrived, Maria Kleeberg was dead. Philip Kleeberg maintained that there was no reason for his wife to have committed suicide. However, during the marriage he apparently had purchased another home on the Upper West Side, for his own use.

In 1915, the Kleeberg property was rented by Dr. William Knipe, one of the first physicians in New York to offer his patients "twilight sleep," a state intended to make childbirth more tolerable. This was typically accomplished through drugs such as scopolamine, a narcotic and amnesiac, along with morphine. As a result, women would fall asleep and wake up unable to remember anything about the birth—thus rendering it "painless."

The mansion became Dr. Knipe's "twilight sleep sanitarium." A year later, neighbors Mary Tier Sutphen, who lived on the corner of 72nd Street and Riverside Drive, and Angie M. Booth of 4 Riverside Drive filed suit to close down the sanitarium, claiming it violated the so-called nuisance covenant to which the street's homeowners had agreed. The courts eventually ruled in their favor.

Gordon Kleeberg, son of the original owner, regained the property in 1943 and by 1951 converted it to a multiple dwelling, with two apartments per floor. In 1995, it was purchased for $10 million by owners who spent nearly eighteen years restoring the residence to a luxurious private home. In 2012, they put the one-family home on the market for $40 million. At the time, it had eighteen rooms, including eight bedrooms and nine bathrooms, nine gas fireplaces (each featuring a different shade of marble and a mahogany mantel), a mosaic and marble lobby, a two-room staff suite, and four terraces. This was in addition to grand mahogany and marble staircases, gilded coffered ceilings, carved mahogany doors and molding—plus an elevator, pool, gym, radiant-heated-floor bathrooms, and state-of-the-art technology including motion detector lighting in each room.

With no buyers interested, the price was reduced to a "bargain" $20 million by 2016. It sold in 2017 for $15.8 million. Happily, the new owners maintained it as a single-family home. However, according to a spokesperson, after consulting historians and architects and concluding that virtually none of the building's original details remained, they restored the exterior while gut-renovating the interior.

In March 2021, 3 Riverside Drive was back on the market, for $25 million, this time with twenty-six rooms—eight more than before—and a grand total of 19,000 square feet. The new owners created the additional eight thousand square feet when they excavated to create a two-level sub-basement. The 2021 listing also noted "approved plans" for, among other features, a half-Olympic-size marble pool, an onyx-walled hot tub, a partial basketball court, and a stadium-seating movie theater. Later that year, the price was reduced to $20 million. Number 3 Riverside Drive was designated a New York City Individual Landmark in 1991.

11 Riverside Drive/73rd–74th Streets: The Schwab Mansion/Schwab House

Here once stood the intoxicating, mesmerizing, completely over-the-top, seventy-five-room French Renaissance Schwab mansion, the Upper West Side's largest and most distinctive private home.[9] Created in 1905 for the steel magnate Charles Schwab, it was—sadly—demolished in 1948. Two years later, the exceptionally boring, red-brick, eighteen-story Schwab House rose in its stead. Like the original, the grounds of its replacement extend the full block from 73rd to 74th Streets, Riverside Drive to West End Avenue. The newer building fills about 60 percent of the original property, with much of the remaining space dedicated to courtyards and gardens. With over six hundred apartments, Schwab House, a co-op, is one of the largest apartment complexes in New York City. A 2010 *New York Times* article referred to the Sylvan Bien–designed building as "quotidian but efficient."[10] At least it has an on-site garage.

22 Riverside Drive/74th Street

In this nineteen-story building from 1931 by Boak & Paris, multitoned bricks top a warm, almost peach-colored cast-stone base. Casement windows sharply edge around the corner, and all of the building's windows are trimmed in a sophisticated and complementary bluish-gray tone. The overall effect of what the Landmarks Preservation Commission terms "eclectic with Gothic and Elizabethan detailing"[11] is inviting rather than standoffish. The condominium building includes a triplex penthouse. A three-bedroom, three-and-a-half bath, 2,100-square-foot apartment on a low floor hit the market for $3.4 million in 2021.

35 Riverside Drive/75th–76th Streets

Each Riverside Drive row house has its own personality—some demure and more polished, others outgoing, maybe even a bit coarse, some devoted to their architectural origins, others more playful about their past.

Thirty-Five Riverside Drive has always called to me with its contrasts. A modern-looking, unadorned wall of windows wraps around classical columns on the top floor, glassing in what was once an open porch. Rough stone throughout the building's façade counters the smoothness of that park-facing upper story, while a delicate oval window peeks out through the rock. Entranceway stairs climb obstinately to the side rather than head straight up. A fetching four-story cylindrical bay ends in a conical roof.

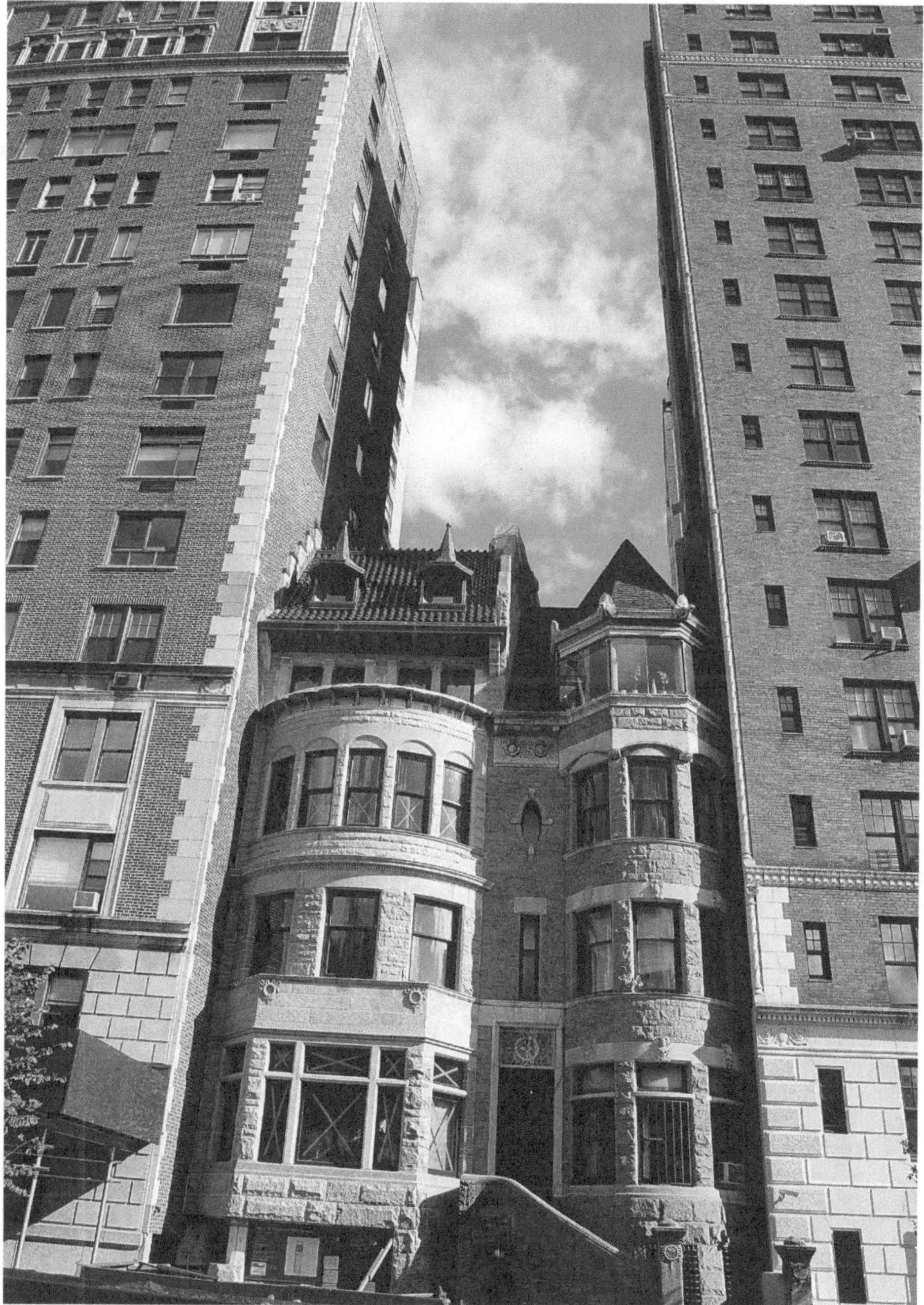

Figure 51. Contrasts charm at 35 Riverside Drive (row house on r.). *Source*: Robert F. Rodriguez.

Carvings of what seem to be knights in armor peer out from above the windows on the main floor.

Designed by Lamb & Rich, the Renaissance Revival and Romanesque Revival row house was built in 1889 and is currently a co-op.

Riverside Park/76th Street: The Robert Ray Hamilton Fountain

Lusciously carved in bright white marble, the Robert Ray Hamilton Fountain is watched over by a giant eagle, wings spread. The fountain was designed by Warren and Wetmore, the architects, along with Reed and Stem, for Grand Central Terminal. Dedicated in 1906, it was intended by its donor, Hamilton, primarily as a drinking fountain for horses.

The front portion faces out from the park onto Riverside Drive, and it was long understood that this represented the complete design. However, a deep dig along the other side of the retaining wall in 2008 discovered a broad marble drinking basin set into the back side of the wall and once fed from a sluice carved into the wall. This served horses traveling through the park. That part of the fountain has since been removed.

A descendant of Alexander Hamilton and a distinguished politician in his own right, Robert Ray Hamilton was plagued by scandal—and really bad luck. Toward the end of his life, he was in the midst of a divorce from his wife, Evangeline, known as Eva. This lovely lady was not only a bigamist but also stole another woman's child

Figure 52. Scandal plagued the Hamilton Fountain's donor, Robert Ray Hamilton. *Source*: Robert F. Rodriguez.

to palm off on Hamilton as his own and later stabbed the baby's nurse. Mrs. Hamilton was imprisoned for "atrocious assault" and variously denounced as an "adventuress," a "morphine fiend," and a "false woman." To escape his troubles, Hamilton left for Wyoming, where at the age of thirty-nine he drowned while attempting to ford the Snake River. His partner, John D. Sargent, was arrested for murder and sent to an insane asylum.

Because they did not wish to have a Riverside Drive fountain associated with the family's black sheep, other Hamiltons opposed having it erected. Clearly, there has been enough drama in the Hamilton family for a Broadway production.

40–46 Riverside Drive/76th–77th Streets

Of all the blocks along Riverside Drive, the one from 76th Street to 77th Street is undeniably the most enchanting. It is the only remaining full block of row houses on the entire avenue, every one of them designed and built by Clarence True. True had no great fondness for the typical, relatively staid New York City row house and preferred the more picturesque, favoring Elizabethan or French Renaissance details. That's abundantly clear here, where each of the pretty residences endears itself in its own unique way, like preschoolers in party dresses all in a row. There are round-arched

Figure 53. Turn-of-the-century view of 76th to 77th Streets, the only extant block of row houses on Riverside Drive. 40 Riverside Drive occupies the corner. *Source*: Library of Congress.

windows and sweet oval windows, bay windows that are angled and bow windows that are curved. There are round columns and flat columns, parapets, dormers, and more. Intricate carvings detail the tops of doorways, and no two of those carvings are alike.

The true belle of this architectural ball is the 1898 Elizabethan Renaissance Revival 40 Riverside Drive, known as the Miner Mansion, on the northeast corner of 76th Street. Considered one of True's grandest designs, it is most noticeable, first, simply because of its size—the five-story building, with thirty-two feet on the Drive, takes a giant step around the corner and has a nearly 11,000-square-foot interior. The home originally held seventeen rooms and an elevator.

Equally attention getting is its striking, four-story, round corner tower, with an unusual open top that serves as a terrace. The tower separates the two sides of the building, each of which ends in peaky gables and is handsomely bordered by quoins. A tall chimney surmounts the mansard roof, along with a pedimented dormer. A lovely two-story oriel extends from the eastern end, capped by a balconet. Buff-colored brick combines perfectly with limestone.

In 1897, native New Yorker Henry C. ("Harry") Miner bought the home for $125,000. Miner's curriculum vitae is dizzying. Starting as a pharmacist, he also "read medicine"; managed a lecturer on medical subjects, then a magician and bird trainer, and later a circus; became a police officer; and ran several theaters. He founded a lithographing company and two different drugstores, held interests in railroads and mining companies, and owned considerable real estate. He also served a term in Congress.

His personal life added even more spice to his CV. Two years after his wife of thirty years died, Miner, then sixty-four, married the much younger Annie O'Neill, an actress. Miner's four grown sons strongly opposed the union, resulting in a falling out between them and their father. In 1900, the couple had a son. Six weeks later, Miner collapsed and died, leaving an estate worth $2 million. Apparently, despite their attitude toward her, Mrs. Miner had encouraged her husband to set aside his grievances toward the sons from his previous marriage. Thanks to those efforts, Miner's adult sons were included in his estate. His newborn, however, was not—Miner had not gotten around to amending his will in the short time between the boy's birth and Miner's own passing. Despite the initial rancor between the grown sons and the new wife, they settled the estate amicably. It was divided equally among Mrs. Miner and the sons, and her young son was also provided for. Mrs. Miner got the Riverside Drive house.

From 1906 until 1938, its owner was Max Brill, of the famous midtown Brill building, where leading songwriters kept offices and studios. It was there that they wrote some of the most popular American songs, especially in the early 1960s. Brill hosted opulent parties at his home, with guests including Lehmans, Guggenheims, and Strausses.

In 1938, the residence became the Riverside School and remained so for many decades. When the institution left, the house was divided into two sizeable apartments. It was a three-unit building in 2013, when Roy Niederhoffer, a hedge-fund manager and former chairman of the board of the New York City Opera, purchased it for $12.99 million. At the time, much original detail remained on the lower floors, while on upper floors, much had been stripped. The owner restored the building to a private residence and in 2018 put it on the market for $15.9 million. Real estate listings highlighted a marble foyer; triple-height living room; five outdoor areas, including a terrace with a fire pit; and a separate apartment for guests. As of fall 2021, however, it was delisted.

52 Riverside Drive/77th–78th Streets

It's the terracotta details that make the difference at 52 Riverside Drive. In warm shades of Wedgewood blue and peach, they surround the entrance door and the center windows on the third and thirteenth floors. Most charmingly, in my opinion, they decorate the front of the stone window boxes on the first floor, with flowers gathered in curly swags. Around the door may be found urns, crowns, and gryphons, shells, and shields. A somber silhouetted portrait faces north above the entrance.

Intriguingly, a nearly identical terracotta design may be found at two other Upper West Side buildings, 243 West End Avenue and 147 West 79th Street. The architectural historian Andrew Alpern has speculated that this same look by three different architects on three different buildings all constructed around the same time may reflect the success of a particularly persuasive terracotta salesman, whose terracotta design catalog, complete with detailed drawings, made its way into each of the architect's libraries.[12]

Erected in 1926, the fifteen-story Renaissance Revival brick and stone 52 Riverside Drive co-op building was designed by Deutsch & Schneider.

Figure 54. Terracotta details enhance doors and windows at 52 Riverside Drive. *Source*: Robert F. Rodriguez.

67 Riverside Drive/79th Street: The Riverdale

Frilly and fabulous from top to bottom, this Beaux Arts meringue of limestone, terracotta, and light brick drips with stone balconets boasting lacey metal railings and elaborate stone brackets. There are charming French-door windows, splayed lintels with keystones atop other windows, substantial swags, and an alluring columned entrance portico. Inside, apartments feature expansive foyers, high beamed ceilings, leaded-glass pocket doors, and herringbone wood floors.

Designed by George Frederick Pelham and built in 1907, the nine-story co-op on the southeast corner of 79th Street had only two apartments per floor of ten rooms each, renting at the time for $2,000 to $3,500 annually.

In 2018, one of those ten-room apartments, with 2,600 square feet, five bedrooms, and three baths, was on the market. With a library/den, pocket doors, two decorative fireplaces, a wood-paneled dining room with exposed wood beams and five Juliet balconies, it sold for $4.2 million.

Unexpectedly, given the lightness of the building's façade and the somberness of the movie's theme, the exterior of 67 Riverside Drive played a role in the film *The Manchurian Candidate*, starring Frank Sinatra.

Figure 55. Lacey metal railings and other elaborate ornamentation distinguish the Riverdale. *Source*: Robert F. Rodriguez.

Riverside Park/79th Street: The Boat Basin and Rotunda

During the West Side improvement project of the 1930s, the Boat Basin on the Hudson River was to be Robert Moses's piece de resistance. His goal was to create a structure fine enough to serve as a grand "river gate" for travelers by sea, a welcoming portal for marine dignitaries not just from the United States but around the world.

While the city at the time had numerous commercial ports and a few private boating clubs, the 79th Street Boat Basin was created specifically for recreational boaters. The largest recreational marina in Manhattan and the only one within Riverside Park, it is also the only marina on New York City parkland that allows people to remain aboard their vessel year-round.

By the 1960s, most Boat Basin slips were occupied by year-round boaters, including the *Mad Magazine* writer Dick DeBartolo, who used a houseboat as his office. The author of *The Godfather* Mario Puzo, Frank Sinatra, and the notorious attorney Roy Cohn all docked boats here.

In early 2021, there were 116 slips, with fifty-two available for year-round dockage. Visitors to the Boat Basin may enjoy the sight of sleek sailboats, envy-generating yachts, and education-focused tall ships reminiscent of times past. The *Clearwater*, the sloop that teaches about Hudson River environmental and pollution issues, often docks here and is the most visible component of the marina's overall education programs for the public.

A number of structural changes were made at the Boat Basin in the first two decades of the twenty-first century. In 2003, a dedicated launch for canoes and kayaks was added, opening the marina to public access (no permits needed). Hurricane Sandy destroyed it, although a standard floating dock replaced it temporarily. In January 2005, ice floes knocked out the marina's two westernmost ice breakers, which were then replaced with steel piling structures. After Hurricane Sandy lifted the marina's most heavily used pier from its pilings, a new one took its place in 2016.

Current plans are to dredge and rebuild the marina, bringing it up to modern design and resiliency standards, including replacing wooden pilings with concrete-filled steel pilings. New berths are anticipated, along with a new dock. With those goals in mind, the Boat Basin closed in November 2021, with construction expected to begin in 2023.

Centered directly across from the marina, in Riverside Park itself, is a multipurpose and rather glamorous Rotunda, which Moses built at the same time as the Boat Basin, in 1937. It's been referred to as the "Bethesda Terrace of Riverside Park." At the lowest level, it houses a garage for the owners of boats docked at the marina. One flight up, its outdoor terrace and courtyard served for twenty-two years as the Boat Basin Café, a popular restaurant where guests could relax over a casual menu while gazing out at the dock and the river beyond.

The restaurant interior was housed under a dramatic arcade, vaulted with Guastavino tiles. This tilework has created some of the city's most stunning spaces, including the

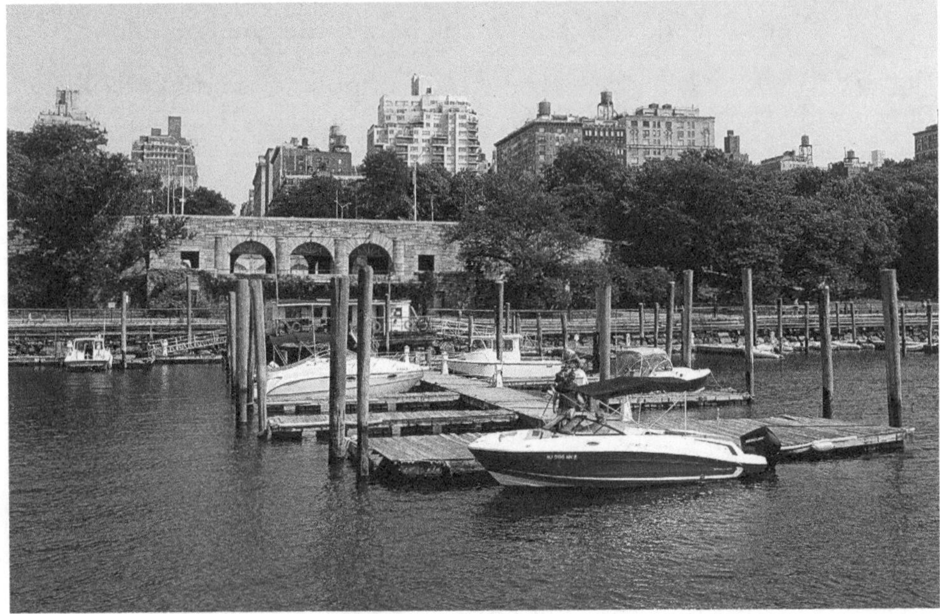

Figure 56. The marina and Rotunda, just before they were closed for repairs. *Source*: Robert F. Rodriguez.

original Pennsylvania Station, Grand Central Terminal, and on the Upper West Side alone, both Riverside Church and the Cathedral of St. John the Divine. Tables spilled outside the arcade to the courtyard, above which sits a busy traffic circle allowing entry and exit from the Henry Hudson Parkway.

The space permanently closed in the fall of 2019 to allow for major renovations of the Rotunda. The plan includes repairs to the traffic circle, Guastavino ceiling, pedestrian path into the park, and the railroad bridge over the tracks at 79th Street, along with upgrades to lighting and restrooms. All levels of the Rotunda will be made ADA compatible, and there will be improved access to the dedicated bicycle route on top of the Rotunda and to dedicated bike lanes connecting at 79th Street. Once completed, the Rotunda will again host a restaurant. Happily, the plan is to also restore the fountain that once proudly stood in the open courtyard, including its bronze turtles. For years, the fountain was covered over and used as a stage for theater performances.

And More . . .

Although the 70s' buildings overflow with charm, there are ugly ducklings among the very soigné swans. Between the precious, deliciously froufrou 1 and 3 Riverside Drives crouches a grossly out-of-place 1963 building of brown and yellow brick, built on a lot that until then had remained vacant. At 60 Riverside Drive, just to the south of the Riverdale on 79th Street, stands a plain white-brick building from 1965, clearly dressed for work at home rather than an evening out like its neighbor. Immediately north of the Riverdale, on the northeast corner of 79th Street, a bland red-brick apartment building, 70 Riverside Drive, takes up space. Next door to it at 74 Riverside Drive is a row house reconfigured to have its own garage, making the first floor seem as if it had been sliced in half horizontally.

On a happier and more musical note, Sergei Rachmaninoff, the Russian composer and pianist, occupied a five-story dwelling at 33 Riverside Drive during the early 1920s that became a home away from home for other Russian artists. Rachmaninoff's sale of that residence made way for an apartment building of the same address that sheltered the famed composers George and Ira Gershwin. From 1929 until 1933, the brothers lived in adjoining penthouses where they hosted glamorous gatherings for Jazz Age entertainers. It was also where the actress and singer Ethel Merman auditioned for a part in the Gershwin musical *Girl Crazy*, which resulted in her stage debut.

The area's musical composition continued at 67 Riverside Drive,[13] home to the violinist Isaac Stern. Jeffrey Seller, a producer of the award-winning musicals *Hamilton*, *In the Heights*, *Rent*, and *Avenue Q*, has also lived in the neighborhood, as has Jacob J. Shubert of the Shubert theater empire.

Chapter 14

The Elegant Eighties

THE 80s FLAUNT a unique blend of extravagance and restraint. They are home to the largest apartment ever built in New York, memorials both modest and magnificent, a Renaissance-style "castle," and an Art Deco star. It's here that a nineteenth-century woman MD led the country's first antinoise campaign, from a villa that became a yeshiva.[1]

The streets from 80th to 89th mark an elegant and inviting neighborhood of curves, cannons, and, in one case, the architectural equivalent of cosmetic surgery. The area has its own historic district, the Riverside Drive–West 80th-81st Streets Historic District. The 80s are also part of the Riverside–West End Historic District, which includes Riverside Drive between 85th and 95th Streets, and the Riverside–West End Historic District Extension I, which encompasses 81st to 85th Streets.

86 Riverside Drive/81st Street: The Carroll Mansion

In the late 1890s, Clarence True acted as both speculator and architect for seven exceedingly comely row houses filling the entire block between 80th and 81st Streets on Riverside Drive, as well as one on the southeast corner of 83rd Street.[2]

The limestone Carroll Mansion, 86 Riverside Drive at the southeast corner of 81st Street, is the dragon slayer among these Elizabethan Renaissance Revival homes. Five stories high and commanding fifty feet along its western front, it's a fever dream of high-pointed gables, pedimented dormers, chimneys, and romantic stone balconets over a rough-cut granite façade—a sixteenth-century castle scaled for urban streetscapes. A stone parapet crowns the captivating round pavilion that circles the corner. A deep and detailed, arched, and gated portico is unlike any other entranceway on the Drive and is topped by a balcony enclosed by a wrought-iron railing. A sharply

Figure 57. 86 Riverside Drive delights with gables, a deep portico, and other romantic adornments. *Source*: Robert F. Rodriguez.

pointed iron fence surrounds it all. True continued this royal fantasy inside, with stunning plastered ceilings and elaborately carved woodwork.

The 8,400-square-foot home was completed in 1898 and sold to William Carroll, a native Canadian and principal of William Carroll & Co., hat manufacturers. The company was best known for its straw-hat selection. Many of its designs were manufactured in unexpected locales, including Sing Sing prison. Apparently, the hat business did not always go smoothly. An 1883 headline observed, "Failure of William Carroll. Prison Contracts Not So Profitable as They Seem." Fortunately, that was long before the family moved to Riverside Drive.

It's easy to imagine refined ladies in floor-length gowns sweeping down the home's intricately detailed carved-wood staircase. Gentlemen might be found swirling after-dinner drinks beneath its tall ceilings while chatting about yachting or cards or their clubs. Perhaps they spent the rest of the evening enjoying music all together in the fourth-floor grand ballroom that ran the full width of the building front or took time out simply to enjoy the park view. The *New York Times* called 86 Riverside Drive "one of the most modern houses on the west side."[3]

The Carroll family sold the residence for $125,000 in 1922. Starting in the 1940s, after a succession of owners, the home was leased to a United Nations of organizations including the Chinese Delegation for International Cooperation and Cultural Relations, the International League for the Rights of Man, and the Woochefee Institute. There were also the Rochdale Institute, the Institute of International Cooperation School, and later the Royal Consulate of Iraq. This was in addition to the Sino-American Amity Fund, the Free Pacific Association, and the East Asian Research Institute. Later, in the 1980s and 1990s, it housed the National Catholic Press and sometime after that was split into apartments.

In 2019, the nineteen-room 86 Riverside Drive was put on the market for $8 million. Realtor photos show that, despite the long chain of institutional residents, remaining original details included coffered ceilings, decorative plaster, tall carved-wood-paneled doors, wainscoting, exquisite original fireplace mantels, and a baronial staircase that travels the entire height of the house.

In 2021, the residence sold for $7.3 million.

103 Riverside Drive/82nd–83rd Streets

From 1898 to 1899, True designed and built a speculative row of five undulating residences, also in his signature Elizabethan Renaissance Revival style,[4] from 102 Riverside Drive to 107–109 Riverside Drive. The Department of Buildings protested True's plans to extend the row houses' stoops and bays beyond the property line into what was considered parkland. However, True moved forward with his original design after obtaining permission from the Parks Commission.

Unfortunately, a neighbor by the name of Charlotte Y. Ackerman claimed that the sprawling row houses devalued her property by obstructing her view, light, and air. She filed a lawsuit and won. As a result, the homeowners had to hire new architects to trim their façades. All that remains of the original bowed fronts and projecting porches is the partial curvature of the corner bay at the southeast corner of 83rd Street.

This unhappy architectural fate applied to the charming, five-story row house built in 1899 at 103 Riverside Drive, one of my personal favorites among Riverside row houses. The L-shaped façade, which originally had a bow front and low stoop, was dismantled and rebuilt by Clinton & Russell in 1910. Fortunately, the revision maintained True's arched, recessed entranceway; original second-story windows; and the arched fourth-story windows with the keystones above them. The new cornice could barely be distinguished from the old, and the peaked red-tile roof was salvaged.

The actor Joseph Jefferson purchased the home in 1902 for $40,000. One of the most famous nineteenth-century American comedians, he was best known for his portrayal of Rip Van Winkle on stage and in silent films. In addition, he was president of the Players Club and listed as a "comedian and litterateur" in *Notable New Yorkers of 1896–1899*. He was also credited with the saying "There are no small parts, only small actors" and for memorably dubbing the Church of the Transfiguration, on 29th Street and Fifth Avenue, "The Little Church around the Corner." A glowing 1905 obituary in the *New York Herald Tribune* ran for three full columns and included a year-by-year chronology of his life and career.

From 1911 until her death in 1927, the home's owner was Amelia Bingham, a popular actress and the first American female theatrical producer, known for decorating the façade of her Riverside Drive house with statues of Shakespeare and his characters. The home was converted into a multiple-family residence in 1929 and returned to a single-family home before 1987.

Years ago, I watched as 103 Riverside's exterior was meticulously refurbished by owners who, along with beautifying the building, added large lighted globes to the tree outside, a lovely, festive touch that, in my mind, enhanced the entire block. Those globes are gone now, perhaps those owners are too, but I still find extremely warm and soothing the mix of rosy accents against tan ironspot brick on the building's Riverside front. The pattern the two make over the round arches of the first-floor window and doorways is particularly pleasing, as is the home's ornamental ironwork and the pedimented windows on the second floor. The result of the design is a sweetness and freshness that separates 103 Riverside from its neighbors like a pink-cheeked blond among jaded brunettes.

In 2012, the building sold for $11.5 million, and it was designated a New York City Individual Landmark in 1991.

107–109 Riverside Drive/83rd Street

Set on a trapezoid-shaped lot on the southeast corner of 83rd Street, this northernmost of True's Riverside Drive houses pops with an array of True-isms. The steeply pitched, red-tile mansard roof of this 1899 "on spec" creation reveals not one but three prominent chimneys, all with bands of limestone striped against red Roman ironspot brick, like out-of-reach, oversized candy canes. There's a charming crenellated

Figure 58. 107–109 Riverside Drive, before and after a lawsuit required its curves to be trimmed back. *Source*: New image: Robert F. Rodriguez; Deconstruction photo: Library of Congress.

parapet—hardly a typical sight on the Drive—its tower also banded. What looks like a heraldic shield on the side of the tower further enhances the Elizabethan Revival theme. The five-story building dominates forty-two feet along Riverside Drive, sprawls over two lots, and to the passerby confusingly looks like at least two buildings rather than one.

On the ground floor, the round-arched entrance, located on the side street just past the intersection, is heavily embellished, with carved stonework, colonnettes, and niches. On that same level, windows capture attention with their own round arches accented with limestone, along with decorative wrought ironwork.

In 1901, Charles Austin Bates and his wife became the building's first owners. Like so many other Riverside Drive residents of the day, Bates, who came from Indianapolis, had a varied career. He first made his mark in the advertising world, establishing the Bates Advertising Co. and writing no fewer than twenty books about the industry. He also organized and was president of the Knickerbocker Syndicate, president of the Rutherford Rubber Company, and vice president of the Crystal River and San Juan Railway, the Colorado Yule Marble Company, and the Colorado Slate company.

The 107–109 Riverside Drive building lost part of its original three-quarter-round corner tower following the 1903 lawsuit. What was once circular now appears shaved down one side, like a large block of hard cheese. The firm of Tracy, Swartwout & Litchfield partially rebuilt the home with the original materials. The ruling did not require changes on West 83rd Street, which presents an asymmetrically placed three-sided, projecting stone section on the eastern half, abutting what remains of the corner tower.

The residence was converted to a multiple dwelling in 1937 and is currently a rental building. In 1991, 107–109 Riverside Drive was designated a New York City Individual Landmark.

Riverside Park/83rd Street: The Warsaw Ghetto Memorial Plaza

Monuments and memorials in Riverside Park come in many different shapes and sizes. The Warsaw Ghetto Memorial Plaza centers on a modest granite plaque placed in the ground and surrounded by a metal fence at the southern end of the park's promenade. The memorial is one of the first Holocaust monuments in the United States. It commemorates the heroic but failed spring 1943 uprising by Jews against Nazi captors in the Warsaw Ghetto, where conditions were such that the mortality rate surpassed six thousand per month. Some 15,000 of the 56,000 Jews who fought in the uprising were killed, and another forty thousand were sent to concentration camps.

The plaque was intended as a cornerstone for a larger memorial, for which funding was never allocated. Over time, the plaque itself became the monument. Two boxes containing soil from concentration camps in Czechoslovakia are buried beneath the plaque, along with a scroll in both Hebrew and English describing the defense of the Warsaw Ghetto and prepared by the Chief Rabbi of Jerusalem.

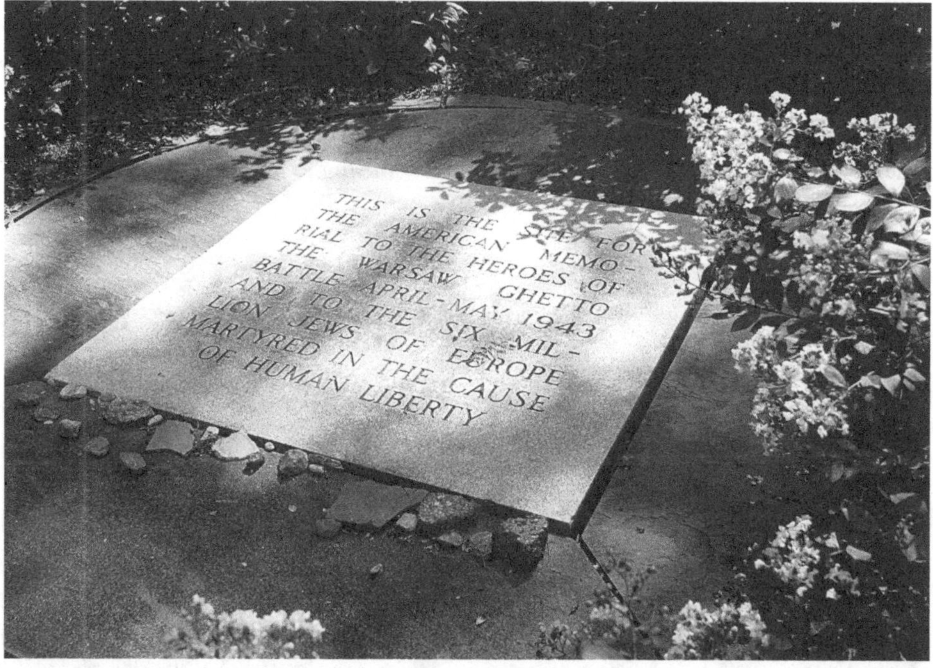

Figure 59. The Warsaw Ghetto Memorial was one of the first Holocaust monuments in the United States. *Source*: Robert F. Rodriguez.

A crowd of 15,000, including one hundred Holocaust survivors, attended the monument's dedication in 1947. On April 19 each year, the anniversary of the Warsaw Ghetto uprising, people gather here to honor those who rebelled against their Nazi captors as well as all six million Jews killed during World War II.

Riverside Park/83rd–84th Streets: Mount Tom

Rocks don't typically get much love, but this one deserves at least a nod of recognition. This tall mound of Manhattan schist is named Mount Tom, after the son of Edgar Allan Poe's hosts at the nearby farmhouse where he spent the summers of 1843 and 1844. It is from Mount Tom that Poe regularly gazed out upon the Hudson, lost in thought. He composed his famous poem "The Raven" while staying at the farmhouse.

120–125 Riverside Drive/84th–85th Streets: 125 Riverside Drive Apartments

This building entices the eye with its voluptuous curved bays that roll one after the other and its Medieval Revival style, unusual for Riverside Drive. One of the Drive's very early apartment houses, the nine-story brick and stone 120 Riverside appeared on the northeast corner of 84th Street in 1900, claiming to be the only fireproof building on the avenue between West 72nd and West 92nd Streets. Pretty, carved rounded arches run across the building above the top-floor windows. There is a flattering, wide stone cornice at the fifth floor and a bracketed stone cornice at the ninth floor. Heavy ornamentation enhances the arched stone entrance on 84th Street. Unfortunately, a row of fire escapes hovers above that entrance for the rental building's length.

In 1907, a twelve-story annex was built to the north of 120, and together they were renamed the 125 Riverside Drive Apartments, offering living spaces of up to twelve

Figure 60. Mt. Tom, where Edgar Allan Poe would gaze out at the Hudson. *Source*: Robert F. Rodriguez.

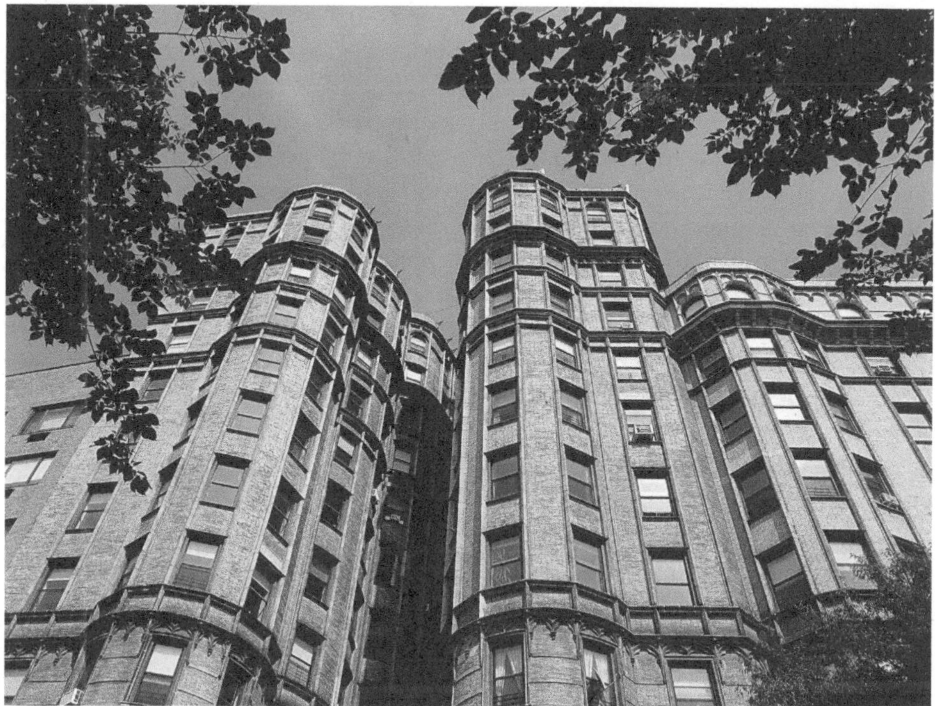

Figure 61. The rolling bays of 120–125 Riverside Drive. *Source*: Robert F. Rodriguez.

rooms. George Keister designed 120 (as well as the landmarked Belasco and Apollo theaters), and L. B. Ogden was the architect for 125. Together the buildings hold about 150 one-, two-, three-, and four-bedroom apartments.

137 Riverside Drive/86th Street: The Clarendon/Hearst Mansion

The media mogul William Randolph Hearst owned not just one building on Riverside Drive but *three*—numbers 137, 331, and 332. The first was for his family—his wife, Millicent, and their sons—the second for his mistress, Marion Davies; and the third for her father.

An impressive marquee distinguishes the 86th Street entrance to 137 Riverside, a twelve-story cooperative apartment building known as the Clarendon. It was built in 1907 on the site previously occupied by the 1856 Episcopal House of Mercy, a home for "fallen women" that was demolished in 1906.

The Neo-Renaissance building designed by Charles E. Birge and built in 1907 has a handsome but relatively simple exterior of red and black brick set in Flemish bond over a limestone base. There's some interesting red and white banding near the top, a few stories below a large mansard roof. "Clarendon" and a large cartouche with garlands are carved above the doorway.

Based on looks alone, it would not be anyone's first guess as to where the vastly wealthy Hearst once lived. On the outside, the Clarendon is no Hearst castle—nor is it a mansion, freestanding or otherwise. In this case, however, it's what's inside that counts. Each floor contained two ten- to twelve-room apartments, all with unusually large living rooms and four bathrooms. In 1908, Hearst negotiated with the Clarendon's developer to have the top three floors combined into a single thirty-room apartment. The agreed-upon annual rent for the colossal space: $24,000.

Along with his family, the space was to accommodate Hearst's ever-expanding art and antiques collection. In 1913, when those acquisitions had already outgrown the original triplex, he bought a particularly large medieval tapestry and wanted to raise the apartment's ceiling height to accommodate his purchase. When the developer refused his request for permission, Hearst promptly bought the whole building, for about $950,000, and proceeded to take over the eighth and ninth floors. In the process, he transformed his already huge home into the first five-story apartment on Riverside Drive and the largest apartment in New York City.

Hearst added a copper mansard roof to the top of the building, on the western side. This allowed him additional space to create the most impressive of all his rooms. The nearly hundred-foot-long gallery, known variously as the Banquet Hall, Gothic Hall, or Tapestry Gallery, rose thirty feet to a cathedral-like vaulted stone ceiling. In this extraordinary space, he displayed his extensive array of medieval tapestries, suits of armor, and stained-glass windows. Hearst also created themed rooms to showcase his vast collection, including an English room, a Julius Caesar room, a Greek room, a Georgian dining room, and a French Empire bedroom. Numerous reports maintain that a private roller skating rink was situated under the mansard roof, although others suggest that was unlikely.

Figure 62. William Randolph Hearst (inset) added a mansard roof to the Clarendon, to make room for his elaborate banquet hall. *Source*: Clarendon photo: Robert F. Rodriguez; Banquet hall and Hearst photo: Library of Congress.

It was at 137 Riverside Drive that Hearst played host to various dignitaries, society members, and celebrities, among them princes, politicians, movie stars, Belmonts, Goulds, Vanderbilts, Chryslers, Astors, Kahns, and even a German spy.

At some point during his residency, Hearst erected an iron walkway to the roof of the apartment house next door, at 340 West 86th Street, which he often used to leave the building and avoid process servers and other unwanted visitors waiting outside the Clarendon.

Over time, Hearst's fortunes changed, and in 1939—long after moving out of the 137 Riverside Drive apartment and relocating to San Simeon in California with his mistress—Hearst lost the Clarendon to foreclosure. In 1940, the building's apartments were divided into smaller spaces. The Clarendon became a co-op in 1985. In 1997, the old Hearst space was converted into a three-floor, seven-thousand-square-foot apartment that included seventeen rooms, seven bedrooms, and seven-and-a-half bathrooms, as well as ten thousand square feet of private outdoor terraces. Ceiling heights in some rooms reached fifteen feet or more.

In 2014, the art and furniture collector Benedict Silverman, who had purchased the space in the 1990s, put his apartment up for sale for $38 million, although a year later he reduced the asking price to a "mere" $24 million. In 2016, the apartment sold to the A. H. 2012 Family Trust for $20 million—a real steal.

140 Riverside Drive/86th–87th Streets: The Normandy

Because most of the buildings on Riverside Drive were built in earlier decades, it hosts but a few Art Deco apartment houses. The glorious Normandy, gracing the entire blockfront from 86th to 87th Streets at 140 Riverside Drive, is surely the most striking. The Landmarks Preservation Commission called it one of "the most outstanding apartment buildings on Manhattan's Upper West Side" and one of "the last great monumental pre–World War II apartment houses in the area."[5]

The Normandy was designed by the esteemed architect Emery Roth. Built in 1939, it has been termed Roth's last great work. Among the other outstanding apartment buildings that Roth either designed or for which he consulted are the Beresford, San Remo, and Eldorado, all of them New York City landmarks and all on Central Park West.

The Normandy, now a co-op, originally comprised approximately 250 apartments and replaced twelve townhouses built on the site in the 1890s. The building uniquely combines Italian Renaissance detail common in the 1920s and early 1930s, design elements for which Roth is perhaps best known, with the streamlining typical of the Style Moderne that became popular in the late 1930s. The Landmarks Preservation Commission identifies it as Neo-Renaissance/Art Moderne.[6]

Roth divided the Normandy into north and south wings, with two identical twin towers of nineteen stories each hugging a recessed midsection. The distinctive towers are light brick over a limestone base striated in a way that evokes Italian Renaissance palaces. Together the towers curve sensuously at each end of the block. Casement

Figure 63. The Normandy's twin towers, rising high above Riverside Park. *Source*: Robert F. Rodriguez.

windows round the corners along with the towers. Terraces ornament the sixteenth and seventeenth floors, and balustraded parapets set off the recessed eighteenth story. Balconies near the top of the building are rounded, and elaborate water towers resembling Roman *campanile*, or bell towers, signal even more visual delights at the rooftop.

The glass-walled sunken lobby, lined with deep-green marble, faces Riverside Drive and an unusual recessed garden. Glistening, intricate mosaics of beige, gold, and blue adorn the recessed, semicircular side-street entrances. Bronze revolving doors lead into the lobby and are shaded by a canopy, also curved.

The Normandy was intended to offer its residents a grand lifestyle, a fitting focus for an architect who once worked on Cornelius Vanderbilt's opulent Breakers "cottage" in Newport, Rhode Island. Original plans for the individual apartments included a bathroom for every bedroom, numerous closets, circular foyers at least fourteen feet wide, multiple terraces at the setbacks, and carved wood and marble fireplaces in the penthouse apartments.

Today, the apartment layouts offer generous living spaces, most including a spacious kitchen, oversized entry foyer, and an abundance of storage and closet space. Along with several penthouse apartments with terraces, duplexes are also available. Wall-to-wall windows found in many of the apartments frame breathtaking vistas of Riverside Park and the Hudson River.

Although evidence is said to be inconclusive, it's considered highly likely that the Normandy was inspired by and named after, in Anglicized form, the celebrated French ocean liner *Normandie.* At the time the "fastest ship on the Western Ocean,"[7] the *Normandie* departed on her hundredth trans-Atlantic voyage on July 13, 1938, just six weeks before plans for the Normandy Apartments were filed at the Buildings Department.

In fall 2021, a two-bedroom in the building was for sale, priced at $2.5 million. The Normandy was named a New York City Individual Landmark in 1985.

Riverside Park/89th Street: The Soldiers' and Sailors' Monument

The Soldiers' and Sailors' Monument is among the most impressive on Riverside Drive, second only to Grant's Tomb. The 89th Street monument was erected in 1902, as part of the City Beautiful movement, to honor the Union soldiers of the Civil War. It cost $275,000. The structure had been a long time coming. Since the Civil War ended in 1865, there had been numerous memorials to its soldiers around the country and various efforts to build monuments in New York. Brooklyn had its own Soldiers and Sailors Arch, dedicated in 1892. Plans for the Manhattan memorial, however, became stuck among disagreements over its design and location.

The Manhattan monument was conceived as a triumphal arch, similar to its Brooklyn counterpart at Grand Army Plaza. Sites under serious consideration included Madison Square (at the intersection of Broadway, Fifth Avenue, and 23rd Street) and the plaza at the Fifth Avenue entrance to Central Park. However, the Fine Arts Federation maintained that the site should be on the waterfront, where the monument would be visible from both land and sea. Riverside Drive met the criteria, although some felt it was too far out of the way.

On December 15, 1895, the *New York Times* commented, "At one end of the drive Grant's tomb is already rising. If the other end were bounded by a military and naval monument visible from afar and easily accessible from close at hand . . . the border of the drive between these two terminal monuments would become the fitting repository of the monuments of individual military and naval heroes."[8] Still, debate continued, and at one point the mayor and parks commissioners announced that the Central Park plaza had been selected, a site much protested by naval officers, who preferred a waterfront location.

In 1897, a design was chosen—not a triumphal arch, but a 125-foot column on a terraced pedestal, by brothers Arthur A. and Charles W. Stoughton. It was to be executed by Frederick Macmonnies and placed at the Central Park plaza, bookending the Columbus statue on the park's western entrance. This plan was immediately vetoed by the National Sculpture Society, whose approval was required by law for monuments planned on land belonging to the city.

A month later, the Riverside Drive site was approved—but this time, there were objections to the design. In response, the Stoughtons together with the French architect

Paul E. M. Duboy presented a significantly revised proposal. The new design was for a ninety-six-foot-high, cylindrical white marble and granite Beaux Arts structure modeled after the ancient Choragic Monument of Lysicrates in Athens and enclosed by a dozen thirty-six-foot-high Corinthian columns.

On December 15, 1900, thirty-five years after Robert E. Lee surrendered to General Ulysses S. Grant, New York governor Theodore Roosevelt laid the cornerstone in a ceremony attended by more than one thousand Civil War veterans. Roosevelt returned two years later, this time as president, for the formal dedication of the monument on Memorial Day 1902. Throughout the early 1900s, Memorial Day crowds of as many as twenty thousand people paraded up Riverside Drive to the site, and it remains the setting of Memorial Day observations to this day.

A mighty eagle perches above a bronze entry door over which "In Memoriam" is inscribed. Plazas with balustraded stone walls lead to the memorial on both the north and south sides while offering up a grand view of park and river. Following World War I, a bronze panel by the sculptor Salvatore E. Florio was added to the monument's door, as a tribute "to the men who died overseas." Three mounted bronze cannons cast in 1865 stand to the south.

Inside the monument is "one of the most astonishing memorial chambers in New York."[9] A fifty-foot-tall rotunda of elaborately carved marble rises high above five huge statuary niches. There is a great dome, ornamented with green mosaic palm fronds

Figure 64. The Soldiers' and Sailors' Monument with 173–175 Riverside Drive to the far right. *Source*: Robert F. Rodriguez.

and topped by an oculus and a cupola of polished marble. In 2015, however, the door to the interior space was locked for safety reasons, because of internal deterioration. Plans to restore it in 2020, at a cost of $36.5 million, were derailed by the pandemic. A chain-link fence currently keeps visitors from getting too close.

The Soldiers' and Sailors' Monument is sometimes confused with the General Grant National Memorial (Grant's Tomb) about thirty blocks north. Both are significant Civil War–related memorials, designed with stately columns, made of white marble, and set within grand plazas. Unlike Grant's Tomb, however, the Soldiers' and Sailors' monument is entirely cylindrical. The Soldiers' and Sailors' Monument was declared a New York City Individual Landmark in 1976.

170 Riverside Drive/346 West 89th St: The Rice Mansion/Villa Julia/Yeshiva Ketana

Directly across from the Soldiers' and Sailors' Monument is the singular home of Yeshiva Ketana, formerly the Rice Mansion. The building is notable for two reasons: first, because it is one of only two freestanding villas remaining on the Drive and, second, because it once belonged to the family of Julia Barnett Rice.

In 1899, Isaac L. Rice bought the land on the southeast corner of Riverside Drive and 89th Street for $225,000. Rice, who came to the United States with his family from Bavaria at the age of six, was a graduate of Columbia University Law School, taught there, and was a corporate lawyer. He also was president of several electricity-related businesses, including the Electric Boat Company.

Benjamin Altman had previously owned the land on which the Rice mansion stands, although like so many of his peers, he eventually chose to live on Fifth Avenue instead. Among New Yorkers of a certain age, Altman is remembered for the once famous and now long-gone B. Altman department store on Fifth Avenue (where I worked my way through college as a dutiful part-timer in the linens department).

According to an 1898 agreement between Altman and William W. Hall, a builder and real estate developer who sold the land to Rice, the plot had to be allocated to "a high class private dwelling house, not less than four stories, and designed for the use of one family only."[10] Rice hired the architectural firm of Herts & Tallant, best known for its theater designs, including the New Amsterdam, the Gaiety, the Helen Hayes (formerly the Folies Bergère), the Longacre, and the Brooklyn Academy of Music. In 1903, the company created a large, freestanding, four-story house that uniquely mixes an overall Beaux Arts style with Georgian and Renaissance elements.

The exterior was dark-red brick with boldly contrasting white marble detail, an unusual combination at the time. The main entrance is at the second-floor level, at the top of a wide stairway. The doors are crested by a pediment and surrounded by a massive marble arch that rises to the third story, making for an especially grand entrance for a private home. The repetition of curves throughout—that arch above the main entrance, the porte cochère on the 89th Street side and the bay above it, the projecting two-story wing on the south side—is particularly noteworthy, as are the roof's deep eaves. The delightful bas-relief on the porte cochère shows the family's six children, including four daughters, who were nicknamed Dolly, Polly, Molly, and Lolly. Columns edge windows throughout the main level, and a limestone balustraded wall borders a terraced front garden.

A highlight of the interior reflected Rice's passion, chess. A soundproof room devoted to the game was carved out of solid rock in the basement. It's here that he organized matches via overseas cable between United States and British chess competitors. He also developed the chess opening called the Rice Gambit.

Rice named the home Villa Julia, after his wife. Despite Isaac Rice's own accomplishments, it's Julia whose story stands out. Julia Rice was a nineteenth-century woman to be reckoned with. She was one of the few women of that era to earn a medical degree, although she never practiced as a physician. Instead, she worked alongside her husband on the literary journal he founded, *The Forum*, and contributed essays to other literary magazines of the time.

And she didn't like noise. She was particularly bothered by the constant din of river traffic, especially from the tugboats that passed beneath her windows on the Hudson River. Their captains would sound steam whistles and sirens for personal messages at all hours, often to summon crews from late night saloon hopping. In 1905, she launched a campaign to keep the noise down. She hired Columbia University students to monitor the river sounds and discovered that the tugs would toot two to three thousand times on a typical night. She focused on the impact of that barrage on hospital areas and received support from hospital and medical authorities. Rice pleaded her case at police stations, the health department, offices of shipping regulators, and finally Congress.

As might be expected, the tugboat operators were not happy with the attention. In response, they gathered their ships together across from Villa Julia, focusing their spotlights on the mansion's windows while blasting their whistles without reserve. But nothing stopped Mrs. Rice, and she eventually succeeded in generating legislation prohibiting unnecessary tugboat noise. Encouraged by her success, in 1906 she founded the Society for the Suppression of Unnecessary Noise, the earliest anti–noise pollution movement in the United States. The group's targets included firecrackers, factory whistles, and boys who clacked sticks along iron fences. It also encouraged schoolchildren to pledge to make as little noise as possible when walking or playing near hospitals. That particular campaign was run by the organization's Children's Hospital Branch, headed by none other than Mark Twain.

In 1907, the Rice family sold their mansion to Solomon Schinasi, a Turkish tobacco baron, for $600,000. The Schinasi family, in fact, at one time lived in what are now the only two remaining freestanding villas on the Drive—Solomon in the old Rice Mansion and his brother Morris a mile north at 351 Riverside Drive and 107th Street.

In 1954, the Rice mansion was sold to Yeshiva Chofetz Chaim. When a developer offered to buy the property in 1979 for $2 million, intending to replace it with a thirty-story apartment building, a fierce battle erupted between the school and those who wanted to preserve the mansion. Early the following year, the Landmarks Preservation

Figure 65. Julia Rice battled noise pollution from Villa Julia, also known as the Rice Mansion. *Source*: Rice portrait: Collection of the New-York Historical Society; Mansion: Robert F. Rodriguez.

Commission designated the building as a New York City Individual Landmark, and in 1988, Yeshiva Ketana took over the site.

173–175 Riverside/89th–90th Streets

This fifteen-story Neo-Renaissance co-op apartment building fills the entire block from 89th to 90th Street. It features a slightly concave shape that embraces the curve of the park and ends with an atypical and eye-catching chamfered corner at its southernmost point. That grand sweep of limestone and tan brick draws attention, as do the high arched windows with diamond-shaped details on the second floor and the similarly patterned lattice grille ironwork beneath them. Quoins, fluted pilasters, rosettes, cartouches, and . . . fish . . . complete the façade, along with four iron-rimmed balconies.

The 1927 building was designed by J. E. R. Carpenter and constructed in two separate units, divided by a firewall perpendicular to Riverside Drive. The two sections connect through the basement. Built with 140 apartments, it now contains approximately 167 units, ranging in size from three to eleven rooms, including several penthouses. Interior details include high ceilings, moldings, hardwood floors, French doors, and oversized formal reception galleries.

The building replaced the Scriven Clark/Bishop Potter mansion built in 1900 and the Cyrus Clark mansion from the 1880s. In 2020, a three-bedroom, three-bath apartment sold for $3 million.

Although it says 173 Riverside Drive on the 89th Street entrance to the building, 175 Riverside Drive appears over the 90th Street entrance.

And More . . .

According to its residents, 173–175 Riverside Drive has been home to numerous individuals who made their name on screen and various stages. They include the singer and actress Lena Horne, singer and actress Diahann Carroll, violinist and conductor Itzhak Perlman and classical pianist Emanuel Ax. The flutist Eugenia Zukerman; violinist, violist, and conductor Pinchas Zukerman; playwright and screenwriter Sir Peter Shaffer (author of *Equus* and *Amadeus*); opera singer Sherrill Milnes; and soprano Nancy Milnes all called the building home. The singer and actor Dean Martin also may have resided at that address. Yankee legend Babe Ruth briefly lived there as well, moving in 1942 to 110 Riverside Drive, his home until he died six years later.

One-Fifty-Five Riverside Drive was the residence of Julius Robert Oppenheimer, the "father of the atomic bomb." The author Herman Wouk resided at 140 Riverside Drive and the theater critic Brooks Atkinson at 120 Riverside Drive.

The actor Ben Stiller owned a four-thousand-square-foot, five-bedroom, five-and-a-half-bath duplex at 118 Riverside Drive. He also grew up in the building, in a 3,700-square-foot, five-bedroom, three-and-a-half bath apartment belonging to his parents, the comedians Ann Meara and Jerry Stiller. In 1965, when they moved in, the building was a rental; they paid $220 per month. They later combined two apartments, and the combined unit appeared on the market in the summer of 2021 for $5 million. It later sold for $1 million above the asking price. The artist Peter Max not only lived in the same building but created a typeface he called—what else?—*Riverside Drive.*

Riverside Drive in the 80s also has provided the exteriors for several popular TV shows. One-Thirty-One Riverside Drive was the setting of Oscar Madison's apartment in the movie version of *The Odd Couple*, 155 Riverside Drive the location of the lead characters' apartment building in the TV show *Will & Grace*, and 160 Riverside Drive the façade of Liz Lemon's condo on TV's *30 Rock*.

Chapter 15

The Very Nice Nineties

LOCATED LARGELY TOWARD the base of a steep slope, the 90s make up in perks what they lack in high viewing ground. It's here that Riverside Drive splits in two, carving out luxuriant front lawns for residents of the buildings that border them. The 90s also boast a beloved garden, favorite playgrounds, a wedge-shaped building extravagant with Native American symbols, and the home of one well-known comedian.

Like the 80s, the 90s are part of the Landmarks Preservation Commission's designated Riverside–West End Historic District, bound by 85th and 95th Streets on Riverside Drive. They also are included in its Extension II, encompassing the Drive from 95th Street to 108th Street.

Riverside Park/91st Street: The 91st Street Garden/Garden People's Garden

Located on the park's promenade level, the 91st Street Garden, also known as the Garden People's Garden, is a generous and much appreciated gift to all Upper West Siders. In 1981, it became the first official community garden inside a New York City park. Maintained by volunteers, it has delighted walkers, bikers, and seekers of peace and beauty. In good weather, the benches alongside the space fill with neighbors enjoying hundreds of varieties of perennial and annual flowering plants, all bursting with color and frequently attracting butterflies.

So appealing is this site that the writer, director, and Upper West Sider Nora Ephron chose it as the setting for the final and most memorable scene of the film *You've Got Mail*, starring Meg Ryan and Tom Hanks.

Figure 66. Volunteers care for the Garden People's Garden, where a famous scene from the movie *You've Got Mail* (with Tom Hanks and Meg Ryan) was filmed. *Source*: Volunteers: Robert F. Rodriguez; Film still: AF archive/Alamy Stock Photo.

Riverside Park/91st Street: The Hippo Playground

Playful pachyderms are the appeal at the Hippo Playground, a personal favorite ever since my then one-year-old, stripped down to a white onesie in the summer heat, made a gleeful dash to its kid-friendly manmade puddles. Tucked among honey locust trees, this simple spot offers shade as well as cooling spray, thanks to a sprinkler-sprouting hippo or two and a water-bubbling boulder. There are jungle gyms, slides, swings, and a sandbox, too. The Hippo Playground also hosts a "legendary" annual Halloween parade. What else could a kid possibly need?

Riverside Drive/91st Street

It's here that the Drive first splits in two, dividing the main road below from a much narrower and more "private" avenue above. In the process, it carves out islands ranging from sweeping lawns dotted by sunbathers to narrow wooded areas. The islands run north to just before 114th Street, with a brief break at the Henry Hudson overpass in the mid-90s, then pick up again for a time around 120th Street.

190 Riverside Drive/91st Street

This sumptuous Beaux Arts apartment building charms with its wonderful rippling façade of three-sided bay windows, stone balconets with balustrades or verdigris railings, and a spikey decorative iron fence. Classically inspired wrought-iron lanterns and stone urns flank the entranceway.

Figure 67. Fun time at Hippo Playground. *Source*: Robert F. Rodriguez.

Designed and developed by Townsend, Steinle & Haskell, the eleven-story buff-brick building with limestone trim was completed in 1910. It rests on the former site of a two-story, wood-framed dwelling and adjacent to a twenty-five-foot-wide alleyway that separates 190 Riverside Drive from the building to its north, number 194. The alley is what remains of a path that once led from the old Bloomingdale Road to Twelfth Avenue and separated the Brockholst Livingston estate from that of its northern neighbor. It was known as Jauncey Lane, after William Jauncey, who bought the surrounding land in 1799.

The building opened with two apartments per floor. When 190 Riverside Drive converted to a condominium in 1999, a number of units were combined to restore their original prewar layouts of 3,300 square feet or more. Many living spaces still include original details such as coffered ceilings, decorative plasterwork, moldings, wood-paneled dining rooms, and inlaid hardwood floors.

Riverside Park/91st–95th Streets: Crabapple Grove

Each spring, I follow the same, never-to-be-missed ritual: a stroll into Riverside Park at 95th Street, where, if the timing is just right, a short stretch south along the path will have burst into full white and pink bloom. Like the season, the exquisite sight is short-lived but sensational. The path is the westernmost part of Crabapple Grove, a four-acre grouping of colorful trees of that name that begins on 91st Street.

Figure 68. Remains of a lane that once led from the old Bloomingdale Road to Twelfth Avenue are visible between 190 and 194 Riverside Drive. *Source*: Robert F. Rodriguez.

194 Riverside Drive/92nd Street

I long ago fell for the lion's-head relief sculptures guarding the entrance at 194 Riverside Drive. The elaborate portico also pairs with stained-glass windows on both sides, glass and wrought-iron doors, and a double set of Corinthian columns made of smooth marble.

Curvy bays round the building's corners, bold horizontal bands enunciate the base, and a balustrade draws the eye to the roof. Stone balustrades accent balconets and balconies on the second and third floors, while pediments complement third-floor openings. Black against white marble in the entranceway presents a sophisticated contrast. A series of attractive arches leads past the lobby.

Like its next-door neighbor at 190, this 1902 Beaux Arts beauty has buff-colored brick with contrasting limestone and terracotta trim. A one-story pavilion unites the two wings of the seven-story building while a wrought-iron fence encloses it. The co-op's interior features beamed ceilings, inlaid hardwood parquet floors, delicately tiled fireplaces, lovely moldings, and charming bay windows.

At its start, 194 Riverside Drive had three thirteen-room apartments per floor and was built on the site of five row houses. According to a recent real estate description, there are currently about forty apartments, including three of the original thirteen-room spaces. In 2021, a three-bedroom, two-bath apartment was on the market for $3.1 million.

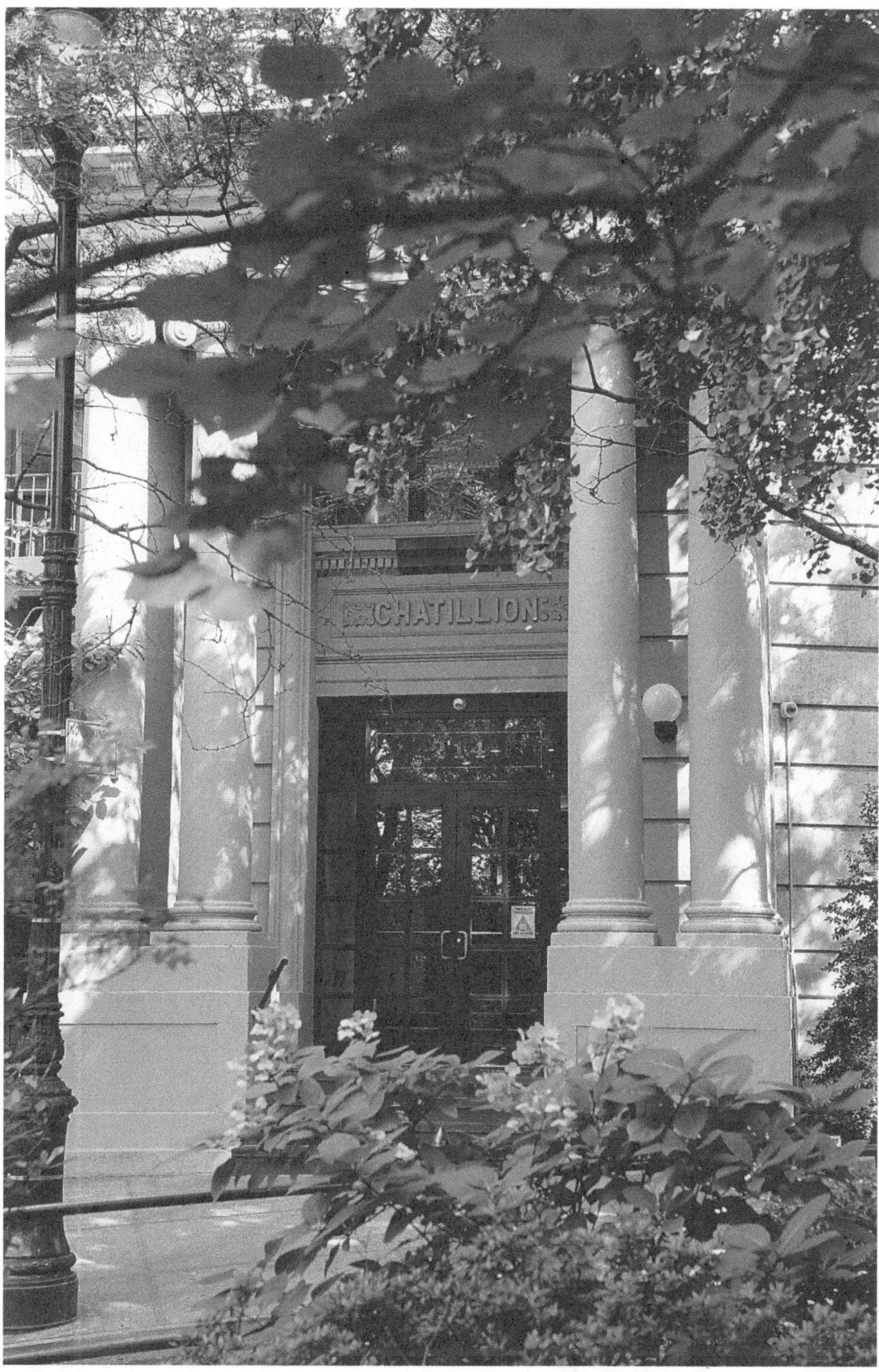

Figure 69. The Chatillion sits at a sharp angle facing Riverside Park. *Source*: Robert F. Rodriguez.

Local folklore has it that architect Townsend, of the same firm as 190 Riverside Drive, lived nearby on a boat in the Hudson River while this building, his first major project, was underway. He later lived at number 190.

Riverside Island/93rd Street: The Joan of Arc Memorial

Early in the twentieth century, the Joan of Arc Memorial became the first New York City park monument dedicated to a real (nonfictional) woman. Like the Eleanor Roosevelt statue at 72nd Street, it is also one of the few park sculptures created by a woman. Considered one of the finest works of art in the Parks Department collection, it rises high on the island between Riverside Drive and Riverside Park.

This inspiring monument honors the fifteenth-century French heroine who led an army, was convicted of heresy, and burned at the stake at the age of nineteen. In 1909, a prominent group of citizens formed a Joan of Arc monument committee to commemorate the five-hundredth anniversary of her death. They chose Anna Vaughn Hyatt Huntington, a young artist and art patron, to create the bronze equestrian statue, which shows Joan sitting tall in the saddle, dressed in armor, holding her sword aloft. Huntington maintained that her goal was to show the spiritual side of Joan rather than the warrior. An early version of the statue won the artist honorable mention at the Salon in Paris in 1910, although the jury was "skeptical that such an accomplished work of art could have been made solely by a woman."[1]

Huntington's design vibrates with naturalistic detail. She conducted research at the Metropolitan Museum of Art's arms and armor division for her subject's armor; to refine the horse's muscular anatomy, she borrowed a horse from her local fire department. Her niece posed sitting astride a barrel, as Huntington modeled the figure of Joan.

The architect John Van Pelt designed the granite pedestal, with its Gothic-style arches and coats of arms. Notably, it incorporates a few limestone blocks from the tower in Rouen where Joan of Arc had been imprisoned.

The 1915 unveiling ceremony, observed by more than one thousand, included a military band and, in the midst of World War I, was attended by the French ambassador. Also on hand was Mrs. Thomas Alva Edison, who was among the guests chosen to pull the cord that revealed the monument.

A few years ago, a group of neighbors created La Fête de Jeanne d'Arc, an annual festival at the site, complete with a French band and macarons.

214 Riverside Drive/94th Street: The Chatillion

Like 194 Riverside Drive, the seven-story Beaux Arts Chatillion was constructed in 1902, making the two apartment buildings among the oldest on Riverside Drive. The Chatillion is set at a sharp angle to the park, in a way distinct from every other building on the avenue. Six towering granite columns outline a dignified portico. Sidelights and a transom complement the entranceway, which is topped by a balcony. A rounded

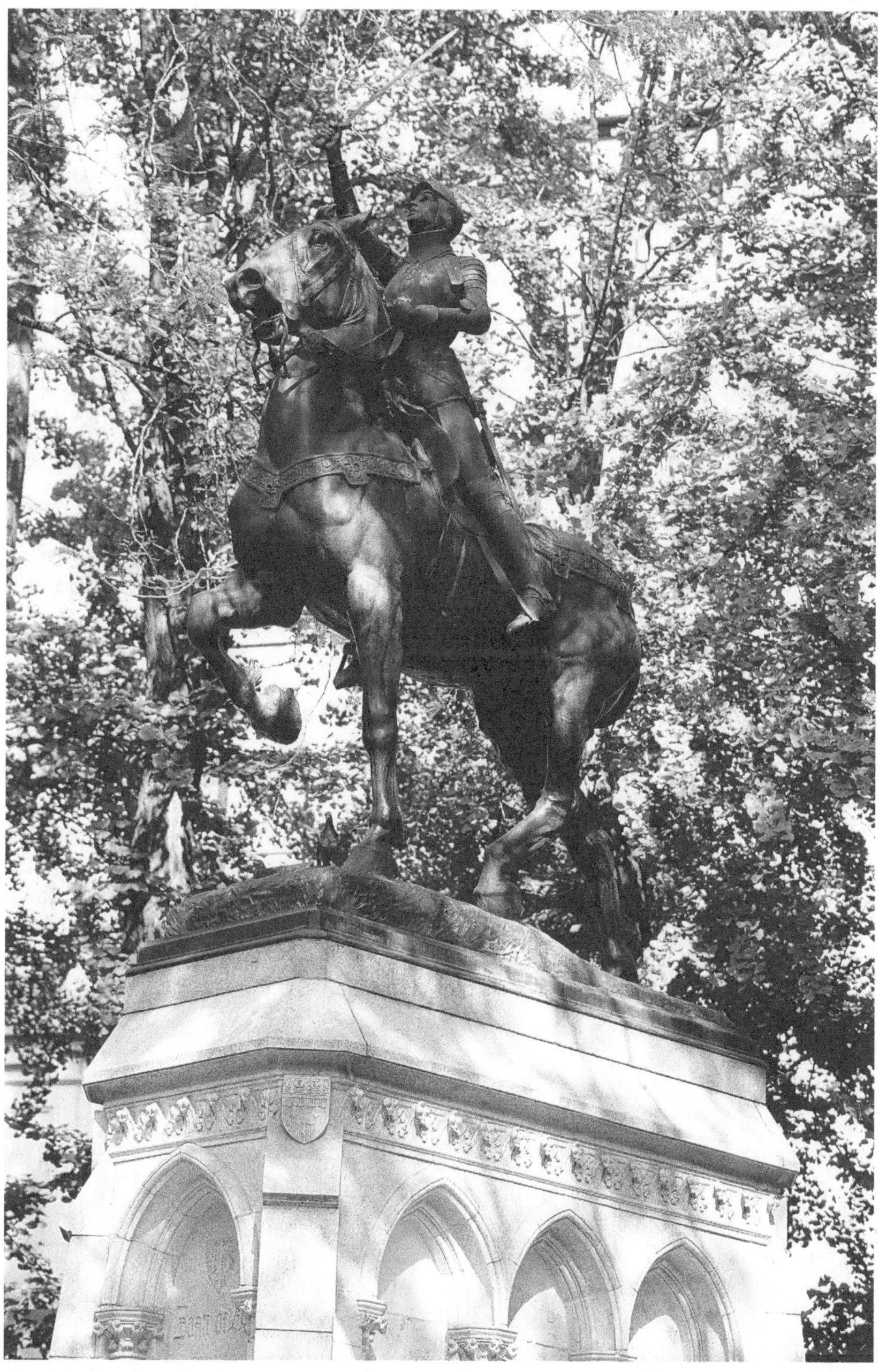

Figure 70. The Joan of Arc statue was the first New York City park statue dedicated to a real (rather than fictional) woman. *Source*: Robert F. Rodriguez.

Figure 71. Spring flowers bloom in Crabapple Grove. *Source*: Robert F. Rodriguez.

bay wraps appealingly around the northern corner of the building, while a stone balustrade circles it beneath third-story windows. Unfortunately, fire escapes scale the wall facing Riverside Drive.

The buff-brick, limestone, and terracotta building is named after a Parisian suburb, and "Chatillion" is chiseled into the limestone above its entrance. The Chatillion, now a co-op, was built with two apartments per floor but since has been divided into fifteen per floor. In 2021, a six-room apartment listed for $1.4 million was under contract.

The site was once part of the grounds of Mount Aubrey, a mansion built by Jacob C. Mott that was destroyed by fire in 1877. The building was designed by architects Stein, Cohen & Roth (as in Emery Roth).

222 Riverside Drive/94th Street

Worth mentioning here because it is the newest building on the Drive, the Postmodern 222 Riverside Drive was built in 1989. Even then and still today, it is an anomaly on this avenue of predominantly nineteenth- and early twentieth-century homes, although not an unattractive one. The twenty-one-story condominium tower was designed by Fox & Fowle and has a red-brick façade with three set-back terraces. A wide column of bowed windows boldly accents the building's Riverside Drive exterior. The lower three floors are clad in Indiana limestone. An iron and glass canopy shields the Riverside Drive entrance.

Figure 72. The old Irving Arms, replaced by Riverside Drive's newest building, 222 Riverside Drive (inset). *Source*: Irving Arms: Courtesy The New York Public Library; Inset: Robert F. Rodriguez.

The building replaced the Westsider Hotel, formerly the Irving Arms, a seven-story apartment building from 1908 on the northeast corner of 94th Street. The site had been the workplace of one "Mme. Marie," a prolific advertiser in 1920s New York newspapers who "for the past twenty years has specialized in the removal of facial blemishes." She could be reached by telephone at RIverside 3376.

243 Riverside Drive/96th Street: The Cliff Dwelling Apartments/Cliff Dweller

Whenever I walk the 90s, I treat myself to a stop at Herman Lee Meader's unique Arts & Crafts–style Cliff Dwelling, built in 1916. This wedge-shaped surprise package, just nine feet wide on its northern end, is uniquely wrapped with design elements associated with Native Americans and Mesoamericans.

Twelve stories high, the orange Flemish-brick and white terracotta exterior delights with a profusion of raised-brick geometric designs as well as carvings of mountain lions, corn, tomahawks, snakes, panthers, and scowling masks. From on high, buffalo skulls glare down on those who dare approach. A wonderful arch centers above a window on the uppermost floor. At one time, there was also a large metal and glass marquee at the entrance.

To make the most of the shallow lot where the building resides, the architect faced all the rooms toward 96th Street and Riverside Drive. The narrow east-facing rear wall housed the stairway, elevators, and a few secondary windows. Unfortunately, fire escapes mar the building's southern wall.

The original lobby carried through the indigenous theme with Navajo rugs; tan, green, black, and blood-red tiles; and zigzag designs on the lamps and elevator cages. Although the rugs are gone, much of the rest remains. Decades later, when its elevators switched from manned to automatic, the building used grillwork from the passenger elevator for the interior front door, turning the design upside down for a more dramatic look.

Not to be confused with the more traditional Cliff *Haven* on the southeast corner of 114th Street and Riverside Drive or the Clif*den* at 99th Street and Riverside Drive, the Cliff Dwelling, sometimes also known as the Cliff Dweller, was originally designed

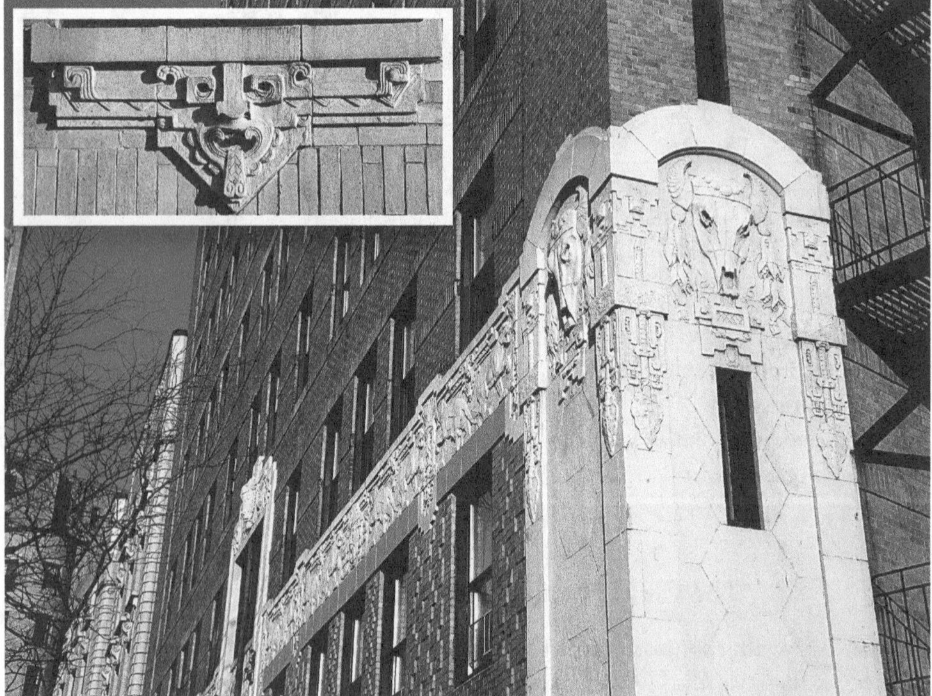

Figure 73. The Arts & Crafts–style Cliff Dwelling, with patterned raised brick and unique carvings. *Source*: Robert F. Rodriguez.

as an apartment hotel, with five one- and two-bedroom suites per floor and a restaurant on the mezzanine to serve residents. The building became a co-op in 1979.

Riverside Park/96th Street: Oscar Hijuelos Clay Courts/Red Clay Courts

This setting along the Hudson River near 96th Street offers the public ten clay courts on which to play tennis with a view. They are maintained and operated by the Riverside Clay Tennis Association, a not-for-profit organization affiliated with the Riverside Park Conservancy. Membership is not required to play, but a tennis permit is. In summer, crowds gather on the grass next to the courts for a series of association-hosted music concerts, from reggae to jazz to classical.

Farther uptown, a set of ten hard courts sits at the base of the steep slope at 119th Street, managed by the 119th Street Tennis Association.

Riverside Park/97th Street: Dinosaur Park

When my son was little, we spent many a hot summer day enjoying the cool spray of the sprinkler in the Dinosaur Park, he bounding from one nozzle to the next as I dipped my toes in the water. The playground, a favorite among many locals, is home to two fiberglass dinosaurs, a triceratops and a hadrosaur, on which all the kids in the neighborhood love to climb. It also includes swings for toddlers and older children, two sandboxes, and climbing equipment with safety surfacing. Is it the most spectacular playground in New York City? By no means, but your budding paleontologist will never know it.

258 Riverside Drive/98th Streets: The Peter Stuyvesant Apartments

Look up—way up—when passing 258 Riverside Drive, the 1909 Renaissance Revival building designed by William L. Rouse. Its decorative wrought-iron entrance door and the intricately carved frame around it are stately. Yet it's the elaborate, vibrant blue-glazed terracotta decoration surrounding the windows on the top two stories that dazzles.

The thirteen-story, fifty-one-unit co-op consists of two separate elevator banks, each one opening to a private vestibule shared by two apartments. Old-world apartment details include wood-beamed ceilings, inlaid herringbone floors, mahogany French doors, dentil moldings, wainscoting, and decorative fireplaces with original mantels. Based on personal experience, at least one apartment has an oval dining room, which alone nearly persuaded me to move in.

The building's developer was James T. Lee, grandfather of Jacqueline Kennedy Onassis. In 2021 a three-bedroom, two-bath apartment here was on the market for $2.5 million.

Figure 74. Glazed terracotta surrounds the Peter Stuyvesant's windows. *Source*: Robert F. Rodriguez.

Riverside Park/99th Street: The John Merven Carrère Memorial

The lovely memorial honoring the distinguished architect John Merven Carrère centers a pink-granite commemorative tablet in a balustraded terrace above a stairway.

A draftsman with the architectural firm of McKim, Mead & White, in the mid-1880s Carrère formed a partnership with the architect Thomas Hastings, who had also worked there. The firm Carrère and Hastings produced some of New York City's most memorable City Beautiful–era designs, including the New York Public Library, the Frick mansion (now the Frick Museum), the Manhattan Bridge approaches and triumphal archway, and Grand Army Plaza in Manhattan.

In 1911, Carrère died in an automobile accident, only two months before the official opening of the New York Public Library. Designed by Hastings, the memorial was a gift to the city and dedicated in 1919. At the time, it was the only memorial to an architect ever erected in the United States.

And More . . .

New York's "boy mayor," John Purroy Mitchel, lived at 258 Riverside Drive during his term in office, a fact acknowledged by an oval plaque to the left of the building's entrance. Mitchel, elected in 1913 by the largest plurality in New York City history

Figure 75. The Carrère Memorial was the only US memorial to an architect. *Source*: Robert F. Rodriguez.

when he was just thirty-four years old, was known to pack his own pistol when he went to work.

The publisher Charles Scribner also resided at 258 Riverside Drive. The novelist John Dos Passos lived at 214 Riverside Drive while he wrote *Manhattan Transfer*, and the humorist S. J. Perelman made his home at 230 Riverside Drive.

In 2016, the comedian Amy Schumer paid $12.1 million for a 4,500-square-foot, glass-walled penthouse in the 90s with five bedrooms, five bathrooms, coffered ceilings, and a wrap terrace with an outdoor kitchen.

Number 194 Riverside Drive has appeared in television shows including *Billions*, *Orange Is the New Black*, and *The Americans*. Woody Allen filmed scenes for the movie *Manhattan* at 265 Riverside Drive near 99th Street. In Cameron Crowe's film *Vanilla Sky*, Cameron Diaz's character deliberately swerves her car out of control on Riverside Drive, sending herself and Tom Cruise careering off the overpass at 96th Street and crashing onto the street below.

Chapter 16

The Happy Hundreds, Part 1

100th–116th Streets

LOCATED A FEW miles north of midtown Manhattan, the 100s are another world. Perched high up on the bluffs, they gaze serenely down on the park and river traffic below. This slice of Riverside Drive is special not only because of its spectacular vistas and distance from city center but also for its exceptional mix of monuments and religious institutions. Here a visitor will find one of the only freestanding private mansions in all of New York City; the tallest building on the entire Drive, as well as the site that once held its smallest; and memorable scenes of murder and mayhem.

The 100s are part of three different historic districts. On Riverside Drive, the Morningside Heights Historic District runs roughly from 109th Street to 119th Street. The Riverside–West End Historic District Extension II encompasses Riverside Drive from West 95th Street to West 108th Street. Lastly, there is the Riverside–West 105th Street Historic District. On Riverside Drive in the 100s alone, there are also eleven locations listed on the National Register of Historic Places, compared to just two elsewhere on the entire Drive.[1]

There is so much to see in the first twenty-nine blocks of the 100s that they are divided here into two chapters. This one explores 100th Street to 116th Street, the next 117th to 129th Street.

Riverside Drive Island/100th Street: The Firemen's Memorial

The attractions of the 100s begin, appropriately enough, at 100th Street, on one of the lush green islands that separate the upper and lower parts of the Drive.

The Firemen's Memorial is a dignified monument to those who gave their lives in New York City's fires. There were many such conflagrations throughout the city's history.

Figure 76. The Firemen's Memorial is the scene of an annual service honoring firefighters killed on 9/11. *Source*: Courtesy FDNY.

Five hundred buildings burned during the Revolutionary War and one thousand in the years 1835 and 1845 combined.

When Deputy Fire Chief Charles W. Kruger drowned in a flooded Canal Street basement while fighting a fire, Bishop Henry C. Potter (the same Reverend who lived on Riverside Drive at 89th Street) proposed a memorial to firefighters who had died while performing their duties. The city granted $40,000 to the project in 1911, and a popular subscription raised an additional $50,500.

Although initially planned for Union Square, the Firemen's Memorial eventually arose on Riverside Drive. The memorial's grand staircase leads upward from the main Riverside Drive to a balustraded plaza. On the park side, a fountain fronts a large rectangular marble monument with an impressive bronze bas-relief of horses drawing an engine to a fire.

On the north and south sides of the monument are moving allegorical sculptures representing *Duty* and *Sacrifice*. One depicts a woman holding the limp body of a fallen firefighter, the other a woman clutching a fireman's cap and embracing a child. Audrey Munson, the sculpture supermodel of her time, is said to have posed for both.

The architect Harold Van Buren Magonigle designed the monument, and its sculptures are by Attilio Piccirilli. Magonigle and Piccirilli had previously collaborated on Central Park's USS *Maine* National Monument, for which Munson also posed.[2] Piccirilli also sculpted the Daniel Chester French–designed statue of Lincoln for the Lincoln Memorial in Washington, DC. In 1927, the American Society for the Prevention of Cruelty to Animals placed a bronze tablet in the plaza beneath the memorial, dedicated to the horses that once pulled the fire department's engines.

The Firemen's Memorial was dedicated on September 5, 1913. Each year since September 11, 2001, Riverside Drive for blocks near the monument has been closed to traffic as throngs of firefighters solemnly pay respects to their brethren who fell on that day at the World Trade Center.

Riverside Park/100th–125th Streets: Cherry Walk

Cherry Walk is my choice for a joy-inspiring, up close and personal experience with the Hudson. This path along the river from 100th to 125th Streets is named for the two thousand cherry trees the Committee of Japanese Residents of New York presented to the city in 1909. The gift was part of the far-reaching celebration recognizing the hundredth anniversary of Robert Fulton's first steamboat expedition up the Hudson and the three-hundredth anniversary of Henry Hudson's discovery of the river. The colorful trees were planted in various parts of Riverside Park, nearby Sakura Park, and Central Park.

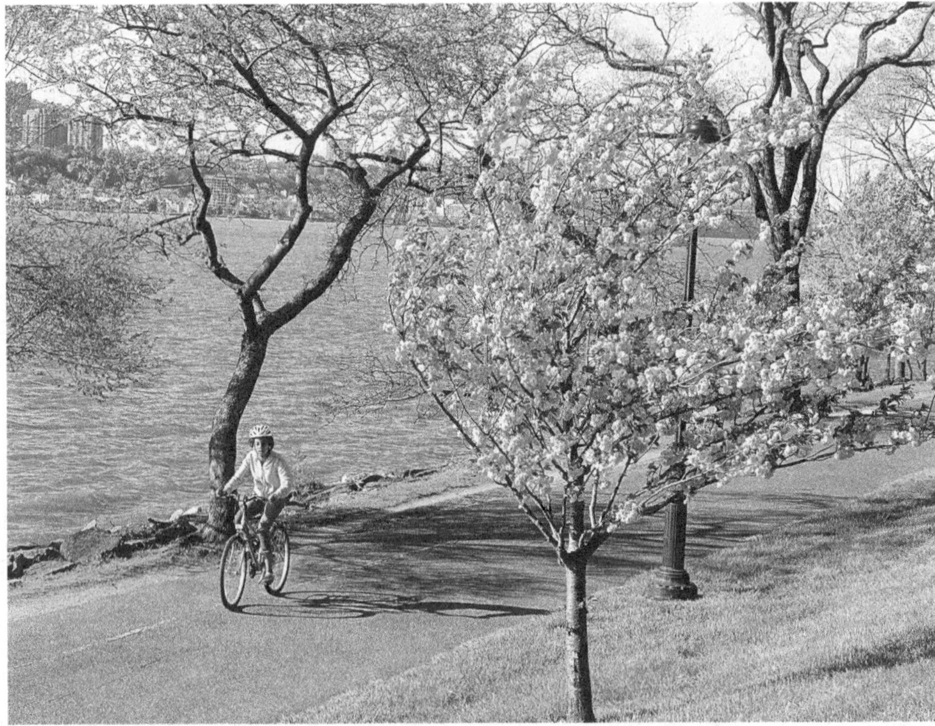

Figure 77. Cherry Walk is a favorite spot for bikers. *Source*: Robert F. Rodriguez.

Thirty-five new cherry trees were planted in Cherry Walk when it was completed in 2001. They line this blissful biking and walking path, which has no fences, railings, or other barriers between people and the rocks along the shore. The path is part of the Hudson River Greenway, which is separated from traffic and runs through a series of parks along the Hudson River and the west side of Manhattan. The greenway itself is part of the 750-mile Empire State Trail.

294 Riverside Drive/101st–102nd Streets: The William and Clara Baumgarten House

Delightfully frilly, this 1901 Beaux Arts limestone home oozes ornamentation, with swirly ironwork at balconies, balconets, and a first-floor window grille. There is even a surprisingly pretty wrought-iron fence. At the entrance to the asymmetrical five-story residence, a columned portico and scrolled brackets alike support a pleasingly ornate balcony across the full width of the building's façade. The original wooden double doors tease the curiosity of passersby with a discreet pair of small, perfectly rounded windows. Tall windows open to the second-floor balcony, while others entice with segmented arches, keystones, or cartouches. Balconets adorn the fourth floor, while a copper dormer to the north and a stone-faced one to the south detail the mansard roof.

The home was commissioned from the firm Schickel & Ditmars by William Baumgarten, a German-born master cabinetmaker. It is one of the few remaining homes on Riverside Drive designed for a specific client rather than built on speculation.

Baumgarten worked for the celebrated and very posh Herter Brothers furniture and interior design company and succeeded Christian Herter as the head of the firm. He later established William Baumgarten & Co., which continued the tradition of high-end interior decoration and furnishings and in 1893 became the first American producer of intricate Aubusson-style tapestries. In 1900, when the average annual wage in the United States was in the mid-hundreds, Baumgarten's tapestries ranged from $500 to $1,000 each.

Baumgarten knew his market. By 1896, his New York City factory had forty employees, a number that would eventually double. His client list featured the elite of the day, among them Astors, Carnegies, Schwabs, Woolworths, and Rothschilds. Examples of the company's work are in the collection of the Metropolitan Museum of Art.

Baumgarten died in 1906, and his family sold the house in 1914. The Landmarks Preservation Commission notes that it was converted into multiple-family use in 1940, although it may have served much earlier, soon after its sale, as an upscale rooming house. Today it is a rental building with nineteen units. The building was designated a New York City Individual Landmark in 1991.

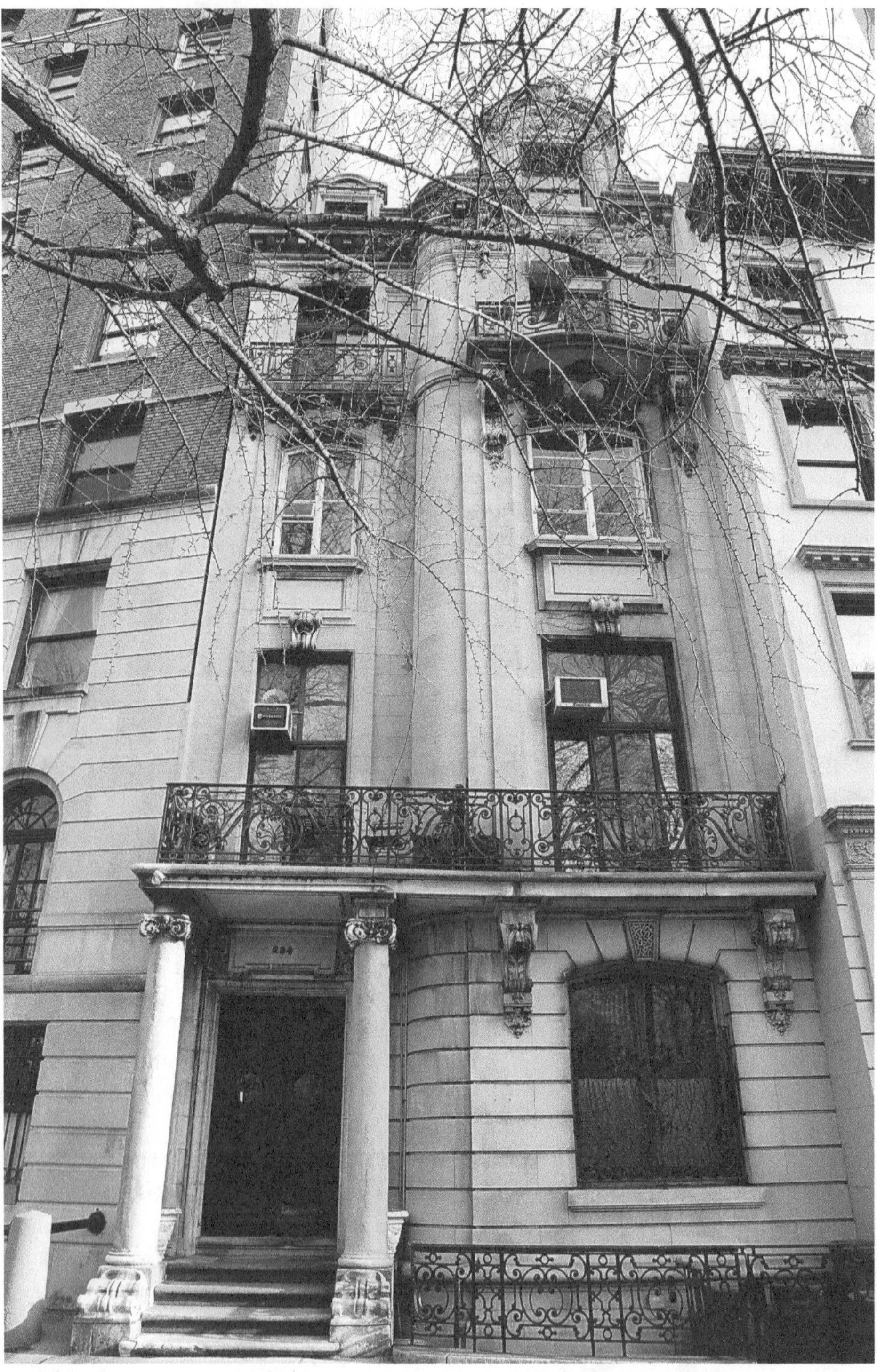

Figure 78. Fanciful ironwork characterizes the Baumgarten house. *Source*: Robert F. Rodriguez.

310 Riverside Drive/103rd Street: The Master Building/Master Apartments

Standing out as the tallest building on Riverside Drive, this twenty-nine-story residence known as the Master Building or the Master Apartments was completed in 1929. It is one of the avenue's few residences in the Art Deco style, and in *Guide to New York City Landmarks*, Andrew Dolkart calls it "among the finest Art Deco high-rise structures in New York City."[3]

It was also the first building in the neighborhood to use terraced setbacks, enabling a number of apartments to enjoy terraces as well as corner windows, said to be the first corner windows in Manhattan. In addition, the building features patterned ironspot brickwork, graded in color dark to light from its base to its distinctive high tower.

Topping that tower is a twenty-five-foot ziggurat-shaped metal stupa, a structure traditionally erected as a Buddhist shrine.[4] The building's boiler chimney extends through the middle, and in the days when the boiler was coal fired and there was an incinerator in the basement, smoke would billow out through the stupa. Clad from the start in light-colored metal, most likely copper, it later was covered with black tar and asphalt, probably to make it less visible during World War II. The Master's top floor was originally a meditation room and is now a small apartment.

The building's front and side entrances are distinguished by a distinctly Deco cantilevered metal canopy and large transom windows with blue leaded-glass sidelights. Original wrought-iron grillwork finesses first-story windows.

In the 1930s, ads for the Master promoted free lectures and recitals for its residents. The Master Building is an outgrowth—a very tall one—of a museum that once resided on the same spot. The Roerich Museum displayed the work of the charismatic Russian painter, philosopher, and explorer Nicholas Roerich, who, among numerous other accomplishments, designed the stage sets for Stravinsky's controversial ballet *Rite of Spring*. He was also known for his efforts to protect art and cultural treasures during wartime. In 1921, Roerich began a school, the Master Institute of United Arts. It was financed and directed by Louis Horch, who hosted the school and the museum in a mansion he owned at 310 Riverside Drive.

By 1928, Roerich had produced three thousand paintings, most of which were displayed in the Horch mansion. That same year, Harvey Wiley Corbett of the architectural firm of Helmle, Corbett & Harrison, with Sugarman & Berger, designed the Master Apartments to house the Roerich operations, tearing down and replacing the old house and "yielding one of the most picturesque skyline ornaments in New York."[5]

At the new building, the first three floors were entirely centered on Roerich's interests. They contained the museum; the school, offering courses in art, architecture, music, literature, and related subjects; two libraries, one containing rare Tibetan manuscripts; and an auditorium for lectures, recitals, plays, and movies.

Figure 79. The Master Building stands out against the Riverside Drive skyline, while an old ad touts its merits. *Source*: Robert F. Rodriguez; public domain.

The building's black granite cornerstone has a monogram, the letter *R* engraved within the letter *M*, for the Roerich Museum. Hidden within that cornerstone is a four-hundred-year-old box of hand-wrought iron with elaborate inlays of gold and silver from northern India, containing photographs from Roerich's expedition to Central Asia.

Over time, Roerich's influence declined, and Horch faced a variety of legal issues. In 1938, Horch expelled Roerich's devotees and replaced all things Roerich with the Riverside Museum, which showed contemporary American and foreign art and sculpture, including the work of emerging artists such as Louise Nevelson, Milton Avery, and Jasper Johns. The museum remained in operation through 1971. The Master Gallery, a space in the lobby where the museum once operated, continues to host events and exhibitions. The building was also the longtime home of the Equity Library Theater.

Other signs of the museum's former presence remain. The words "Riverside Museum" are visible above the no-longer-used Riverside Drive entrance, which leads to a grand staircase where there hangs a replica of a Roerich painting, *Treasure of the Angels*. The original occupied the same space when it lived at the Roerich Museum. Roerich's supporters relocated the Nicholas Roerich Museum to a row house at 319 West 107th Street, near the corner of Riverside Drive, where it remains today.

Sadly, Horch's son Frank Horch, the building's part-owner and manager who lived there with his family, became a victim of the crime that so badly afflicted the city during the 1970s. In 1975, he was shot to death in the building's basement when he went to check on the boiler room.

When it was converted to a cooperative in 1988, the Master had 320 apartments. Since then, a number of its many one-room studios, designed to attract artists, have been combined to produce about 285 spaces, some with multiple terraces and exceptional views. A 2020 ad featured a studio with seventeen-foot-high ceilings. The Master was designated a New York City Individual Landmark in 1989 and added to the National Register of Historic Places in 2016.

Riverside Park/105th Street: Ellington in the Park

All the walking, biking, running, and skating that Riverside Park goers enjoy is enough to make anyone hungry. An outdoor restaurant that spans two levels and overlooks the Hudson provides a welcome respite from all that activity, along with simple food and drinks. It's a fun, casual setting for enjoying a summer sunset or for following the action on the sand-filled volleyball court and "swing-a-ring" area on the lower level. Ellington is also directly across from one of the park's many dog runs, meaning that guests are likely to be both human and canine.

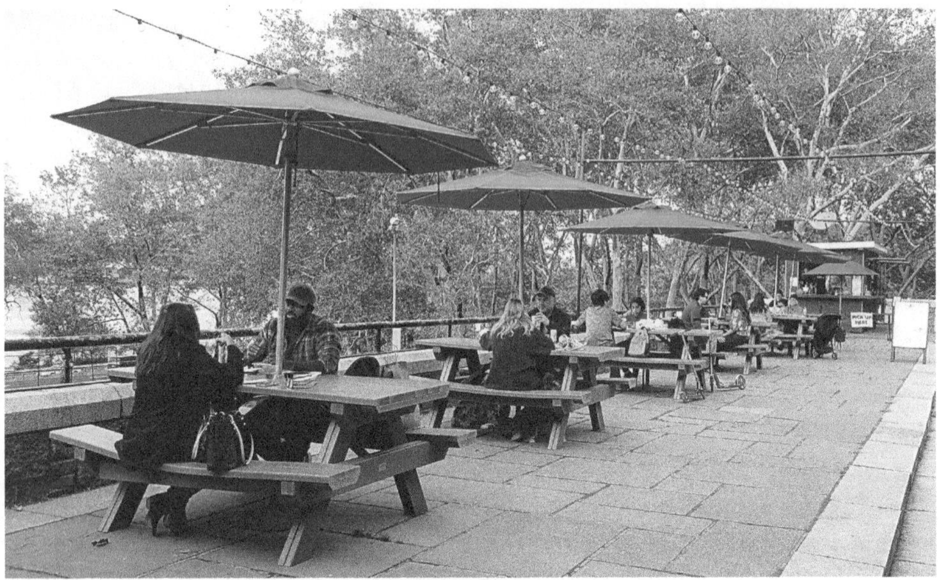

Figure 80. The Ellington draws park goers in need of sustenance. *Source*: Robert F. Rodriguez.

330 Riverside Drive/105th Street: The Davis Mansion/Riverside Study Center

The five-story Davis mansion is the southernmost building on what was once a full block of distinguished private residences, 330 through 337 Riverside Drive, the remaining homes referred to as the Seven Beauties.[6] Running from 105th Street to 106th Street, they comprise part of the Riverside–West 105th Street Historic District, known as "Paris on the Hudson." The block is also celebrated, according to a *New York Post* headline, for an interior life of "crime, sex and tragedy."[7]

Four of these homes, numbers 330, 331, 332, and 333, were constructed on speculation in 1902 and designed by Janes & Leo. The Beaux Arts buildings represented "all that is latest in fashionable dwelling construction, and are furnished with all the devices for insuring the convenience and comfort of their occupants, besides being designed with artistic correctness and finished with taste."[8] Further, "The location and houses are worthy of each other."[9]

The Davis mansion at 330 Riverside delights not only with its cultured appearance but also its scandalous past. Stepping grandly around the northeast corner of 105th Street, the nearly 14,000-square-foot, originally twenty-five-room building smartly pairs carved limestone with buff-colored brick. It keeps its more public Riverside Drive face relatively simple, even demure, saving its architectural surprises for its side-street profile. Here, entrance and window accents instantly draw the gaze. Large console brackets surmount the doorway and support a stately balconet. Windows bedazzle with arches, pediments, and cartouches, along with brackets, stone balustrades, and balconies adorned with ironwork. A mansard roof with multiple rounded-arch dormers deliciously tops off the scene. On the 105th Street side, a pediment embellishes an alluring, verdigris conservatory on the second floor.

If mansions were fashionable women, this one would be a rich man's sophisticated wife, dressed in a simple off-white sheath, makeup minimal, hair pulled back into a graceful bun—neck and wrists dripping with diamonds.

As they did more than a century ago, guests proceed today through a charming oval entrance, then are met by a cozy fireplace flanked by inviting upholstered benches. To the left was the billiard room, now a library, still wainscoted in oak, with built-in wood and glass cabinets and a lovely pair of fluted oak columns. A large globe, from the home's early days, stands proudly to the side of the doorway.

To the right, the stairway leads upward under an exceptionally beautiful stained-glass skylight, foliate in design, its leaves bright green against clear glass, its deep pink accents perhaps representing berries. Twisty spindles support railings while delicately carved swags top wainscoting along the wall. Leaded-glass windows shine between floors. On the spacious second-floor landing with floor-to-ceiling windows, marble columns once supported classical statues, and vases displayed generous bouquets of fragrant flowers. Imposing double doors, curved at the top, bordered by glass transoms and sidelights and headed by lively cartouches, continue to dominate both sides of the landing.

One pair leads to what was originally a music room and is now a chapel. The other opens to the old drawing room, followed by a richly detailed dining room, its wainscoted walls warming the large space. Here mahogany furniture, original to the house, includes a dining table with six extension leaves, dining room chairs (reupholstered over time), and a heavily carved sideboard. A peaceful woodland scene covers the walls below beamed ceilings and above bullseye-glass windows and leaded-glass cabinets. Fireplaces are everywhere in the house, brick in one room, oak or stone in another. Ceiling carvings range from delicate to bold. Tall windows look out on Riverside Park and Drive.

Robert Benson Davis was 330 Riverside Drive's first owner. Born in Pompey, in upstate New York, he was the founder of the Davis Baking Powder Company, a brand (think orange tin, red label) still found in many pantries today. At age thirty-eight, he married teenager Jennie Weed, with whom he later had one child, Lucretia.

Over time, the story goes, Mrs. Davis became less interested in her aging husband and more in his money. In 1908, she attempted to have Davis judged incompetent. In response, not so surprisingly, he sued for divorce. Delphin M. Delmas, who defended Harry K. Thaw in his first trial for the murder of the celebrated architect Stanford White, represented Mrs. Davis. Later that same year, Davis fell ill and informed the court that when he did so his wife "usurped his business . . . and surrounded him with spies that made his home a prison."[10] He further claimed that she even intercepted his mail and kept him locked in the bedroom.

Davis concocted an unusual escape plan. He dropped a letter addressed to a friend from the bedroom window; astonishingly, it was found by a passerby and delivered.

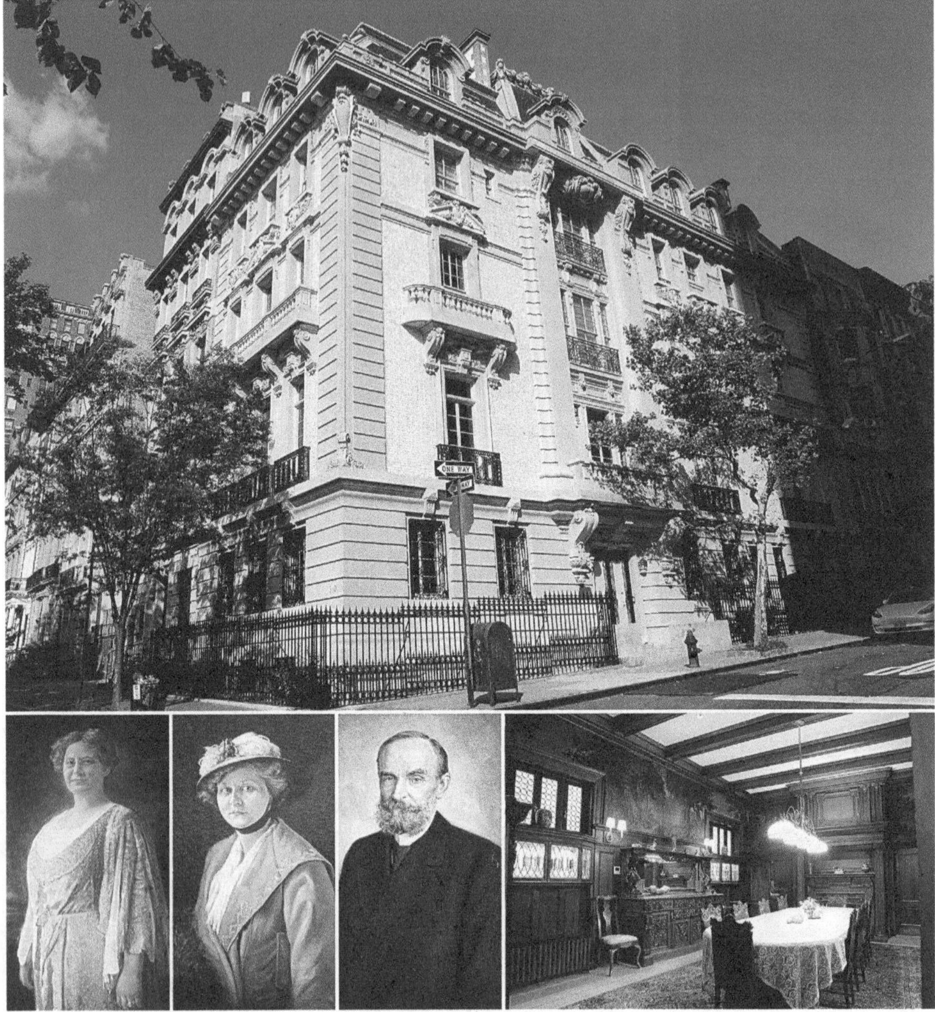

Figure 81. An ornate exterior and interiors such as this still intact dining room concealed family drama at 330 Riverside Drive. Original owners Jennie Weed Davis and her husband R. B. Davis flank their daughter Lucretia (insets). *Source*: Portraits: Courtesy Hillcrest Jephson Estate; Other photos: Robert F. Rodriguez.

When the servants were removing dinner dishes from his room, Davis escaped to a waiting car. At least, that's one version of the tale. Alternatively, the escape was the equally inventive one (from the family's other home, in Summit, New Jersey) that later appeared in the *New York Times*. "Disguised as a physician and accompanied by two nurses in uniform, it is said, Mr. Davis eluded the hired caretakers."[11] To complicate matters further, it appears that Davis may have had a romantic relationship with his nurse.

When Mrs. Davis discovered that her husband had altered the terms of his will, and not in her favor, she threatened him with allowing their daughter Lucretia to become—gasp!—an *actress* if he did not change his plans, saying that he would be "responsible if she falls into the many pitfalls of that career and becomes a low woman."[12] (Even though one of those "low women" owned a home a few doors down on the same luxurious street.)

The domestic drama goes on, with Davis taking off to California for several years, leaving Mrs. Davis behind in New York. Some of her descendants feel that there was another, sadder story behind the headline-making variety—that because of an illness, Davis had been acting strangely, and between that behavior and the rumored relationship with the nurse, Mrs. Davis feared being abandoned by her husband of thirty years. She was concerned about her future and that of other members of her family, whom she was helping to support. It was an era, after all, when women had few options.

Ironically, just three months after Lucretia married, Jennie Weed Davis died—five years before her much older husband. Lucretia's husband, George Jephson, later bought the adjoining mansions on Riverside Drive, numbers 331 and 332. After George's death, Lucretia sold 330, 331, and 332 to the Hansair Realty Company, which resold all three in 1955. She also, in her sixties, married her chauffeur, a suspect relationship in terms of the younger man's motivations and one that was quickly ended. Apparently, according to the family, 330 may have been sold to provide the chauffeur with a cash settlement.

The Brothers of the La Salle Provincialate, a group of parochial school teachers, purchased 330 Riverside Drive and remained there until 1978. They sold it to the Heights Foundation, a charity associated with Opus Dei, an international organization within the Catholic Church whose mission is to help people come closer to God through their work and everyday life. Opus Dei was founded in 1928 by Josemaría Escrivá, a Spanish priest whom Pope John Paul II canonized, calling him a saint of ordinary life.

In 1989, the foundation transferred ownership to the nonprofit Riverside Study Center, which operates the building as a hub for Opus Dei, organizing activities such as retreat classes and personal spiritual direction. The building also serves as a residence for celibate men active in the organization and can house up to fifteen people. Current residents range from a retired tax-law professor to a United Nations NGO staff member to a Columbia University doctoral student, along with a few priests.

Unlike many of its neighbors, happily, the Davis mansion has never been broken up into apartments. A major renovation began in 2017 and was completed in 2021, primarily to update heating, electrical wiring, and plumbing systems, many of which had not been changed for more than a century. Its current owners tend carefully to the building, inside and out.

In keeping with the apparent religious-ownership theme in this part of Riverside Drive, 331 and 332 Riverside Drive were sold to the American Buddhist Academy.

331 Riverside Drive/105th–106th Streets

The Davis feud wasn't the only scandal on this block whose quiet façade has hidden a good bit of tumult. In 1918, William Randolph Hearst, founder of Hearst Communications, bought 331 Riverside Drive, but he never lived there. Instead, it was in this

Beaux Arts mansion designed by Janes and Leo and completed in 1902 that the married Hearst ensconced his mistress, the Broadway chorus girl and silent film actress Marion Davies, who was thirty-four years his junior. Hearst spent over $1 million to remodel the twenty-five-room home, installing a large fountain in the sitting room and an impressive library of books that apparently were never read. Hearst also bought the home next door—number 332—creating an apartment there for Davies's father. The mogul himself lived on 86th Street and Riverside Drive with his family.[13]

According to Daniel Wakin's *The Man with the Sawed-Off Leg*, "Hearst and Davies hosted leading cultural figures of the day at the home. Anita Loos, author of the novel *Gentlemen Prefer Blondes*, lunched with the illicit lovebirds one afternoon and, that night, dined with Hearst and (his wife) Millicent at their digs on West 86th. She claimed that Hearst turned to her and said, 'Well, young lady, we seem to be sitting next to each other in rather diverse locations, don't we?'"[14]

Although Hearst and Davies remained a couple until his death in 1951, their living arrangements changed after a Hearst enemy leaked news of the affair, resulting in broad coverage of the scandal in New York's non-Hearst newspapers. Hearst sold 331 Riverside, and after 1925 the two lived in an even more imposing residence, his 115-room castle in San Simeon, California.

332 Riverside Drive/105th–106th Streets: The New York Buddhist Church

The original 332 Riverside Drive was damaged by fire and torn down years ago. It was replaced in 1963 by a squat modern building that, set back amid the endearing row houses, is as jolting aesthetically as a missing front tooth on a beauty contestant. Both 331 and 332 Riverside Drive are home now to the New York Buddhist Church. A larger-than-life-size bronze statue of the Jodo Shinshu sect's founder, Shinran Shonin, stands in the space once graced by the block's eighth "Beauty." The statue had been located on a hilltop overlooking Hiroshima, where it survived the world's first deployed atomic bomb, exploded over the city. A carved stone plaque on the wall below the statue describes it as "a testimonial to the atomic bomb devastation and a symbol of lasting hope for world peace."

335 Riverside Drive/105th–106th Streets

This 1902 home is the Seven Beauties' nonconformist sister, the rebel in the family. More American (Colonial Revival) than French (Beaux Arts) in style, and designed by Hoppin & Koen, it is an engaging combination of rosy-red brick and bright-white fluted columns, quoins, and other accents among all that reserved pale limestone. It's also, apparently, the one sibling on a diet, as it's the narrowest of all the buildings on the block. The home's name, West River, is visible above the door.

Figure 82. "The Seven Beauties" between 105th and 106th Streets. The gap toward the right is today the location of a squat Buddhist temple. The second house from the right was the home of the actress Marion Davies. *Source*: Davies photo: Library of Congress; Row: Robert F. Rodriguez.

337 Riverside Drive/106th Street: The River Mansion

Things get especially interesting again, architecturally and otherwise, on the northernmost corner of the block at 106th Street, home to 337 Riverside Drive, also known as River Mansion.

If the Davis mansion on the block's southern corner were a reserved and refined wife, the River Mansion would be the more playful mistress—equally attractive, but more vivacious, even flamboyant. Long said to be owned by the deeply dimpled Julia Marlowe,[15] at the time America's most famous Shakespearean stage actress, the building was, suitably enough, a showstopper.

The architect Robert D. Kohn designed the five-story, 8,550-square-foot Beaux Arts home, along with its next-door neighbor at 322 West 106th Street, both completed in 1902. Kohn was also responsible for Temple Emanu-El on Fifth Avenue, Riverdale's Fieldston School, and the Society for Ethical Culture's hall on Central Park West. He collaborated with Carrère and Hastings on the adjoining Ethical Culture school building.

The side-street residence is a quiet, buff-colored brick. The corner house, meanwhile, beguiles with bricks in lipstick red set against bold limestone surrounding the windows and quoins laddering the corners. Intricately carved limestone columns frame a marvelous entrance and are topped by a small stone balconet fronting a window. A lively mansard roof embraces an array of dormers, while a protective iron fence encases the property.

Marlowe supposedly purchased the home in 1903 for $68,000 but sold it in 1906. The buyers were the Faber family, of pencil fame and later Faber-Castell art supplies. It was likely not until years later, probably 1921, that the name "River Mansion" was

Figure 83. The River Mansion graces the corner across from the Franz Sigel monument. *Source*: Robert F. Rodriguez.

carved above the doorway. One of Marlowe's greatest commercial successes during the course of her career was the play *When Knighthood Was in Flower*, which she both starred in and directed. The playwright Paul Kester wrote it around the turn of the century while staying at the old Furniss mansion on the corner of 100th Street and Riverside, a half-dozen blocks south. This was the very same story that, in movie form, later became a silent movie hit of the same name for a future resident of Marlowe's own Riverside block, Marion Davies.

Of all the buildings on Riverside Drive between 105th and 106th Streets, 337 has led the most lives. Over time, as a private home, it had numerous successive owners, then was converted into furnished rooms, which it remained for decades, then back to a private dwelling that served as a music school, then a two-family home, and now a private home, owned, fittingly, by an actress. Sherry Bronfman, then Sherry Brewer, is best known for her role in the movie *Shaft*. She bought River Mansion with her now former husband, Edgar Bronfman, previously CEO of Warner Music Group and the Seagram Company.

Riverside Drive/107th Street

With elegant early twentieth-century mansions surrounding it, the southeast corner of 107th Street was once the surprising site of a single-story, five-room prefabricated dwelling, made of two-by-four-foot steel panels. Perched atop a jagged boulder, the structure was designed by William Van Alen, known for a somewhat more notable project, the Chrysler Building, and built by the developer Charles Paterno.

The home was meant to be a demonstration model for National Houses Inc., which was promoting this inexpensive housing alternative for low-income buyers. A news article at the time noted that the house was "resistant to fires, winds, lightning, termites and earthquakes."[16] Designed to sell for $3,000, the home was erected in 1937.

Paterno's original plan to build an apartment house on the site was blocked by an 1897 deed restriction requiring that the first building on the lot be a private house. The little prefab satisfied that requirement at minimal cost. Yet after it was demolished, another developer built 345 Riverside Drive there instead.

351 Riverside Drive/107th Street: The Morris and Laurette Schinasi Residence

On the northeast corner of 107th Street rests the residential jewel in the crown of Riverside Drive, the stunning Schinasi villa. It is the only remaining freestanding, privately owned mansion on the Drive and one of the last in all of Manhattan.

For years, under a variety of owners, it was nearly obscured by scaffolding. Neighbors would wonder aloud: Who bought it? How much did it sell for? What are they *doing* in there under all that scaffolding? And does anyone live there yet? I for one would regularly stop and stare, as, most recently, the owners replaced crumbling marble balustrades with new stone, upgraded windows, and repaired roofing. I always called it the Mystery Mansion, although it is better known as the Schinasi Residence.

The gleamingly white Schinasi, built in 1909, is the brightest of smiles on the face of Riverside Drive. This delicious four-story wedding cake of a residence was designed by William Tuthill, the architect of Carnegie Hall, on property previously owned by Samuel Bayne.[17] The French Renaissance limestone confection encompasses 12,000

Figure 84. The last remaining privately owned villa on Riverside Drive, the Schinasi residence has changed little over time. *Source*: Inset: Morris Schinasi; Historic photo: Irving Underhill, Museum of the City of New York, X2010.28.118; Current: Robert F. Rodriguez; public domain.

square feet, what was originally thirty-five rooms, and 3,500 square feet of outdoor space. At the time of a twenty-first-century sale, it had twelve bedrooms and eleven bathrooms. The original cost in the early 1900s: $180,000.

A marble wall punctuated by balusters and topped with high newel posts surrounds a grand stairway to the entrance, once guarded by a pair of fierce-faced lions. Elaborate stone balconies on the second floor frame the iron and glass doorway below. A three-sided copper oriel window surprises and enchants at the rear of the building. Stained-glass windows throughout enhance the turn-of-the-last-century setting.

To protect against the "incorrigible vandal"[18] of New York's polluted air, its original owner installed water taps around the outside of the house to enable frequent washing.

The steeply pitched mansard roof bewitches with its green terracotta tile, exceedingly ornate dormer windows, and two spikey finials up front. There is also a tall stone chimney. In the spring, a magnolia tree blooms brightly just outside, warming the stark whiteness with its blush. The *Real Estate Record and Builders' Guide* called 351 Riverside Drive "exquisite from any side."[19]

In the early days, a tunnel ran from the building's basement under Riverside Drive to the banks of the Hudson River.[20] The tunnel has since been sealed off—much to my disappointment.

And the interior! Original descriptions celebrate a wealth of polish and shine, of marble and mosaics, as well as a staircase hall of white oak, gilded panels, and rose silk wall covering. Although there have been numerous alterations over time, most of the mansion's original and exquisite historic detail has endured. Twenty-first-century photos show stunning carved woodwork on ceilings, walls, staircases, and fireplace mantels, along with marble walls and original tilework.

Rooms at various times over the years have included a teak-paneled library with a lacquered gold oval dome along with a fireplace and built-in window seat, a smoking room with ceiling frescos and gold leafing, a formal wood-paneled dining room with stained-glass windows, and a drawing room with carved ceilings. The vestibule boasted striking veined marble and a faience tile ceiling. That's in addition to an English basement and two kitchens.

The exquisite mansion was built for the Turkish tobacco baron Morris Schinasi, born Musa (or Mussa) Eskenazi in the Ottoman Empire to relatively poor Sephardic Jewish parents. When, the story goes, he contracted diphtheria as a child and was treated successfully by a Muslim physician named Şinasi, his parents renamed him Morris Sinasi in gratitude. Other sources say he was born Mussa Schinasi and simply changed his name to Morris on arriving in the United States.

As a youngster, he had to leave school and worked in a Jewish cemetery as a guard. At fifteen, he moved to Egypt, where he learned the tobacco business and lived until he was nearly thirty. In 1890, he borrowed money from a friend to immigrate to the United States. Three years later, Schinasi exhibited cigarettes made with his patented cigarette-rolling machine at the 1893 Chicago World's Columbian Exposition. Until then, cigarettes had always been hand rolled, and his invention generated interest. Soon after, his brother Solomon joined him in New York City, and they established the Schinasi Brothers Company, which featured premade cigarettes rolled with imported Turkish tobacco, made in their factory on nearby West 120th Street and Broadway. Appropriately enough, in the home's "ornamental carvings there is a consistent use of the foliage of the tobacco plant."[21]

Despite his home's opulence, Schinasi refused to pay his architect, Tuthill, $5,655.65 in fees the architect claimed was owed to him. Tuthill sued. By 1907, both Schinasi and his brother were millionaires. In 1916, they sold the cigarette factory and all commercial rights to the business to the American Tobacco Company for $3.5 million.

Despite his success as a businessman, Schinasi never learned to read. When asked what he might have become had he been literate, he responded, referring to the job from which he was fired as a teenager, "A good cemetery guard."[22] His daughter Altina, meanwhile, invented the Harlequin eyeglass frame, a must-have fashion of the late 1930s.

Schinasi lived at the Riverside Drive mansion for almost twenty years until his death in 1928. Two years later, his heirs sold the house for $200,000. It served first as the Semple School, a finishing school for girls. In 1960, Columbia University turned it into a daycare center known as the Children's Mansion. A decade later, the mansion housed a Columbia/Barnard coed residential program called the Experimental College.

In 1979, the university sold the mansion to the Columbia law professor Hans Smit for $325,000. It was then that the grand villa finally returned to its original purpose as a residence. Smit initiated an interior restoration that took twenty years to complete. He never actually lived there, although his son and his son's family did until 2013. Smit also used the mansion for Columbia Law School gatherings and small parties.

In 2006, he put 351 Riverside Drive up for sale, unsuccessfully, for an asking price of $31 million. It reappeared on the market several times and was listed for $15 million in the fall of 2011. Two years later, in 2013, it sold for $14 million to Mark Schwartz, a vice chairman at Goldman Sachs. The building was designated a New York City Individual Landmark in 1974 and was added to the National Register of Historic Places in 1980.

352 and 353 Riverside Drive/107th–108th Streets

The Schinasi mansion's neighbors immediately to the north of the block are twin Beaux Arts charmers, 352 and 353 Riverside Drive, completed in 1901. A pair of rubies complementing Schinasi's luxurious string of pearls, the nine-thousand-square-foot mansions were designed by Robert D. Kohn, the architect behind River Mansion on the southeast corner of 106th Street. Like that delectable domicile, these are bright-red brick and limestone.

At both five-story locations, rusticated limestone bases support a two-story, full-width rounded bay. A cartouche carved with the address enhances the iron and glass double-door entrance. The second floor opens to a romantic balconet with a decorative wrought iron railing; a stone balustrade shapes a balcony on the fourth floor. Multiple

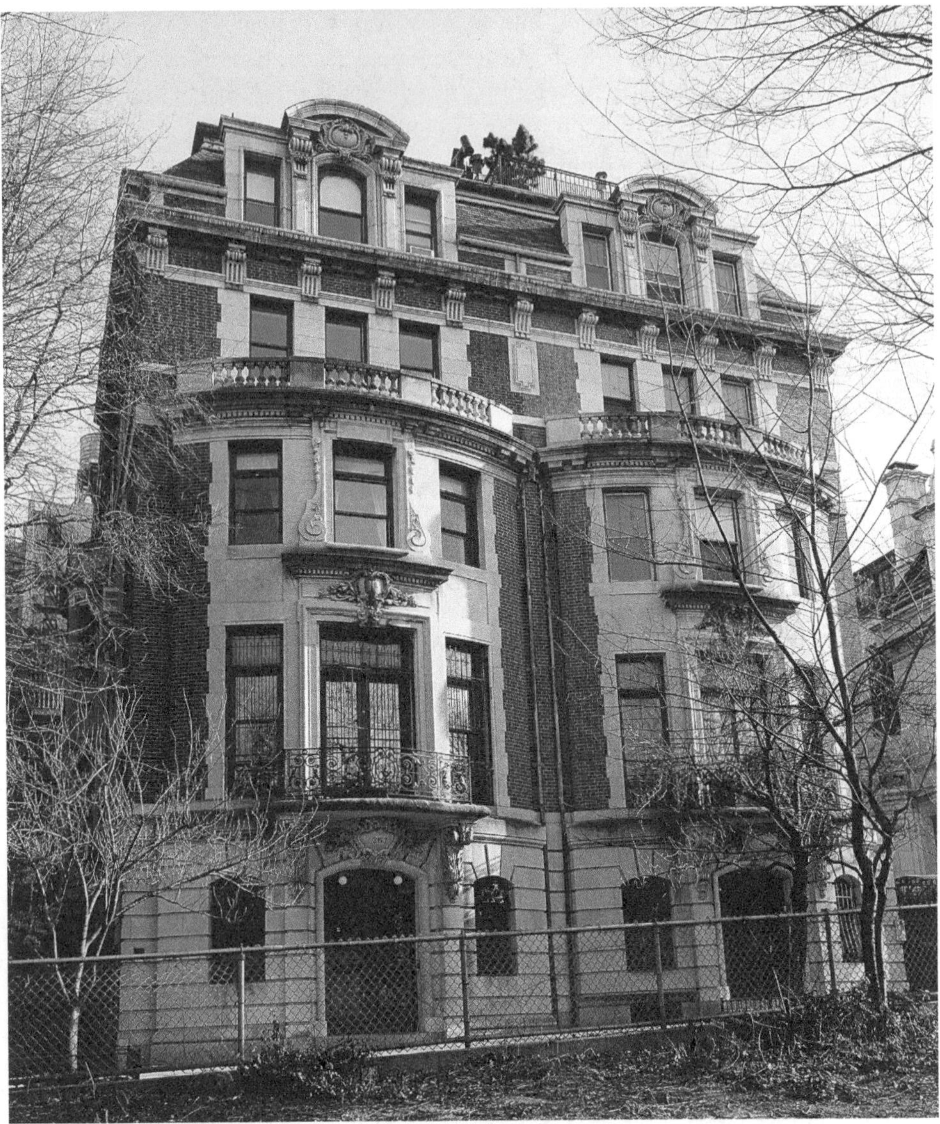

Figure 85. Twins 352 and 353 Riverside Drive grew up very differently. *Source*: Robert F. Rodriguez.

dormers ornament the mansard roof while a two-story, copper-clad oriel window enchants from the sidewall.

Inside, at 352 Riverside Drive, remaining architectural details within the past decade have included a striking mahogany-paneled staircase leading the way below what's said to be an original Tiffany glass skylight, as well as a dining room with beamed ceilings and intricate plasterwork. Eight wood-burning fireplaces, leaded-glass windows, wood paneling, original moldings, coffered ceilings, and pocket doors upped the opulence level. A wood-paneled elevator and a garden with a fountain completed the scene. This is in addition to nine bedrooms and eight bathrooms.

Unfortunately, money and the lifestyle it affords aren't always enough, even on Riverside Drive. That was the case for the building's first owner, Adolphe Openhym, a prosperous silk merchant who moved in with his family in 1901. Like his neighbors the Schinasis, he purchased the land from Samuel Bayne. On March 30, 1903, rather than heading downtown to his office, Openhym headed north to the High Bridge, the tall stone crossing above the Harlem River linking Manhattan and the Bronx. There, he jumped to his death. Openhym's body was found a few days later. The funeral services were held in the parlor of number 352.

By 1943, 352 and 353 Riverside Drive belonged to an order of Jesuit priests, who operated them as Woodstock College. The 352 building served as the school, while 353 was a dormitory. Thirty-four years later, the order sold 352 Riverside Drive to Jim Rogers, a former hedge fund broker who had cofounded Quantum Fund. Rogers paid $107,300 for the property, which retained most of its original detail. In 2007, he sold it to Helen LaKelly Hunt, the daughter of the oil magnate H. L. Hunt, for $15.75 million. She listed it for $19.8 million in 2015 and sold it in 2018 for $11.6 million. It sold again in 2021, still a private home, for $15.25 million.

Its doppelganger at 353, however, served in the 1920s as a venue for weddings and other events and was converted into apartments in 1935. In 1977, it began selling co-op apartments, for $15,000 to $40,000 each, including a duplex. Monthly maintenance charges were $175 to $325. It remains a co-op building today. Both 352 and 353 Riverside Drive are listed in the National Register of Historic Places.

Riverside Park/108th–109th Streets: Riverside Park Skate Park

While there are dozens of recreational facilities in Riverside Park, including multiple baseball fields and basketball courts, there is only one skate park, remodeled in 2020 to accommodate skaters of all levels safely. Upgrades included the addition of a new street-style skating area and an eleven-foot-deep bowl.

380 Riverside Drive/110th–111th Streets: The Hendrik Hudson

The Hendrik (sometimes spelled Hendrick) Hudson apartment building intriguingly angles its Italian Renaissance Revival bulk around the northeast corner of 110th Street, also known as Cathedral Parkway, across Riverside Drive and back up a good part of 111th Street. The broad parkway curls just past the building's entrance downward to the "lower" Drive, creating an island of trees in between. Rouse and Sloan were the architects for the 1907 residence, designed with seventy-two apartments.

The striking, rounded-arch windows at the base of the Tuscan-villa-style building are made to look double height and have unusual pressed-metal detailing. Balconets, some all of stone and others with iron railings, project here and there, adding still

Figure 86. The new skate park sees lots of action. *Source*: Robert F. Rodriguez.

more texture to the building's eight floors (plus penthouse) of brick, limestone, and terracotta.

Over the recessed and arched main entrance on 110th Street, the carved head of Bacchus peers down upon visitors. It is flanked by large, elaborate figures supporting a projecting cornice and balustrade, where "HH" is carved onto a central shield. The arched entry is reportedly modeled closely after the 1656 design for the town hall in Toulon, France. A railed "dry moat" surrounds the exterior.

Up on the roof, a pair of square towers once had open Palladian arches on all four sides, balconies, and panels detailed with terracotta. A balustraded and trellis-covered promenade, for the tenants' use, linked the two towers together, while huge bronze brackets supported an enormous Spanish-tile roof that projected over the walls. Over time, all of these features except for the southern belvedere were removed. When the old roof was stripped, an extra floor of apartments was added to the top of the building. A large and generously embellished oval window below the base of each tower, however, continues to gaze out toward the Drive and park.

Inside, the Hendrik Hudson's original amenities were legion, among them a café, billiard parlor, barbershop, and ladies' hairdressing salon, exclusively for residents and their guests. In the marble lobby, the original bronze torchères and stone benches and tables are no more. The coffered ceiling, however, remains, while just past the doorman's desk, a small fountain now greets residents and visitors. Ranging from seven to nine rooms in size, the original apartments included walnut paneling, wood-beamed ceilings,

Figure 87. Two towers originally topped the Hendrik Hudson (inset), while lower-floor windows were made to look double height. *Source*: Current photos: Robert F. Rodriguez; Historic: Courtesy The New York Public Library.

mahogany doors with glass knobs, and porcelain bathroom fittings. The rents for all of this in the early twentieth century: $1,500 to $3,000 per year.

Like many others in the city, the building underwent some hard times in the 1960s, functioning as the Hendrik Hudson Residence Hotel. Single rooms were rented to entire families for as little as $7, bathrooms and kitchens were shared, overcrowding was severe, and the building became rat infested. It was also where a fourteen-year-old boy was crushed to death in an elevator accident. The once desirable 380 Riverside Drive became known in the media as "the slum with a view."

Under new ownership, the building converted to modern apartments with bathrooms and kitchens, where rents for three rooms started at $125. The building went co-op in 1970 and currently has about 146 apartments, as well as its own basement parking garage. A first-floor, ten-room, four-bedroom, three-and-a-half-bath apartment was listed in 2021 for $2.1 million. Upon 380 Riverside Drive's completion, its architects were commissioned to design the building's twelve-story annex next door, on 110th Street between Riverside Drive and Broadway.

404 Riverside Drive/113th Street: The Strathmore

In 1887, William Waldorf Astor purchased the land on which the Strathmore now stands. It might have become the site for his planned new mansion, but like so many of his class at the time, Astor decided to build on Fifth Avenue instead.

Figure 88. The Strathmore, with its lovely marquee, stands directly across from the Lajos Kossuth Monument. *Source*: Robert F. Rodriguez.

This regal twelve-story Beaux Arts building, on the southeast corner of 113th Street, was designed by the architects Schwartz & Gross and completed in 1909 for a cost of about $300,000. The exterior is best known for its gracefully curved, originally glazed-iron and glass marquee,[23] a type common in Europe but rare in New York. A lovely pair of filigree-iron scrolled brackets support it, while a bounteous stone garland, ripe with fruit, curves above it. Glass and ornamental iron doors enhance the entrance, along with a transom and sidelights. Imposing multiglobed torch lights on either side welcome visitors. The tall base is limestone, followed by Flemish-bond dark-red brick, and topped by limestone, terracotta, and a massive copper cornice at the roofline. During a severe storm with high winds not many years back, large chunks of that cornice came toppling down, fortunately hurting no one but leaving the building shrouded in black netting like some elderly Italian widow until the broken sections could be replaced.

The original floor plan of 404 Riverside shows two ten-room apartments per floor, of about 3,500 square feet each. Each had a foyer, living room, dining room, library, kitchen, three bedrooms, three bathrooms, and two staff rooms. At the time, they rented for $2,500 to $3,900 per year.

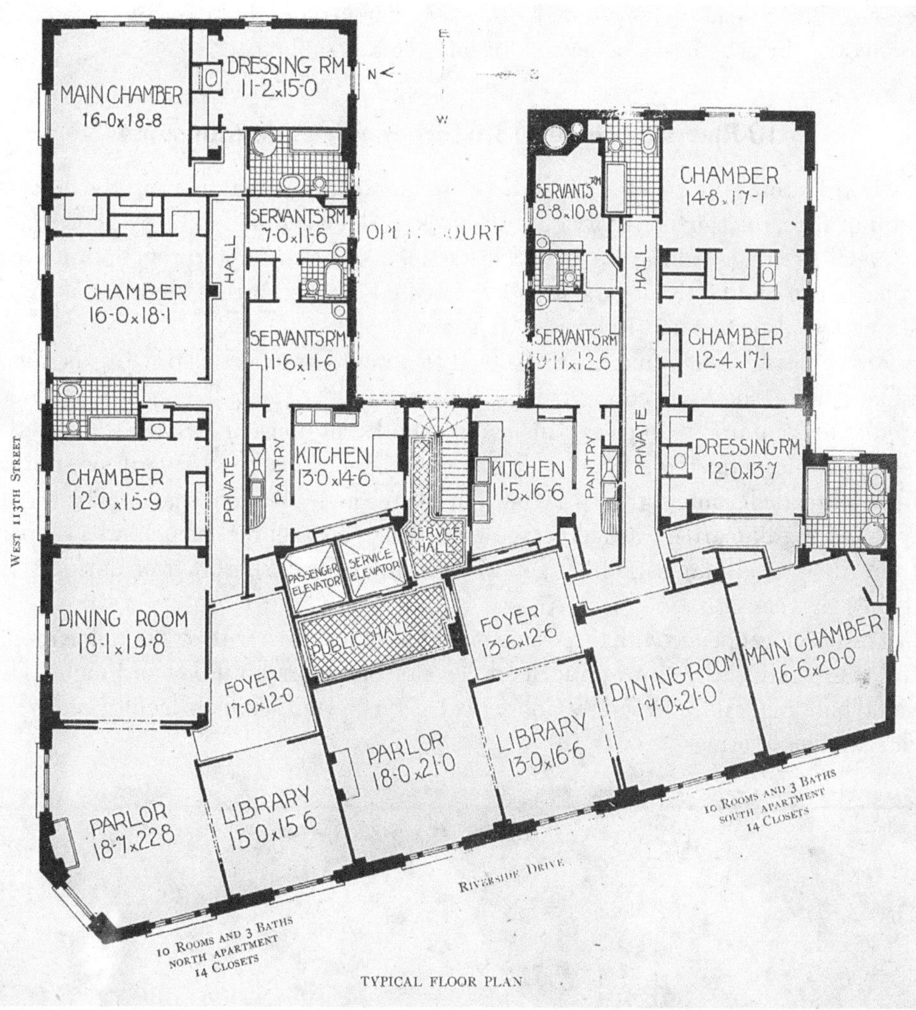

Figure 89. The original floor plan for the Strathmore featured apartments with ten rooms, three baths, and fourteen closets. *Source*: Courtesy The New York Public Library.

Among the design elements were walnut paneling, parquet floors with inlaid borders, high ceilings, coffered ceilings in dining rooms, and plaster moldings. These were accented by mahogany doors, crystal doorknobs, and leaded-glass transoms. The bathrooms were particularly notable, with bathtubs built for two and circular stall showers with chrome water pipes designed to reach multiple angles of the body.

In the 1930s, like many of the other buildings on Riverside Drive, the Strathmore's apartments were cut into smaller spaces, and at one point it had double the number of apartments with which it started. Yet, amazingly, some of the original layouts remain, including the building's only duplex. When the Strathmore went co-op in 1967, a ten-room apartment cost $30,000. In 2021, an apartment of that size—with five bedrooms and three baths—was posted for sale at $4.95 million.

410 Riverside Drive/113th Street: Riverside Mansions

My favorite things at 410 Riverside Drive are the top of the building and the bottom. Built in 1910, the thirteen-story granite, brick, and terracotta building was designed by Neville & Bagge in the Chateauesque style, a look that reinterprets both French Renaissance and Gothic characteristics. Located on the northeast corner of 113th Street, it is also known as Riverside Mansions.

At the base, three grand openings lead to an outdoor court clad with rough-cut ashlar granite blocks and covered with red-brick flooring. The building entrance doors are ornamental iron with glass panels, crowned by an unusual and arresting green, red, and white stained-glass curved hood. Around the globe-lit courtyard, substantial and well-tended planters greet passersby. Inside the lobby, luscious shades of blue-gray and gold streak marble walls along with a fireplace mantel tucked behind a shapely arch. Above it all, fantastic high gables with finials peak sharply over dormers set against the mansard roof.

The building opened with three apartments per floor, each with eight or nine rooms and three baths, as well as uniformed elevator operators both day and night. The rental building is now owned by Columbia University and serves as faculty and graduate student housing.

Figure 90. The porte cochère and a stained-glass hood above the entrance set apart Riverside Mansions. A historic photo (inset) shows the building's many roof gables. *Source*: New photo: Robert F. Rodriguez; Historic: Courtesy The New York Public Library.

434 Riverside Drive/115th–116th Streets: St. Anthony Hall

Designed by Henry Hornbostel of Wood, Palmer & Hornbostel and built in 1899, this Beaux Arts building is home to the Fraternity of Delta Psi, Alpha Chapter, and is known as St. Anthony Hall. Many of its early members were scions of the country's wealthiest families.

The entrance to the four-and-a-half-story red-brick and limestone building appears, on its own, in a one-story side section. Elsewhere, there are flared lintels and keystones over windows, arched windows, and bracketed balconets with iron railings. Slate shingles, dormers, and a pediment with a cartouche bearing Greek letters further distinguish the diminutive building. Inside, visible past tall windows on the main floor, a piano seems always to await players.

Number 434 Riverside Drive is listed on the National Register of Historic Places.

435 and 440 Riverside Drive/116th Street: The Colosseum and the Paterno

A 1910 *New York Times* article called the Colosseum and the Paterno, on opposite corners of 116th Street, "two of the stateliest apartment houses in the city."[24] Completed in 1910, the brick, limestone, and terracotta buildings were designed by the architectural firm of Schwartz & Gross.

The Renaissance Revival residences feature uniquely curved façades. The Colosseum's curve begins on Riverside Drive and turns east on 116th Street, while the

Figure 91. The Paterno and Colosseum uniquely curve around the northern and southern corners, respectively, of 116th Street. *Source*: Robert F. Rodriguez.

Paterno's starts on 116th Street and meets Claremont Avenue, one block east. Together, the buildings nobly bookend the broad 116th Street approach to the Columbia University campus on Broadway.

Why the curve in the buildings and the road? That depends on the source of information. Most say that the curved façades simply follow the direction of the old Bloomingdale Road. Some indicate they were created to present a grand gateway along 116th Street to the campus. Others note a plan to expand Riverside Park by adding the area bound by Riverside Drive and Claremont Avenue from 116th to 122nd Streets, because it was the location of the Revolutionary War Battle of Harlem Heights. Still others suggest this addition was to make the area from 116th Street north a kind of forecourt or open area leading to Grant's Tomb, although that may also have been the point of incorporating the historic battle site.[25]

According to an August 15, 1999, *New York Times* article by the respected architectural historian Christopher Grey:

> On Dec. 31, 1897, the city's Board of Street Opening and Improvement voted, for "the public interest," to redraw the 116th Street corners to the present curved configuration. The official record offers no justification for the change, but a report in *The New York Daily Tribune* said it was to "connect Claremont Avenue with the Riverside Drive," indicating that the curves were meant to provide a gateway not east, up 116th Street to the Columbia campus, but north, up Claremont Avenue and in the direction of Grant's Tomb.[26]

The city, however, declined to buy the land, meaning that neither the park extension nor the 116th Street gateway was built and that the Riverside-Claremont block was sold off for speculative development.

The Colosseum and Paterno complement each other in style and detail. Both present rusticated limestone bases and attention-getting groupings of windows, three or four across. The buildings' curved centers both feature elaborately decorated windows as well as balconies. Terracotta designs accent additional windows on both façades, as do bracketed balconets. Stone quoins brace both buildings.

The thirteen-story Colosseum, with its authentic Roman-amphitheater spelling, stands on the smaller plot of the two. Its entrance, on the corner, rests directly beneath a central triple-window section whose sides are bound together by a zipper-like pattern above the three-story limestone base. A balustraded balcony topped by columns and a pediment extends over the entrance, which is bordered by lanterns. Keystones and splayed lintels ornament the windows above the base.

An early advertisement for the building highlighted that it was "an absolutely fireproof apartment house of the highest class . . . surrounded by equally high-class apartment houses and private residences, the magnificent and famous institutions of Columbia University, etc." Today, Columbia owns the building, which provides faculty and graduate student housing.

The Colosseum opened with just sixteen apartments, each with eight, ten, or twelve rooms, some taking up a full floor. It also offered three duplexes, with parlor, library, dining room, and kitchen on the lower floor and bedrooms and dressing rooms on the floor above. Each apartment had three or four bathrooms, wall safes, and abundant closet space. The parlors and libraries were finished in "ivory enamel" and had mahogany doors, while high wainscoting and beamed ceilings adorned the surfaces of dining rooms. Upon the building's opening, there was a chauffeur's room on the main floor. The Colosseum's four-bedroom apartments with uninterrupted views of the Hudson River rented at the time for $150 to $175 a month.

A plaque near the building's entrance acknowledges a former resident, Harlan Fiske Stone, who lived at the Colosseum from 1920 to 1925. Stone was dean of the Columbia University School of Law from 1910 to 1923 and later served as chief justice of the United States.

Before Stone's years at the Colosseum, it was the four-bedroom home of Clara Peck and Arthur Waite. It is also where, within the space of two months in early 1916, Waite poisoned his mother-in-law and then his father-in-law, Hannah and John Peck, to get quicker access to Clara's inheritance. His method was atypical at best: Waite added diphtheria and influenza germs to Hannah's food. When the same tactic proved less effective with John, Waite tossed helpings of tuberculosis and typhoid into the mix to move along what would appear to be a natural death. Finally, impatient for his efforts to succeed, Waite dosed Peck with arsenic.

Although he took courses in dentistry and claimed the title of doctor, Waite was never a registered physician in New York City. Nor did he ever practice there, although many of his friends erroneously believed he was performing oral surgery at various hospitals around town. In fact, at the time of his arrest, he apparently had no profession whatsoever.

While the bacterial poisons he used could not be traced in autopsy, arsenic could. Convicted of double murder, Waite was electrocuted in 1917.

Across the street from the Colosseum, meanwhile, the twelve-story Paterno stands out from other buildings not only because of its curvaceous physique but also its exquisite semicircular porte cochère, where grand carriages might once have discharged richly attired passengers. The porte cochère is reached through three romantic arches crowned by a ceiling boasting lovely terracotta details, with a herringbone-patterned brickwork floor below. Beyond that is the recessed entrance with an arched transom displaying wrought-iron grille work and, in the expansive lobby, a marvelous stained-glass ceiling.

From the Paterno's mansard roof, a wonderfully elaborate water tower presides above it all. The Paterno's "great curved façade faces south and west and is open to the pleasant breezes of summer, protected from the north winds of winter," said an advertisement of the day.[27] The building opened with ninety-eight apartments. Eight-room homes there rented for $150 to $175 per month. In 2020, a four-bedroom, two-and-a-half-bath co-op apartment sold for $3.9 million.

While buildings are only occasionally named after those who built them, in this case the affectation is understandable. Members of the Paterno family built thirty-seven buildings in the Morningside Heights section of the Upper West Side alone.

Paterno paterfamilias John Paterno was a builder in his native Italy who immigrated with his family to New York. After his death, his small contracting business was taken over by his sons Joseph and Charles, who had just completed his medical degree at Cornell University. The façades of some of their buildings are emblazoned with P for Paterno, JP for Joseph Paterno, or PB for the Paterno Brothers. Joseph, in fact, called the Colosseum (not the Paterno) home.[28]

Notably, in the Morningside Heights area where the Colosseum and Paterno were located, unlike in other parts of New York, Italian and Jewish builders, developers, and architects predominated. Speculative construction work was available to immigrants because it did not require social connections, as building private homes for the wealthy would. While the Paternos were the most prolific builders in the area, Jewish developers operating under their own names or corporate names, such as Carlyle Realty Company and Carnegie Construction Company, were also highly active. Schwartz & Gross was one of the dominant Jewish architectural firms within the Morningside Heights Historic District.

And More . . .

Just across from the Colosseum and Paterno is the 116th Street entrance to Riverside Park, with a steep slope below. It is near the top of this slope that parents, myself included, have stood so many winters, watching their children squeal with delight on their way from top to bottom across a new snowfall, on sleds ranging from fancy flyers to hastily flattened cardboard boxes. The kids, unlike the shivering parents, never want to leave.

At the center of that park entrance stands a lovely carved marble drinking fountain designed by Bruno L. Zimm and dedicated in 1910 to commemorate the twenty-fifth anniversary of the Woman's Health Protective Association of New York City. The organization was created, as its name suggests, to increase awareness of women's health issues. It cost $8,000.

Indeed, the 100s form a neighborhood of monuments. Between the Firemen's Memorial at 100th Street and the fountain on 116th, there are three more worth noting.

On the island at 106th Street and Riverside Drive stands the General Franz Sigel Monument, a bronze equestrian statue dedicated in 1907. Born in Germany, Sigel fought a number of decisive campaigns as a major general in the Union Army and is credited with encouraging many German-Americans to fight for the Union. The monument was created by Karl Bitter, known for designing sculptures for such wealthy private clients as the Vanderbilts and Astors, as well as many public works of art.

Six blocks north, on the island at 112th Street, the Samuel J. Tilden Monument honors a former governor of New York and 1876 Democratic nominee for President. Tilden won the popular vote but lost the presidency.[29] The statue was sculpted by William Ordway Partridge and dedicated in 1926.

Just north of that, at 113th Street, is the Lajos Kossuth Monument, in memory of the Hungarian patriot. The bronze tableau portrays the struggle for Hungarian independence in 1848. On March 15, 1928, a crowd of 25,000 gathered to dedicate the monument, designed by the Hungarian sculptor Janos Horvai. On that date for many years since, Hungarian Independence Day has been celebrated on its steps.

The 100s are also where about thirty sports facilities are located, more than anywhere else throughout the park, including baseball fields, basketball courts, handball courts, soccer fields, volleyball courts, tennis courts, and the 108th Street skate park.

Along with attracting devotees of monumental sculpture and aspiring athletes, the neighborhood has been a magnet for celebrated thinkers and doers of many types, especially those in the arts and entertainment fields. Residents have included actors such as Francis X. Bushman, one of the biggest stars of the 1910s and early 1920s (435 Riverside Drive), James Coco (315), Hayley Mills (320), and Isabella Rossellini (404).

The 100s have also housed the dancer and choreographer Tommy Tune (310 Riverside Drive); musician Billy Strayhorn, composer of "Take the A Train" (310); Marcus Loew of Loew's theaters and MGM (380); and Samuel "Roxy" Rothafel, founder of Radio City Music Hall and father of the Rockettes (420). Elliott Cook Carter Jr., the two-time Pulitzer Prize–winning American composer (also 420), and the movie producer David O. Selznick (449 Riverside Drive) have also been residents. The jazz singer Nina Simone and the singer/songwriter Carole King resided at 336 and 390 Riverside Drive, respectively. The artist Jasper Johns lived at 340 Riverside Drive.

The 100s have also been home to the writers Susan Sontag (340 Riverside), William Burroughs (360), Saul Bellow (333), Damon Runyon (440), Grantland Rice, and Walter S. Trumbull (both 450). The fashion journalist and critic Bernadine Morris (375), chef and food and travel author Anthony Bourdain (420), and playwright and screenwriter Murray Shisgal, who cowrote the screenplay for the movie *Tootsie* (310), have all called Riverside Drive in the 100s home. The book publisher and philanthropist George Thomas Delacorte also lived in the neighborhood (404). So has the comedian Samantha Bee, who purchased a $3.7 million, four-bedroom co-op in 2017.

Other notable residents have included the Nobel laureate Elie Wiesel (310 Riverside Drive), the political theorist Hannah Arendt (370), the suffragist Carrie Chapman Catt (404), Manhattan district attorney Frank S. Hogan (also 404), and the philosopher and social activist Simone Weil (549).

In the late 1950s, the famed musician "Duke" Ellington purchased 333 Riverside Drive between 105th and 106th Streets as headquarters for his Tempo Music publishing company and as a home for his sister, Ruth, the company's president. He also owned 334 Riverside. In December 1977, the city named West 106th Street "Duke Ellington Boulevard."

Polly Adler also lived on Riverside Drive (possibly in the 100s) beginning in 1920. According to *Smithsonian Magazine*, she was "the most celebrated brothel keeper in New York's (and arguably the country's) history."[30] The gangsters "Lucky" Luciano and Dutch Schultz, boxer Jack Dempsey, Mayor Jimmy Walker, and members of the Algonquin Round Table, including Dorothy Parker and Robert Benchley, were all friends of Polly. "She strove to cultivate an atmosphere that was more clubhouse than cathouse, where clients were just as likely to close a business deal or hold a dinner party as retire to an upstairs boudoir." She later wrote a memoir, *A House Is Not a Home*, upon which a film of the same name was based. Shelly Winters portrayed her. In fact, the 100s are perhaps better known for the characters in movies and on TV shows filmed here than for its real-life residents.

The Strathmore (404 Riverside Drive) may be most familiar today as the home of Midge and Joel Maisel and her parents in the Emmy Award–winning Amazon Prime series *The Marvelous Mrs. Maisel.* TV shows often use the exterior of a structure but design a set for the interior that bears no relation to that building's reality. *The Marvelous Mrs. Maisel*, on the other hand, not only showed the Strathmore's entrance and lobby but shot the show's pilot in one of its extremely spacious apartments, which was later replicated to the last detail on a set.

The Schinasi mansion (351 Riverside Drive), or at least its exterior, was "home" to conman Neal Caffrey, played by Matt Bomer, in the popular USA Network show *White Collar.* His apartment on the upper floor included a vast terrace and a city view. In reality, the terrace was built in the studio, and the only view from the downtown-facing side of the house is the apartment building across the street. The residence also appeared in TV shows including *Royal Pains*, *Damages*, and *The Mindy Project*, as well as in the movie *Bullets over Broadway*.

Two episodes of the TV show *Elementary* featured 330 Riverside Drive. It was also the setting for the scene in Madonna's movie *Who's That Girl*, where a co-op board interviews (and rejects) her character for an apartment. In real life, the material girl once lived at 270 Riverside Drive (between 99th and 100th Streets)—as did a bright star of another age, Mary Pickford.

The Paterno (440 Riverside Drive) may be seen in the film *Enchanted*, starring Amy Adams and Patrick Dempsey, and in the recent Netflix series *Inventing Anna*, where it played the role of a French luxury hotel.

Among those who actually lived in the neighborhood, however, there was one story as dramatic as any TV or movie script. In August 1944, at the foot of Riverside Drive and 115th Street, part of that very hill on which today's children sled in winter to their hearts' content, Lucien Carr, nineteen, the Beat Generation's "charismatic, callow swami"[31] and muse, knifed to death David Kammerer, thirty-three, his stalker since childhood.

The previous winter, Carr, then a Columbia student, introduced his fellow Columbia student Allen Ginsberg to Kammerer and William Burroughs. The latter two had been schoolmates in St. Louis and lived near each other in Greenwich Village. Kammerer later met Jack Kerouac, another Columbia student. By that point Ginsberg and Carr were living at Warren Hall Residence Club, a dorm at 404 West 115th Street (now a parking lot). Kammerer visited on occasion.

On a sweltering summer night, Kammerer and Carr left the West End (also known as the West End Gate) bar at 3 a.m., heading downhill to Riverside Park for some cool air. According to the *New York Times*, Kammerer made "an offensive proposal" to Carr. The article continued: "Carr said that he rejected it indignantly and that a fight ensued. Carr, a slight youth, 5 feet 9 tall and weighing 140 pounds, was no match for the burly former physical education instructor, who was 6 feet tall and weighed about 185 pounds." "In desperation," the account added, "Carr pulled out of his pocket his Boy Scout knife, a relic of his boyhood, and plunged the blade twice in rapid succession into Kammerer's chest."

Rather than hurrying to the police station, Carr then rolled the body to the river's edge, "bound the limbs with shoe laces, stuffed rocks in the pockets, and watched his longtime lurker sink."[32] He then headed to Greenwich Village and reported the event to Burroughs, who advised him to tell the police he was the victim of a sex fiend. Instead, Carr woke Kerouac, who recounted the following in his book *Vanity of Duluoz: An Adventurous Education*: "Well," Carr said, "I disposed of the old man last night." The two men walked up West 118th Street to Morningside Park, where Carr buried Kammerer's eyeglasses, which apparently he had pocketed as evidence of his feat. Later, they dropped the Boy Scout knife into a subway grate on 125th Street. They also visited the Museum of Modern Art and a hot dog stand in Times Square and watched a movie before Carr confessed the killing to the authorities. The next day, Kammerer's body bobbed up in the Hudson off West 108th Street.

Years later, the film *Kill Your Darlings* retold the story, with everyone's favorite wizard, Daniel Radcliffe, playing Ginsberg.

Chapter 17

The Happy Hundreds, Part 2

117th–129th Streets

At Riverside, on the slow hill-slant
Two memoried graves are seen
A granite dome is over Grant
and over a child the green.

—Anna Markham, "An Amiable Child"

WITH THE COLOSSEUM and Paterno standing sentry at each corner and its broad sweep up the steep hill from Riverside Drive to Columbia University's main gates, 116th Street is a logical location to split the story of the 100s in two. Most of the buildings up to this point have been residential. Above 116th Street, with a few exceptions, the focus becomes distinctly more religious, institutional—and monumental. Among the park's deep dips and the Drive's open spaces, the observant wanderer will discover the tallest church steeple in North America, the city's only "God Box," a famous tomb that's not a tomb, and the dearest of all Riverside monuments, the discreetly situated memorial to an "Amiable Child."

Riverside Drive from 109th Street to 119th Street belongs to the Morningside Heights Historic District.

Riverside Park/116th–124th Streets: Forever Wild/Riverside Park Bird Sanctuary

Who knew? Riverside Park has sixty acres of forest. Forever Wild, running from roughly 116th Street to 124th Street, is part of the Parks Department's citywide effort to protect and preserve the city's most ecologically valuable lands as natural sites rather than as landscaped areas. It is also home to the park's bird sanctuary.

In 1926, the Women's League for the Protection of Riverside Park planted sixty-five trees here, dedicated to an unknown soldier from each state and in memory of leaders such as Peter Minuit and George Washington. The area was intended both to honor these men and create a haven for birds.

As Riverside Park's fortunes ricocheted up and down over time, so did the fate of the sanctuary and its intended inhabitants. By the late 1980s and early 1990s, deterioration made it less of a draw for birds and other wildlife. Things began looking up by the late 1990s, when the sanctuary saw the removal of invasive species and the addition of bird-friendly native plants, along with the Bird Drip, a manmade water source where birds could drink and bathe. All of this has made the site once again appealing to migrating, overwintering, and nesting birds, an average of about 120 species per year. Avian activity is in full flight during the spring and fall migration seasons.

At street level, meanwhile, the area between 102nd and 122nd Streets on Riverside Drive is a prime spot for sighting peregrine falcons, one of the world's fastest birds and most skilled hunters. They have taken up residence high in the bell tower of Riverside Church between 120th and 122nd Streets. Their presence today is particularly notable: By 1972, there was not a single peregrine falcon east of the Mississippi, never mind in New York City's urban canyons.

Birds are not the only "wildlife" in this part of the city by far. In 2019, twenty-four goats, special guests from Dutchess County, New York, trekked the Forever Wild hills, devouring invasive species of plants. In the process, they delighted Upper West Side adults, children, and dogs, all of whom would routinely watch them in action. The charming spectacle repeated (with fewer goats) in 2021. Given the number of goats

Figure 92. Goats recently grazed on invasive plant species in the park's Forever Wild section. *Source*: Robert F. Rodriguez.

that once populated this part of the city, this approach to lawn maintenance was particularly appropriate.[1]

452 Riverside Drive/118th Street: The Mira Mar

Fanciful, flirtatious, and just plain fun to look at, the nine-story Renaissance Revival Mira Mar was completed in 1910 and remains a personal favorite. This U-shaped, white-glazed brick, limestone, and terracotta building is exuberant with embellishments. There is a two-story rusticated limestone base, with upper floors adorned by elaborately carved bracketed balconets, some of stone, others outlined with wrought iron. Then come slender Corinthian columns along the sides, segmented and rounded terracotta arches around windows, elaborately decorated panels, quoins scaling up and down the corners, an arcaded frieze, and a bracketed modillioned cornice. Kind of like ice cream with a dollop of sugar on top. Here and there throughout the façade, the letter *C* is mysteriously carved—perhaps for the builders, B. Crystal and Son.

A newspaper ad for the then-new fifty-four-unit Mira Mar called out apartments of nine and ten rooms, complete with parlors, foyers, and libraries "separated by portiere [(curtained]) openings and sliding doors." The parlors, libraries, and reception rooms were "finished in white enamel with solid mahogany casement doors. The dining

Figure 93. The Mira Mar enchants with myriad stone, terracotta, and wrought-iron details, along with a mysterious *C* on its façade. *Source*: Robert F. Rodriguez.

rooms are wainscoted in oak and Cuban mahogany, have paneling, plate shelf and beam ceilings. The floors are of parquet with inlaid borders. Each room has an artistic chandelier and four wall brackets to match." The bathrooms were "handsomely tiled and equipped with needle and shower baths." Each apartment had a built-in vacuum cleaning system and, "for free use," clothes dryers as well as storage compartments in the basement. On a practical note, the apartment doors were "burglar proof, being made of pressed steel."[2]

The Mira Mar is one of dozens of Upper West Side buildings (including my own, much simpler in style) by the architect Gaetan (or Gaetano) Ajello (pronounced eye-YEL-low), who once had worked on the infamous Schwab mansion. Early Ajello designs such as the Mira Mar "shimmer like marble quarries in the Mediterranean sun, quite different from the red and earth tones typical of the time."[3]

A Sicilian immigrant, Ajello's first major commissions were four Italian Renaissance–style buildings north of 116th Street for the developer Bernard Crystal, including the Mira Mar. A few years later, in 1912, Ajello connected with the Paterno and Campagna families, two of the city's most prolific apartment house developers. Like the Paternos, Ajello made a point of "signing" his buildings, which commonly carry a cornerstone with the carved legend "G. Ajello, Architect," an autograph that may be found on the Mira Mar.

475 Riverside Drive/120th Street: The Interchurch Center ("God Box")

In complete contrast to the bodaciously ornamented Mira Mar, we come to a building as plain as—well, a box. Built with near-zero prettification, the stark and spare limestone cube hasn't got a cornice, pediment, or rusticated stone to its name.

Officially known as the Interchurch Center, it is referred to in the neighborhood (not always with affection) as the God Box. The nineteen-story office building was created to bring various Protestant denominations under one roof, assist their work, and promote cooperation among them and with other charitable, religious, missionary, and educational organizations.

Though Protestant groups continue to dominate the tenant list, Jewish, Muslim, and Catholic organizations have also worked in the building. The Interchurch Center was recently the home of over seventy organizations representing community development, educational initiatives, and intercultural and religious exchange. At the time of the building's construction, ecumenism was still a novel concept, and the Interchurch Center was viewed as the most tangible symbol of that goal.

The building rests on land that once held the Barnard College tennis courts. The $21 million Interchurch Center was built with gifts by John D. Rockefeller Jr. and other donors, together with a consortium of religious denominations. In a ceremony that packed Riverside Drive, President Eisenhower laid the cornerstone in 1958. The building was officially dedicated two years later.

490 Riverside Drive/120th–122nd Streets: Riverside Church

The Rockefeller heritage in this part of Riverside Drive continues, in a big way, directly across the street from the God Box. Here stands lofty Riverside Church, spanning two full blocks between 120th and 122nd Streets at one of the highest points on all of Riverside Drive. Its grand twenty-four-floor tower, the tallest steeple in North America, rises far above mere mortals on the avenue below and is easily visible from afar.

Modeled largely after the thirteenth-century Chartres cathedral in France, Riverside Church was completed in 1930 and designed by Henry C. Pelton and Allen & Collens in the Neo-Gothic style. Any buttresses here are purely thematic; steel frames support the limestone-clad building. Burnham Hoyt designed the church interior.

According to its website, Riverside Church, which is associated with the American Baptist Churches USA and the United Church of Christ, is "an interdenominational, interracial, international, open, welcoming, and affirming church and congregation." It is also a church with an intriguing origin. In 1924, John D. Rockefeller Jr. donated $500,000 to the Episcopal Cathedral of St. John the Divine,[4] located on Amsterdam Avenue and 112th Street, just a short walk from where Riverside Church stands now. His wish was for the cathedral to become progressive and inclusive. Yet despite this financial support, the Episcopal Bishop denied Rockefeller, as a Baptist, membership on the cathedral's board. Not, it turned out, a wise move.

In response, together with Harry Emerson Fosdick, a progressive Presbyterian minister, Rockefeller decided to establish a new, nondenominational church, to which he ultimately donated somewhere between $8 million and $10.5 million. Like the cathedral, it was to be located in Morningside Heights. Riverside Church was also conceived from the start as a social services center. Throughout its history, it's been a bastion of activism and political debate.

Worshippers have welcomed an impressive array of world leaders to the pulpit, among them former President Bill Clinton, the Rev. Dr. Martin Luther King Jr., Cesar Chavez, Fidel Castro, Kofi Annan, and the Dalai Lama. Nelson Mandela made Riverside Church the first stop on his visit to New York following his release from prison in South Africa. The Rev. Jesse Jackson gave the eulogy at Jackie Robinson's funeral service here in 1972. Paul McCartney's only US service for his wife, Linda, was held at the church. At one time, the *New York Times* printed articles weekly about Riverside's Sunday sermons.

Riverside Church's architecture is as grand as the personalities that have passed through its doors. On the Riverside Drive façade, the main entrance is carved not just with religious figures, as would be the norm for a church, but also leading scientific and philosophical ones, including Ralph Waldo Emerson, Immanuel Kant, Pythagoras, Charles Darwin, Louis Pasteur, and Albert Einstein. The Jewish Einstein, it's said, was surprised to be included on the portal of a Protestant church. From atop a platform on the church's northern roof, the tall bronze *Angel of the Resurrection* silently blows a trumpet.

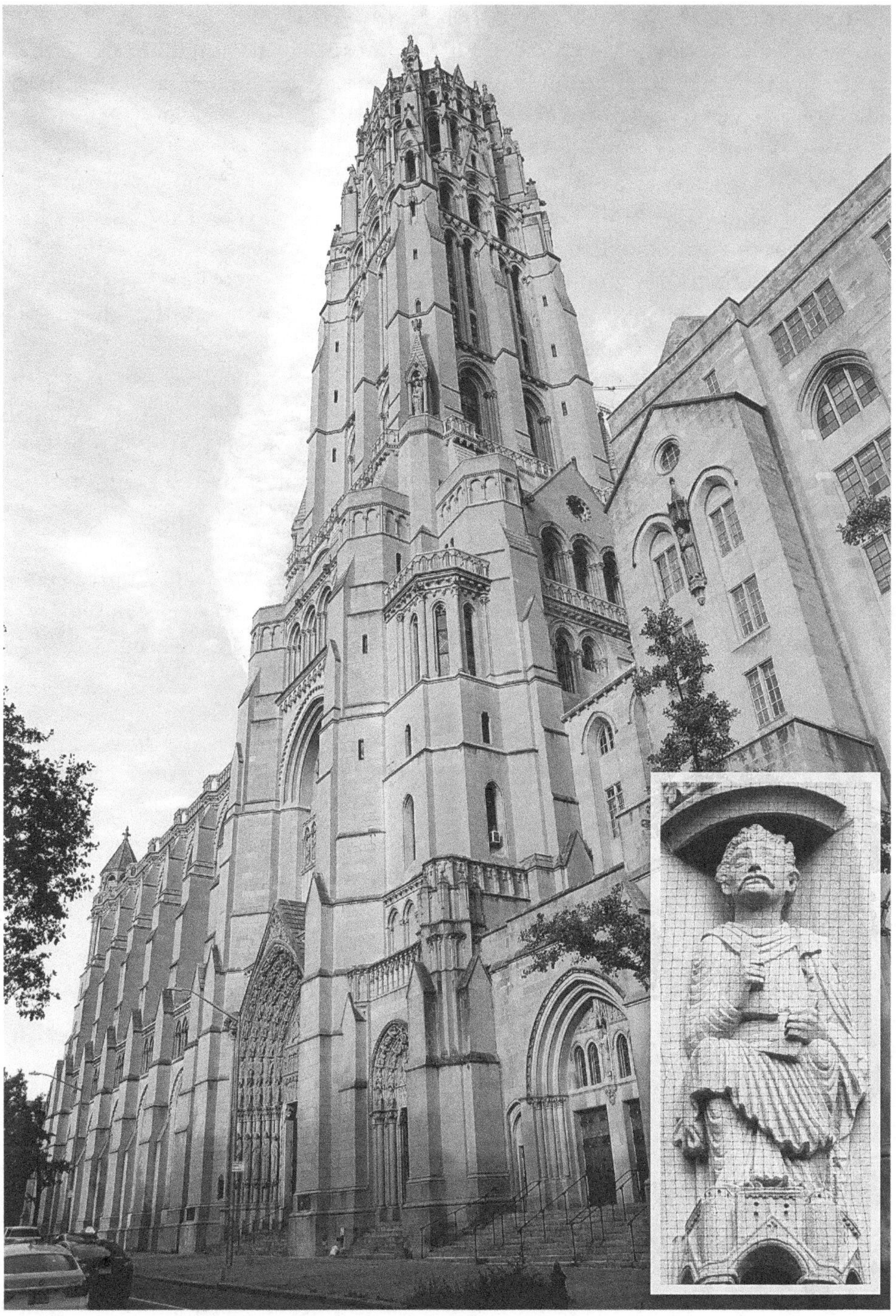

Figure 94. Riverside Church boasts the tallest church steeple in North America, along with carvings of philosophers and scientists, including (inset) Albert Einstein. *Source*: Robert F. Rodriguez.

Inside, the ceiling of the hundred-foot-tall nave, or central part of the church, is lined with Guastavino terracotta tiles. Eight impressive lanterns illuminate the main section of the nave, and four similar ones do the same for the upper gallery. In the chancel, the part of a church near the altar and reserved for the clergy and choir, a carved wooden canopy presides over the pulpit. The back of the chancel holds an elaborate stone screen depicting influential individuals such as Johann Sebastian Bach, Abraham Lincoln, and Michelangelo. There are fifty-one stained-glass windows throughout the main building, including four from a sixteenth-century cathedral in Belgium. The *New York Times* once referred to the cathedral's interior as a "tightly executed visual pageant."[5] Apparently, there was also once a bowling alley in the basement, for use by Columbia University students.

Yet it's the exquisitely detailed bell tower, rising to a height of 392 feet, that is the most memorable of Riverside Church's architectural features. A feast of delicate finials pierces the sky, arches hug windows, and gargoyles stonily safeguard its exterior—Gothicism galore. The tower holds, near its top, the seventy-four-bell Laura Spelman Rockefeller Memorial Carillon, dedicated to John D. Rockefeller Jr.'s mother. At the time of its installation, it was the largest carillon in the world. The tower's twenty-ton, 122-inch-diameter bourdon bell remains the world's largest individual tuned bell.

The outdoor gallery at the top of the tower offers 360-degree views of the city, with close-ups of the carillon on the way. It is here, high up in that tower many years ago, that the man I loved proposed. On Sunday mornings from our apartment, we can hear the bells pealing.

The *AIA Guide to New York City* called Riverside Church "easily the most prominent architectural work along the Hudson (River) from midtown to the George Washington Bridge."[6] Riverside Church replaced the 1880s Kittel and Gibbons mansions and three early twentieth-century apartment buildings.[7] The New York City Landmarks Preservation Commission designated the church as an Individual Landmark in 2000. It was listed on the National Register of Historic Places in 2012.

Riverside Drive Island/122nd Street: The General Grant National Memorial/Grant's Tomb

First, let's get the old riddle out of the way:

Question: Who's buried in Grant's Tomb?
Answer: No one. Grant and his wife, Julia, are *entombed*, in aboveground sarcophagi, not buried.

North America's largest mausoleum, Grant's Tomb, stands tall and with great dignity diagonally across from Riverside Church, overlooking the Hudson River.

Widely celebrated for the Union's win in the Civil War, Ulysses S. Grant was elected the eighteenth president of the United States and served two terms. A West Point graduate, he fought in the Mexican War before leading Civil War victories in the

Figure 95. A 1903 postcard shows a pathway to Grant's Tomb, also pictured as it is today. Inset: President Grant. *Source*: Historic: Courtesy The New York Public Library; Current: Robert F. Rodriguez; Grant photo: Library of Congress.

battles of Vicksburg and Chattanooga and accepting Robert E. Lee's surrender at Appomattox. In 1866, Congress awarded Grant his fourth star, making him the first full general of the armies.

Grant's accomplishments also included signing the act that established Yellowstone, the country's first national park. In 1879, after his presidency, Grant settled in New York City, where he died six years later. While he could have been buried in Washington, DC, or any number of other cities, his wish was that he and his wife remain together after death, and New York acceded to that request. Grant is the only US president laid to rest in the city. He was initially interred for twelve years in a temporary vault just north of where the current monument now stands, while the permanent memorial was designed and built.

Over one million people attended the parade and Grant's Tomb dedication ceremony on April 27, 1897,[8] what would have been his seventy-fifth birthday, and buildings throughout the city were draped in black. At the time, it was the largest display of public grief in US history, with attendees that included generals from both the Union and Confederate armies. The funeral march stretched for seven miles.

The General Grant National Memorial is modeled in part after the Mausoleum of Halicarnassus in Turkey, one of the Seven Wonders of the ancient world. Grant's monument used eight thousand tons of granite, and its $600,000 cost was financed by contributions from ninety thousand donors from around the globe, at that time the largest public fundraising effort in history.[9] For many years, Grant's Tomb was one of the most popular attractions in the city, receiving more visitors than the Statue of Liberty.

The imposing Neo-Classical granite monument, designed by J. H. Duncan, rises 150 feet tall. It features a high conical roof that slopes downward to a circular colonnade atop a rotunda. Grant's words "Let us have peace" are inscribed between two allegorical figures on the outside wall, representing *Victory* and *Peace*. Monumental bronze doors front the entrance within a portico supported by massive columns. Eagle statues flank the approach to the memorial.

Inside, where the mood is solemn and the space too often empty, stained-glass windows cast light upon white marble. Overhead, mosaic murals depict important scenes from Grant's military career and figures carved in relief represent four chapters of the General's life: his youth, military experience, civil life, and death. In the center of the main hall, visitors can look down through a circular opening to the twin red-granite sarcophagi below containing the remains of General and Mrs. Grant. They can also take the stairs down to the crypt, where lifelike bronze busts of Grant's senior generals surround the sarcophagi.

A spacious plaza leads to the monument's steps. To the delight of some and disbelief of others, four hundred feet of undulating, Gaudi-esque mosaic benches were installed alongside the memorial in 1972 to honor the hundredth anniversary of the creation of Yellowstone National Park. The colorful works, created as part of a project to empower local residents through art, are in vivid contrast to the monument's reserved design. The project involved six professional artists and over three thousand members of the community.

A visitors' center across the street in Riverside Park offers an exhibit gallery and informative video addressing key events in Grant's life. A classically columned viewing pavilion nearby offers vistas of the Hudson and a place for quiet reverie.

In 1909, ships from around the world engaged in a grand naval parade on the Hudson River for the Hudson-Fulton anniversary celebration, which featured replicas of Hudson's *Half Moon* and Fulton's *Clermont*. The greatest international fleet of war vessels ever seen together in one port gathered opposite Riverside Park, each one outlined at night in a blaze of electric lights. During the celebration, a glorious ceremony included fireworks and the illumination of Grant's Tomb, along with the Statue of Liberty and the Soldiers' and Sailors' Monument. So many turned out for the event that the crowds "blackened the slopes of the park in the vicinity of the tomb so that the lawns were obscured."[10] As part of the celebration, at a time when air travel was in its early stages, the aviation pioneer Wilbur Wright flew from Governor's Island to Grant's Tomb and back, an event witnessed by as many as a million people, most of whom had never seen an airplane before.

The Grant Memorial was declared a New York City Individual Landmark in 1975 and listed on the National Register of Historic Places in 1966.

500 Riverside Drive/123rd Street: International House

Built in 1924, this thirteen-story Italian Renaissance building by Louis E. Jallade and Marc Eidlitz and Sons appeals with a two-story Palladian entrance paired with equally tall banded columns, on the northern end of Sakura Park, just east of Riverside Park, with an additional entranceway on Riverside Drive itself.

The building's purpose, however, is even more impressive than its design. The private, nonprofit International House, also known as I-House, was created to build leadership, mutual respect, empathy, and moral courage by bringing students from around the world to live and learn together. The organization promotes interaction through programs designed to foster diversity of thought and experience, as well as through residential life. International House was the first global community of its kind, predating the United Nations. The Rockefeller family, clearly a major force in this part of town, and descendants of automobile mogul John Francis Dodge founded the organization in 1924.

Each year International House hosts seven hundred graduate students, interns, trainees, and visiting scholars from more than one hundred countries, about one-third of whom are Americans, who study, train, and conduct research at more than one

Figure 96. International House was the first global community of its kind, predating the United Nations. *Source*: Robert F. Rodriguez.

hundred academic and professional institutes in New York in a broad range of fields. International House actually consists of two buildings. The South Building at 500 Riverside Drive has dormitory-style living, while the North Building, next door at 520 Riverside Drive, has more traditional apartment living.

Among I-House's most notable former residents are the opera singer Leontyne Price, poet and songwriter Leonard Cohen, Academy Award–winning actor Burl Ives, writer Jerzy Kosinski, *New York Times* journalist Flora Lewis, and architect I. M. Pei. That's in addition to a US ambassador, the presidents of Tanzania and the European Parliament, a Belgian prime minister, a UN undersecretary general, and a Labour cabinet minister. The chairmen and CEOs of Morgan Stanley, Citigroup, and Eli Lily, as well as Nobel Prize winners in economic sciences and physics, add to the list. In 1999, International House was named to the National Register of Historic Places.

Riverside Park/124th Street: The Amiable Child Memorial

The visual opposite of the imposing and famed Grant's Tomb—and, to me, the most moving site on the Drive—may be found a mere hundred yards or so past its northern end. A few steps down from the sidewalk along Riverside Park is a grave, marked by a discreet granite monument in the shape of an urn and surrounded by a simple wrought-iron fence. An inscription reads, "Erected to the Memory of an Amiable Child, St. Claire Pollock, Died 15 July 1797 in the Fifth Year of His Age."

Young St. Claire lived on the old Claremont estate on the high hill just above the site where he now rests, and on that summer day so many years past he fell to his death from the cliffs to the rocks below. George Pollock, who was either his father or his uncle, depending on the source, and owned a home there in the early 1790s, decided to bury the child where he fell (or possibly, where he had been playing just before he fell). Around 1800, Pollock sold his estate. He asked the new owners to care for the grave, writing, "There is a small enclosure . . . within which lie the remains of a favorite child, covered by a marble monument. You will confer a peculiar and interesting favor upon me by allowing me to convey the enclosure to you so that you will consider it a part of your own estate, keeping it, however, always enclosed and sacred."[11]

Remarkably, the grave remains, even though the property changed hands many times before the city acquired it for Riverside Park. Visitors still pay their respects, sometimes leaving flowers, wreaths, and other mementos, especially near the date of St. Claire's death. The humble site is believed to be one of only two single-person private graves on city-owned land in New York City.[12]

Several other memorials also acknowledge important people, places, and events in the 100s. At 125th Street, the Claremont Inn Tablet marks the playground that replaced the famous inn. Just north of Grant's Tomb is the Chinese Tablet/Li Hung Chang commemorative plaque with its raised Chinese characters, together with the gingko tree that China presented in gratitude for Grant's help in preventing a war between China and Japan. At 122nd Street, to the left and right of the approach to the tomb, one flagpole and pedestal honors Major General Frederick D. Grant,

Figure 97. Visitors leave stones, flowers, and other mementos at the tomb of the Amiable Child. *Source*: Robert F. Rodriguez.

President Grant's eldest son, while another is dedicated to General Horace Potter, Grant's personal secretary.

The Armed Forces Plaque and the Chaplains Memorial are both located at 121st Street. The Battle of Harlem Heights Marker, also at 121st Street, designates the area where the historic encounter occurred during the Revolutionary War and where Washington won his first battlefield victory in that war. After the Revolution, when New York City was briefly the country's capital, he suggested that the US Capitol building be erected on that hill. It was not.

Chapter 18

The Rest

ALTHOUGH THE FOCUS of this book is the original Riverside Park and Riverside Drive, from 72nd to 129th Streets, there is more to both and to their stories. Since opening in 1880, the park has expanded all the way north to 155th Street (where it meets Fort Washington Park) and south to 59th Street (the start of Hudson River Park), with several noteworthy and sometimes controversial developments along the way.[1]

Over time, the northernmost parts of Riverside Park had received less attention than the southern sections, leading to more limited access, fewer amenities, and greater overall decline. In 1985, the North River Wastewater Treatment Plant was built on the Hudson River adjacent to the park between 137th and 145th Streets. Many in West Harlem, a primarily African American and Hispanic community, were not pleased, protesting the choice of an uptown location for a sewage treatment facility and objecting to the odors that emanated from the plant to nearby streets. As a concession to the community, in 1993 Riverbank State Park was built on top of the treatment plant, providing twenty-eight acres of additional recreation space in the neighborhood. The $129 million park was the first in the United States situated on top of a sewage plant and the first state park to be built in Manhattan. It was also said to be the only park in the Western Hemisphere modeled after Tokyo's rooftop gardens.

Local residents gained further access to the Hudson River waterfront in 2009 when a parking lot was converted into the West Harlem Piers Park, running along the river between St. Clair Place and 135th Street. The $20 million, two-acre park connects West Harlem to the Hudson River Greenway bicycle and pedestrian path and features a docking pier, a fishing pier, and landscaped open space with a public art display.

Figure 98. West Harlem Piers Park features a park area, bike path access, public art, and open views of the Hudson River. *Source*: Robert F. Rodriguez.

In other northern Riverside Park developments, 2017 marked the opening of a sleek new pedestrian bridge at 151st Street.[2] It replaced a tunnel and a long staircase, providing easier entry to the park. In 2020, the Riverside Park Conservancy increased its focus on the north park area. Recent work upgraded a dog run at 142nd Street and improved pathways to a popular community garden at 138th Street and at 148th Street. In late 2020, plans were announced for new adult fitness equipment and playground equipment in the northern section of the park, as well as for three years of public events. Scheduled repairs included the stairway and footbridge at 148th Street.

Meanwhile, in 2008, Columbia University began to build its new $6.3 billion Manhattanville campus, a seventeen-acre site running in part from 125th to 133rd Streets, between Broadway and Twelfth Avenue, alongside the iconic arches of the Riverside Drive Viaduct. The new campus is north of the University's Morningside Heights main location. After a decade-long battle, several Columbia buildings on Twelfth Avenue replaced long-standing if well-worn industrial structures and, in the process, gas stations, auto repair shops, laundromats, stonecutters, and dozens of other mom-and-pop businesses housed there, as well as residences. The new campus displaced an estimated five thousand people.

Developments south of the park were as notable and controversial as those to the north. It is at 72nd Street that Riverside Drive ends and Riverside Boulevard begins. In 1985, Donald Trump bought the abandoned Penn Central railyard between 59th

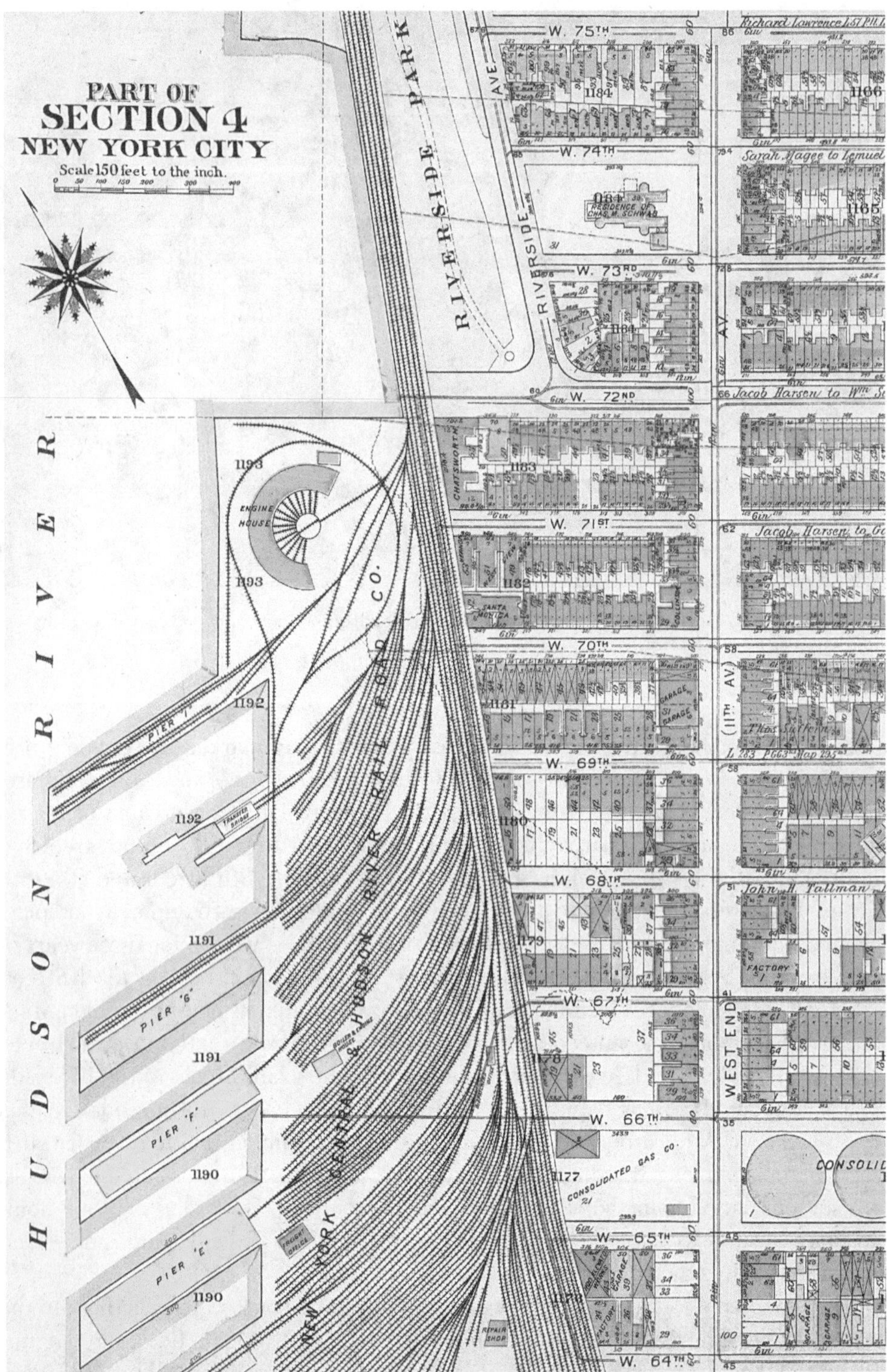

Figure 99. A 1911 map showing the New York Central and Hudson River Railroad train yard south of 72nd Street, now Riverside Park South. *Source*: Courtesy The New York Public Library.

and 72nd Streets. His original intention was to build Television City (later called Trump City), a thirteen-block development that would hold the city's tallest skyscraper, 150 stories high, along with two office towers, sixteen apartment buildings including six seventy-six-story towers, a television studio, a huge shopping mall, and almost ten thousand parking spots.[3] Trump would live in the skyscraper's penthouse.

This idea did not go over well. Local community organizations vigorously opposed the original plan. As an alternative, they proposed reducing the scope of the building project from thirteen blocks to eight, eliminating the shopping mall, building smaller buildings, and creating a new park, Riverside Park South. This park would be similar in design to Riverside Park and incorporate portions of the railroad yard. A new bike path was to connect Riverside Park with Hudson River Park to the south. Trump, who was in the midst of a major cash-flow problem, agreed to this vision in 1990, and in 1991 the city approved the plan. The first buildings in Riverside South, also known as Trump Place, opened in the late 1990s.

Riverside Park South was constructed in six separate phases, beginning in November 1998, with the first phase opening to the public in 2001. Developments to date include improved bike paths; basketball, handball, and volleyball courts; a soccer field; and a reconfigured dog run. This is in addition to two plazas, lawns, new walking paths and stairs, a playground, and swings. New trees have been planted. A more substantial seawall was built, an augmented riprap shoreline (one with rocky material that helps prevent against erosion) constructed, and the shoreline pathway reconstructed.

Figure 100. The transfer bridge in Riverside Park South once helped move freight from the former railyards to river barges. *Source*: Robert F. Rodriguez.

Pier 1 at 70th Street was rebuilt and reconfigured and now hosts public events. A café across from it is the perfect spot for an after-work drink. A train locomotive, a reminder of the railyard's history, serves as the centerpiece of the plaza at 62nd Street, while at 69th Street, a transfer bridge that once helped move freight from the former railyards to river barges is listed on the National Register of Historic Places.

The sixth and final phase of Riverside Park South launched in summer 2021, between 59th and 65th Streets. The final work includes a pedestrian promenade; a large, multiuse athletic field; basketball courts; new ADA-compliant entry points at 62nd and 64th Streets; and an improved 59th Street entrance. Work was expected to take two years. Riverside Park South's completion adds thirty-two more acres to Riverside Park.[4]

In related developments, after the 2016 presidential election, residents of Riverside South/Trump Place removed the large gold letters identifying it with the Trump name, after intense and expensive legal battles with the Trump Organization. Although he helped develop it, Trump does not actually own Riverside South. Because of his financial problems, he sold the controlling interest to investors from Hong Kong long before it was finished and simply licensed his name to the property, for the lordly sum of one dollar.[5]

Chapter 19

The Final Chapter

And I'm Telling You I'm Not Going

I HAVE LIVED on Riverside Drive for more than thirty years, first as a newlywed, then as a mother, and now as an empty nester. Over time, Riverside's face has shown its age far less than my own. Today, as forever, children chase puddles and pigeons along the park's wall, while the elderly slowly make their way to favorite park benches. Bikers, runners, strollers, skaters, parents with baby carriages, and dog walkers all share the park paths, most amicably.

Above the park, carvings and cornices, mansard roofs and stylish water towers shape the skyline. Below, tugboats and their wards pass by slowly or stop overnight midriver. The Hudson at a given hour or season may be quiet, polite, gently rippling, or rudely aggressive, hurling up waves or shoving slow-moving ice floes out to sea.

In between the heights and the river, park paths that were once rutted and trash strewn are now well paved, monuments at one time blackened by graffiti are prettified, and even once-barren islands are filled with lovingly tended foliage.

In winter, snow smoothes the park's rocky surfaces and snuggles Riverside Drive beneath its cover. On the coldest days, howling wind makes the eyes tear on every dash back down the hill from Starbucks on Broadway. Braving the trip without a tightly wrapped scarf qualifies as a major wardrobe malfunction.

Spring blossoms in pinks from blush to bold, while fall explodes with foliage the color of rich metals.

In summer each year, a band plays jazz at the bottom of the park's nearby hill, and all I need to do is open the window.

Regardless of the season, airplanes and low-flying helicopters above the Hudson collage the ever-shifting arrangement of clouds.

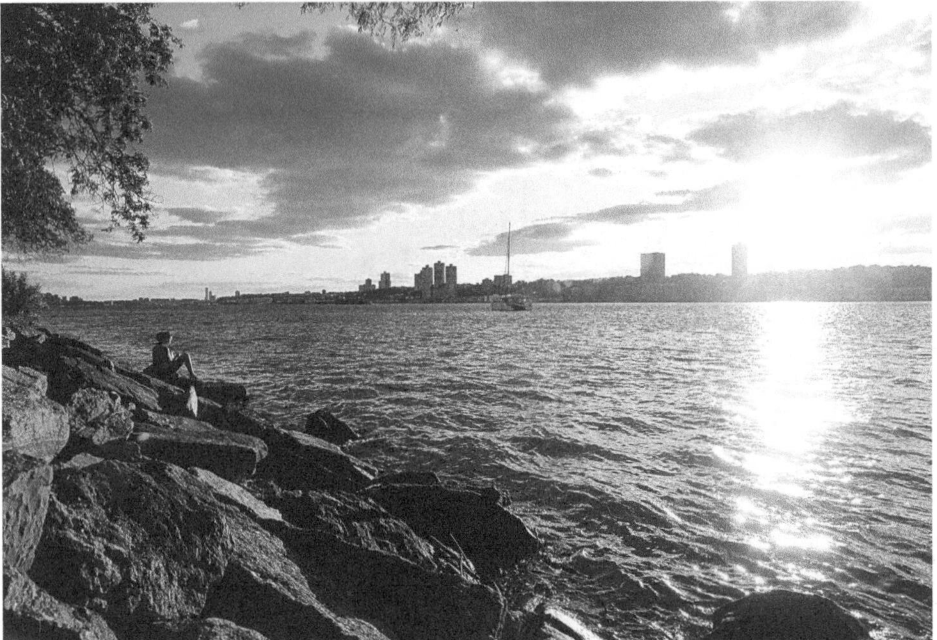

Figure 101. Sunset over the Hudson, from Riverside Park. *Source*: Robert F. Rodriguez.

Light here plays an endlessly varying tune. To the west of the park, sun glistens on the river's surface like sparklers on Independence Day. To the east, it glints off apartment windows, laser focused.

Late in the afternoon, shadows pattern my apartment walls. On the park's retaining walls, some shallow, others seemingly as high as ramparts, schist glitters, from one century into the next. In the evening, visitors flow toward the river to watch the sun set over the Palisades and streak the sky in gold and scarlet hues.

Over time, there have been multiple Riverside Parks. In the nineteenth century, Olmsted's version was devoted to the pure enjoyment of nature. At the turn of the twentieth century, the City Beautiful's park focused on monumental aesthetics. In the 1930s, Moses introduced the Riverside Park of recreation.

In the twenty-first century, Riverside Park serves up all of the above, a sumptuous feast open to the public. It is a joyful jumble of woodland and lawn, formal allée and friendly community garden, monuments and ball fields, playgrounds and parkways. It shares a boulevard for promenades, a platform for scenic vistas, places to play and picnic. Once separating citizens from the river, it now welcomes them to it.

There is the Riverside Park from 72nd to 129th Streets, the one north to 155th Street, the newest one south to 59th Street, each with its own very specific personality and appeal.

There also has been the sad Riverside Park of a financially defeated city and the fortunate one of improved economies and caring neighbors. For those of us who live nearby, it has most recently been the Riverside Park of respite from COVID, an opportunity to get some air and exercise or find a quiet bench and breathe, even with our masks on.

Like the park itself, there have been many Riverside Drives, of expansive farms and garden-filled summer estates, exquisite mansions and elegant apartment houses. Early denizens favored all things Beaux Arts, while their descendants showed great fondness for Renaissance Revival. Alongside these homes today, there are yeshivas and mosques, Buddhist temples and world-renowned churches.

Each time I walk the park or the Drive, I discover something new.

For most people these days, the Upper West Side is no longer the wrong side of town. Yet for many, still, Riverside Park and Riverside Drive remain both a secret and a revelation. It's said that out-of-towners and East Siders who do venture across town still choose Central Park West, while West Siders who move prefer Riverside.

The people who live here now are not so different in background from those who settled Riverside Drive when it opened in the nineteenth century. Back then, they were largely businessmen, typically presidents or vice presidents, in fields from banking to beer, oil and steel to soda water. They were men who created their own businesses or ran others', or they were professionals—engineers, lawyers, doctors, and educators. Often, the homeowners were women, some with family wealth, others self-made, typically through careers in the arts. From one era to the next, Riverside Drive, it seems, has been very popular with actors, writers, and musicians.

Riverside Drive residents over time have been predominantly upper-middle class. Often enough, as with the Schinasis and Schwabs among others, they were honest-to-goodness millionaires, and they had succeeded in life without established names or family fortunes. They were not the ultrawealthy—the Rockefellers, Mellons, and Carnegies, the Morgans, Vanderbilts, and Astors—who remained on Fifth Avenue. Today, the Bloombergs, Murdochs, and Lauders, the Perlmans, Kravises, and Soroses are still more likely to be found on the Upper East Side or perhaps Billionaire's Row than behind doors on Riverside Drive.

Today, my building alone shelters company presidents and retired Columbia professors; authors and journalists; attorneys, architects, and financial advisors; engineers and advertising executives. There are photographers, psychiatrists, and television producers, as well as a travel consultant, opera singer, CFO, crossword-puzzle designer, and a married couple who are both doctors.

There are, also, the mom who always dressed herself and her three young girls all in white, the old-timer who once claimed the entire basement as his personal storage space, the *New Yorker* artist who drew a portrait of my two-year-old son, and the electrician who turned our old elevator parts into sculpture. That's in addition to the longtime doormen, past and present, whom we have known and loved, even if we can't always understand their accents.

Those of us who bought here decades ago, when the Upper West Side still *was* the wrong side of town, probably couldn't afford to do so now.

Here, on Riverside Drive and in Riverside Park, is where we all raised our children, hosted family and friends, fought the fierce wind in winter, welcomed the river breeze in summer, and laughed together year round. It's where, as I've informed my friends and family, I'm staying put—genes, fate, and medical intervention not withstanding—until it's time to leave behind this temporary place of peace for a permanent one. They already know where to scatter my ashes.

GLOSSARY: ARCHITECTURAL TERMS CHEAT SHEET

Arcade. A series of arches supported by columns or other vertical elements.

Architrave. A main beam on the tops of columns in Classical architecture, or a molded frame around a doorway or window.

Ashlar Granite. A block of granite with a rough exposed surface, cut to sizes that permit patterns, shadows, and textures.

Balconet or **Balconette**. A false balcony or very narrow balcony or railing outside a window or French doors. Often referred to as Juliet balconies, they are typically not large enough for a chair.

Balcony. A platform enclosed by a wall or balustrade on the outside of a building, with access from an upper-floor window or door.

Baluster. A vertical support similar to a small column.

Balustrade. A railing comprising a row of balusters supporting a rail.

Balustrade

Bay. A principal section of the walls, roof, or other part of a building; any section of a building between vertical lines or planes.

Bay Window. A window that projects outward from an outside wall and has three openings, projecting at an angle.

Belvedere. A structure built in an elevated position to provide lighting, ventilation, and a view. It is roofed but open on one or more sides and may be situated on top of a building or stand apart as a separate structure.

Bow Front. A front that curves outward.

Bow Window. A window that projects outward from an outside wall, usually has four or five openings, and is curved, creating a rounded appearance.

Bracket. A projection from a vertical surface that structurally or visually supports overhanging elements such as cornices, balconies, and eaves.

Cartouche. A decorative oval surrounded by scrollwork, used ornamentally or containing an inscription.

Caryatid. A stone carving of a draped female figure, serving as a pillar to support a building.

Chamfer. A sloped or angled edge or corner.

Conical. Usually refers to a roof shape that is circular on the bottom and rises to a point, like an upside-down cone.

Console Bracket. A type of bracket or corbel, particularly one with a scroll-shaped profile.

Corbel. A projection that juts outward from a wall to support a structure above it.

Cornice. A decorative molding around the wall of a room just below the ceiling or where the wall meets the roof on a building's exterior.

Crenellated. The top of a wall that has open spaces, originally so that people could shoot guns and cannons.

Dormer. A small window that projects from a sloping roof.

Dormer

Dry Moat. Space around a building bordered by a railing.

Eaves. The projecting edge of a roof that hangs over an exterior wall.

English Basement. A high basement, usually mainly above ground, often used for living quarters or domestic offices.

Entablature. Horizontal moldings and bands above the columns of Classical buildings or similar structural supports in non-Classical buildings. It consists of an architrave, frieze, and cornice.

Faience Tile. Glazed or unglazed ceramic tile with variations in the face, edges, and glaze that give a handcrafted, decorative effect.

Fanlight. A small rectangular or semicircular window over a door or window.

Finial. A distinctive ornament at the top of a roof, pinnacle, canopy, or similar structure.

Flemish Bond. An arrangement with alternate bricks having short sides and long sides facing outward.

Foliate. Decorated with leaves or leaf-like motifs.

French Door. A door with glass panes extending for most of its length. It also can be referred to as a French window.

Frieze. A broad horizontal band, either painted or sculpted, especially on a wall near the ceiling, or the middle of an entablature, above the architrave and below the cornice.

Gable. The vertical triangular portion of an end wall, or a gable-shaped canopy over a window or door.

Gable

Hip Roof, **Hip-Roof**, or **Hipped Roof**. A roof where all sides slope downward to the walls.

Iron-spot Brick. A brick whose surface is speckled with dark spots.

Keystone. The wedge-shaped stone at the top of an arch.

Lattice Grille. Metal open-work generally used to enclose or protect a window.

Lintel. A horizontal support of timber, stone, concrete, or steel across the top of a door or window.

Loggia. A gallery or room with one or more open sides, often with one side open to the garden.

Mansard. A roof that has four sloping sides, each of which becomes steeper halfway down.

Marquee. A structure over the entrance typically of a hotel or theater.

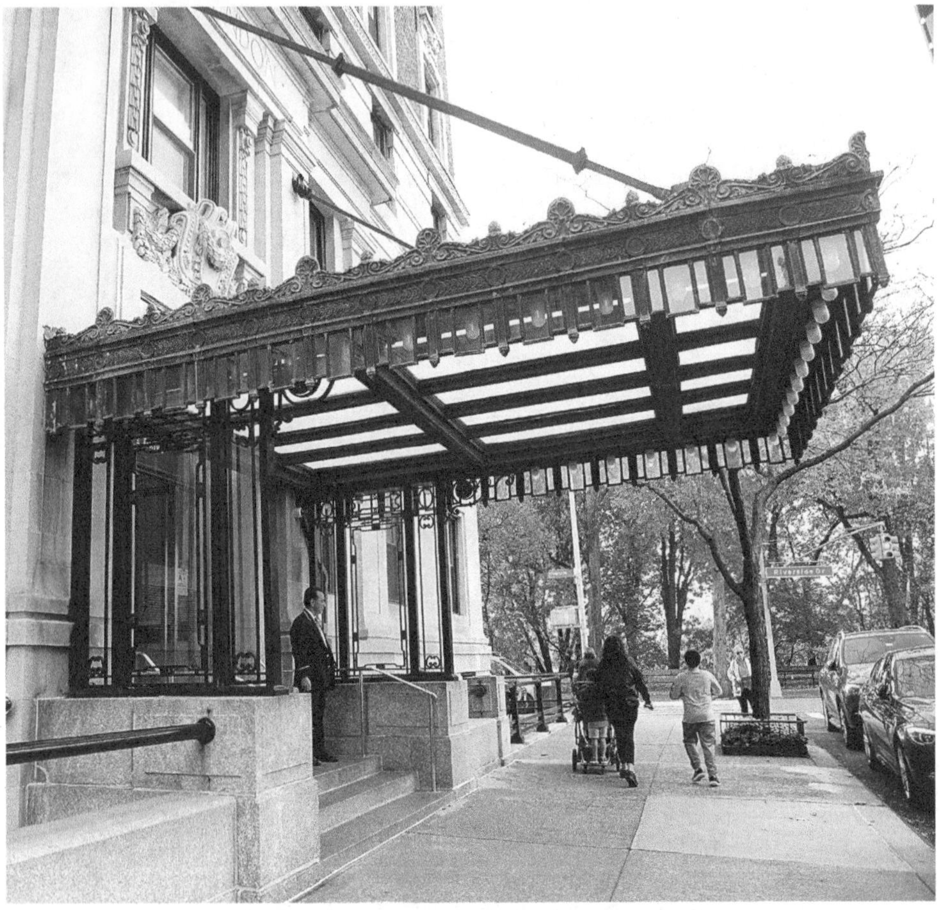

Marquee

Modillion. An ornate block or horizontal bracket used in a series under a cornice.

Obelisk. A stone pillar, typically with a square or rectangular cross section and a pyramidal top, set up as a monument or landmark.

Oculus. A round window, usually a small one.

Oriel. A bay window, often rectangular or semihexagonal in shape, that starts from the first floor.

Palladian Window/Door. An opening topped by a rounded arch, with narrower glass running vertically on each side.

Parapet. A low protective wall on the edge of a roof, terrace, balcony, walkway, or other structure.

Pavilion. A summerhouse or other decorative building used as a shelter in a park or large garden, or a building usually with open sides that is used as a place for entertainment.

Pediment. The triangular upper part of the front of a building, typically above a portico of columns, or the same shape above a door, window, or other part of a building.

Pediment

Pilaster. A shallow nonstructural rectangular column, attached to and projecting only slightly from a wall surface.

Pinnacle. A relatively small, upright structure, commonly terminating in a gable, a pyramid, or a cone, rising above the roof of a building or capping a tower.

Portico. A roof supported by columns at regular intervals, typically attached as a porch.

Porte Cochère. A covered entrance large enough for vehicles to pass through, typically opening into a courtyard.

Quoin. A stone block or brick at the corner of a wall.

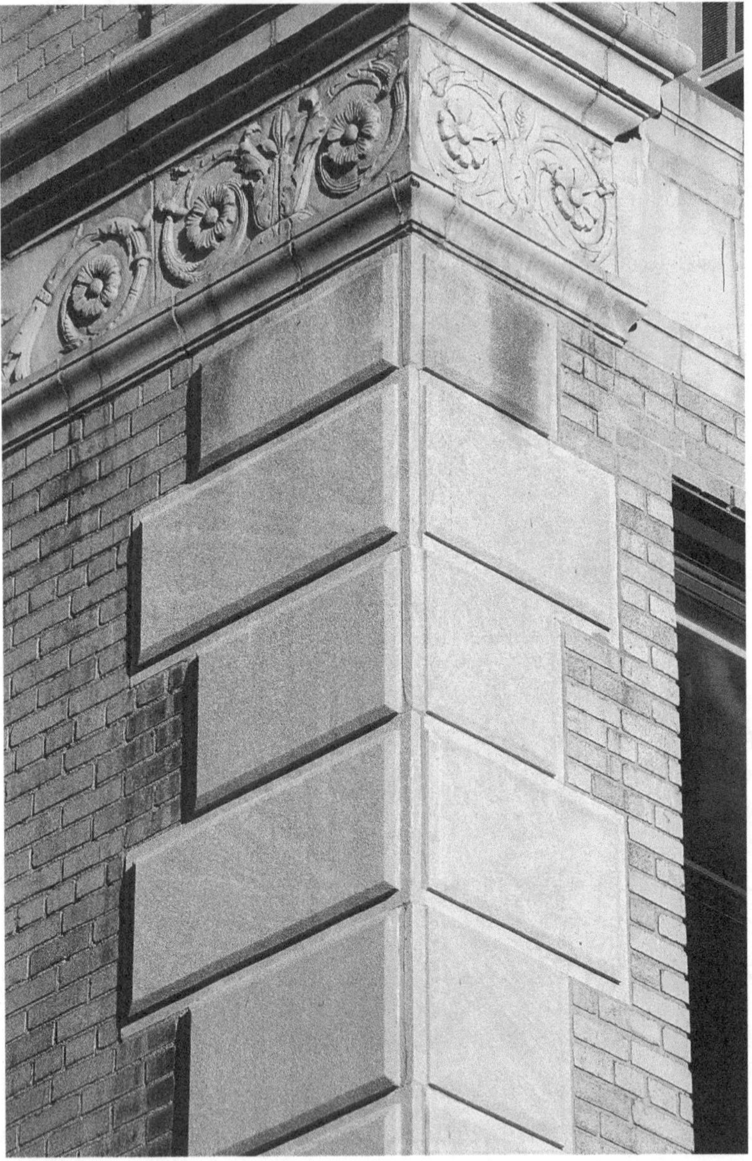

Quoin

Rotunda. A round building or room, especially one with a dome.

Rustication. A type of decorative masonry in which edges of stones are cut back to a plane surface while the central portion of the face remains either rough or projects noticeably.

Segmental or **Segmented Arch**. An arch with a circular arc of less than 180 degrees.

Sidelight. A narrow window or pane of glass bordering a door or larger window.
Splayed Lintel. A lintel with each end slanting down toward the center line of the window.
Stepped-End Wall. A stone or brick parapet wall with a stairstep pattern at the top.
Surround. A decorative trim around a window or opening, normally referring to all the trim pieces around it.
Swag. A carving of stylized flowers, fruit, foliage, and cloth, tied together with ribbons that sag in the middle and are attached at both ends.
Turret. A small tower such as those seen in castles.
Verdigris. A bright bluish-green encrustation or patina formed on copper or brass by atmospheric oxidation.

ACKNOWLEDGMENTS

WRITING THIS BOOK and learning so much about the neighborhood I love has been a joy to me, and I hope that reading it brings some of the same to fellow West Siders, other New Yorkers, and all "New Yorkers at heart."

I'd like to express my gratitude to all who helped me along this happy journey.

First, my thanks to the residents, doormen, superintendents, and handymen of Riverside Drive who answered my many questions, especially Carol Papper, Belmont Freeman, and Michael Trencher. I'm particularly grateful to Brian Finnerty of the Riverside Study Center for welcoming me into his home and Brenda Steffon for sharing its family history.

A very special thanks to the historian Gilbert Tauber for sharing his encyclopedic expertise and to the authors Jim Mackin and Matthew Spady, for their advice on publishing and publishers. Additional thanks to Matthew and to Robert Pigott for their insightful and helpful prepublication comments on the book. Also to George A. Thompson, for educating me about nineteenth-century Hudson River traffic; Marie Bingham, for her tips on researching real estate sales; Gina Barnett, for her collection of Riverside Park and Riverside Drive postcards; and Ken Cobb, for assuring that I received that last, crucial graphic before my deadline. And of course, to Fredric Nachbaur of Fordham University Press, for his interest in this first-time author.

On a more personal note, I could not have completed this labor of love without the love and support of those nearest and dearest.

To my dear friend Lois Dorman, for her unwavering and enthusiastic interest throughout the research and writing process and for insisting that she would buy the first copies and give them to all her friends. To my other wonderful friends Heidi

Kaner, Estelle Hauben, and Lisa Krizman, for always asking about the book and encouraging me along the way.

Most of all, as always, thank you to my husband, Robert F. Rodriguez. Along with assuming far more than his fair share of kitchen duties during this project and otherwise supporting me in every way, he also took the photographs for this book. There would be no Heaven on the Hudson without him.

NOTES

Introduction: My Riverside

1. A single office building far uptown, a rehabilitation and nursing facility that was previously a hotel, and one current hotel.

1. In the Beginning: Into the Woods

1. According to the February 19, 1980, Landmarks Preservation Commission Designation Report, Riverside Park and Riverside Drive are officially a scenic landmark between 72nd Street and St. Clair Place, "approximately 129th Street."

2. Some sources refer to the Riverside Park boundary in the 100s as 125th Street, others as 129th Street. The difference relates to the very confusing way the streets angle, intersect, or have been renamed near the park. A short stretch of West 129th Street nearest Riverside Park is called St. Clair Place. There it crosses 125th Street to create a triangle in which 125th Street is north, rather than south, of 129th Street. The fact that 125th Street is a major thoroughfare and St. Clair Place is lesser known may also contribute to the 125th Street reference.

3. By one measure, Riverside Park ranges from a mere hundred feet wide in some spots to five hundred feet in others (or no more than roughly an eighth of a mile), while Central Park is a half-mile wide. Riverside is one of the city's narrowest parks.

4. In a city known for its diversity, few Lenape can be found today.

5. The same Isaac Bedlow (or Bedloe) was given a grant to the island where the Statue of Liberty now stands, called Bedloe Island.

6. "West Side Is Itself a Great City," *New York Times*, March 10, 1895, 20–22, https://www.nytimes.com/1895/03/10/archives/west-side-is-itself-a-great-city-quarter-north-of-fiftyninth-street.html.

7. The grand country seats along the Hudson River employed slave labor, including footmen, maids, and coachmen. In colonial times, as many as 20 percent of the city's residents were enslaved Africans, and 41 percent of its households owned slaves, compared to 6 percent in Philadelphia and 2 percent in Boston. For more than two centuries, New York City was the capital of slavery in the United States.

8. New York confiscated the De Lancey property after the war. The estate was broken up, with part of it going to the Livingston family.

9. Peter Salwen, *Upper West Side Story: A History Guide* (New York: Abbeville, 1989), 29.

10. Salwen, *Upper West Side Story*, 29.

11. H.D.R., "Furniss Mansion an Interesting Souvenir of Older New York," *New York Times*, July 9, 1905, 42, https://timesmachine.nytimes.com/timesmachine/1905/07/09/101328813.html.

12. "$40,000,000 Estate in a Legal Tangle," *New York Times*, March 5, 1912, 7, https://timesmachine.nytimes.com/timesmachine/1912/03/05/100523388.html.

13. H.D.R., "Furniss Mansion," 42.

14. Unless otherwise noted, all dollar figures are of their period. Equivalent worth today for late 1880s/early 1900s dollars, with inflation, would be approximately twenty-three to thirty-three times higher, depending on the year indicated.

15. "A Bit of Old New York Gone," *Sun*, December 5, 1909, 28, https://www.newspapers.com/image/78231295.

16. "Builders Take Another 'Country Estate,'" *New York Times*, October 31, 1909, 65, https://timesmachine.nytimes.com/timesmachine/1909/10/31/106778232.html.

17. A Bit of Old New York Gone," 28.

18. Robert A. M. Stern, Thomas Mellins, and David Fishman, *New York 1880: Architecture and Urbanism in the Gilded Age* (New York: Monacelli, 1999), 737.

19. During this period, the Upper West Side was often referred to simply as the "West End."

20. See Chapter 8.

21. This was once approximately the site of Nicholas DePeyster's country estate. In 1784, he and his brother James purchased a vast plot of land between the Hudson River and Harlem, from what now would be 107th to 124th Streets, from the Dutch farmer Adrien Hooglandt (sometimes spelled Adrian Hoaglandt), who had bought it from Jacob DeKey (or DeKay) in 1735. Fire destroyed Nicholas DePeyster's home in 1835.

22. "The Real Estate Field," *New York Times*, January 5, 1911, 17, https://timesmachine.nytimes.com/timesmachine/1911/01/05/105018796.html.

23. "New York's Future," *New York Daily Herald*, March 10, 1879, 3, https://www.newspapers.com/image/329777288.

24. "New York's Future," 3.

25. Geographicus.com, https://www.geographicus.com/mm5/cartographers/viele.txt.

26. "Egbert Ludovicus Viele," Find a Grave, https://www.findagrave.com/memorial/21843/egbert-ludovicus-viele.

27. Others maintain that the first resident was George Pollock; that he purchased the land in 1796; and that the house, Claremont, had multiple owners before being sold to Hogan. For more about the Pollocks and their family tragedy, see Chapter 17.

28. Defined as a tavern, inn, or club on a country road.

29. Marjorie Cohen, "The Claremont Inn: A Lost Treasure on the Banks of the Hudson," *West Side Rag*, February 7, 2012, https://www.westsiderag.com/2012/02/07/the-claremont-inn-a-lost-treasure-on-the-banks-of-the-hudson.

30. Cohen, "The Claremont Inn."

31. Cohen, "The Claremont Inn."

2. Post–Civil War: Veterans and Visionaries

1. Dillon J. Carroll, "New York City after the Civil War," Gotham Center for New York City History, September 28, 2017, https://www.gothamcenter.org/blog/new-york-city-after-the-civil-war.

2. "1860s," The Living City, http://www.tlcarchive.org/htm/framesets/decades/fs_60s.htm.

3. Elizabeth Cromley and Gail T. Guillet, "Riverside Park and Riverside Drive," Landmarks Preservation Commission, February 19, 1980, 4.

4. Eleventh Avenue is called West End Avenue from 59th Street to 107th Street, where it merges with Broadway.

5. Andrew Alpern, *Luxury Apartment Houses of Manhattan: An Illustrated History* (New York: Dover, 1992), 83.

6. *The Growth of New York* (New York: George W. Wood, 1865), 42.

7. Stephen Birmingham, *Life at the Dakota* (New York: Random House, 1979), 18.

8. "Andrew Haswell Green," New York Preservation Project, https://www.nypap.org/preservation-history/andrew-haswell-green/.

3. Olmsted's Plan: Parks for the People

1. Andrew Jackson Downing, the "Father of American landscape gardening," introduced Olmsted to Vaux, initiating a decades-long professional relationship between the two. Downing died along with scores of other passengers when the steamboat *Henry Clay* exploded into flames on the Hudson River in 1852.

2. "Frederick Law Olmsted: Death of Leading Landscape Architect of the World," *Hartford Courant*, August 29, 1903, 8, https://www.newspapers.com/clip/37984854/hartford-courant/.

3. Also in 1873, the city commissioned Olmsted to create Morningside Park, just a few blocks east of Riverside Park and bordered by 110th Street, 123rd Street, Morningside Avenue, and Morningside Drive. It opened in 1895.

4. The final plan incorporated a bridle path on Riverside Drive.

5. Andrew S. Dolkart, *Morningside Heights: A History of Its Architecture and Development* (New York: Columbia University Press, 1998), 24.

6. Elizabeth Cromley and Gail T. Guillet, "Riverside Park and Riverside Drive," Landmarks Preservation Commission, February 19, 1980, 8

7. Cromley and Guillet, "Riverside Park and Riverside Drive," 10.

8. Dolkart, *Morningside Heights*, 24.

9. Cromley and Guillet, "Riverside Park and Riverside Drive," 10.

10. Cromley and Guillet, "Riverside Park and Riverside Drive," 10.

11. This refers to the unattractive commercial structures along the waterfront, not the future villas of Riverside Drive.

12. Charles E. Beveridge, Ethan Carr, Amanda Gagel, and Michael Shapiro, *The Papers of Frederick Law Olmsted: The Early Boston Years* (Baltimore, MD: Johns Hopkins University Press, 2013), 8:270.

13. "The Design Principles of Frederick Law Olmsted," National Association of Olmsted Parks, https://www.olmsted.org/the-olmsted-legacy/olmsted-theory-and-design-principles/design-principles.

14. *Riverside Park Master Plan*, October 2016, New York City Department of Parks & Recreation, 66, https://www.nycgovparks.org/planning-and-building/planning/conceptual-plans/riverside-park-master-plan.

15. *Riverside Park Master Plan*, 66.

16. Charles E. Beveridge, "Olmsted—His Essential Theory," National Association for Olmsted Parks, https://www.olmsted.org/the-olmsted-legacy/olmsted-theory-and-design-principles/olmsted-his-essential-theory.

17. *Riverside Park Master Plan*, 73.

18. It was the practice for landowners who benefited from public improvements to share in the cost of those improvements through an assessment. For the development of Riverside Park and Riverside Drive, costs were shared roughly 50:50 with the city.

19. "Letters to the Editor/Morningside and Riverside Parks and Avenues," *New York Times*, March 26, 1876, https://timesmachine.nytimes.com/timesmachine/1876/03/26/81689266.html.

20. "Riverside Avenue: Report of the Examining Committee on the Contract Work," *New York Daily Herald*, December 28, 1878, 9, https://www.newspapers.com/image/329863725.

21. "Tearing Down Barricades. Midnight Movements of Many Workmen on the Riverside Drive," *New York Times*, May 8, 1880, 8, https://timesmachine.nytimes.com/timesmachine/1880/05/08/98898789.html.

22. "The High Fashion of 19th-Century Cycling," *The Week*, https://theweek.com/articles/445249/high-fashion-19thcentury-cycling.

23. In the 1930s, an eighteen-foot-wide promenade, flanked by benches; ten-foot lawn strips dotted with trees; and small play areas replaced the old bridle and biking path.

24. Bruce Weber, "Overlooked No More: Annie Londonderry, Who Traveled the World by Bicycle," *New York Times*, November 6, 2019, https://www.nytimes.com/2019/11/06/obituaries/annie-londonderry-overlooked.html.

25. "Want the Lines Fixed: Riverside Park, Residents Urge, Should Extend to the Bulkhead Line," *New York Times*, November 16, 1893, 4, https://timesmachine.nytimes.com/timesmachine/1893/11/16/109733056.html.

4. Expansion: Up and Over

1. After 1920, when Manhattan Street was renamed to become part of West 125th Street, the name "Manhattan Valley" faded away. It reemerged in the late twentieth century as a name for the neighborhood around Manhattan Avenue.

5. Getting Ready: Build It and They Will Come . . . Maybe

1. Charles Lockwood, *Bricks and Brownstone: The New York Row House, 1783–1929* (New York: Abbeville, 1972), 245.

2. It is also just a few doors from the fourth-floor walkup where former president Barack Obama lived soon after graduating from nearby Columbia University. The movie director Cecil B. De Mille once lived on the same block as well.

3. Hannah Fairfield, "City Lore: The Rock That Gives New York Its Face," *New York Times*, September 24, 2000, 3, https://www.nytimes.com/2000/09/24/nyregion/city-lore-the-rock-that-gives-new-york-its-face.html.

4. *West End Avenue, Riverside Park in the City of New York* (New York: West End Association, May 1888), 18.

5. "West Side Is Itself a Great City," *New York Times*, March 10, 1895, 20–22, https://www.nytimes.com/1895/03/10/archives/west-side-is-itself-a-great-city-quarter-north-of-fiftyninth-street.html.

6. "To Go to White Plains," *New York Times*, May 19, 1888, 5, https://timesmachine.nytimes.com/timesmachine/1888/05/19/103182396.html.

7. Omnibuses, also called horsecars, were oversized stagecoaches with metal and wood wheels, pulled by horses along a designated route, resulting in an uncomfortably bumpy ride over the city's cobblestone and garbage-strewn streets. Streetcars are similar to an omnibus but ran with steel wheels over a steel track, resulting in a smoother travel experience.

8. Edwin G. Burrows and Mike Wallace, *Gotham: A History of New York City to 1898* (New York: Oxford University Press, 1999), 931.

9. "Settling the West Side: New Dwellings Springing Up by Hundreds," *New York Times*, September 11, 1886, 8, https://timesmachine.nytimes.com/timesmachine/1886/09/11/103979006.html.

7. Custom of the City: Society Rules

1. *King's Handbook of New York City: An Outline History and Description of the American Metropolis* (Moses King, 1892), 56, https://www.google.com/books/edition/King_s_Handbook_of_New_York_City/cKkUAAAAYAAJ.

2. "Mrs. Astor's 400," *Quest*, August 11, 2000, 144, https://issuu.com/questmag/docs/qt0811_issuu3/146; "The Secret Splendors of New York's Gilded Age," webinar, New York Adventures, November 9, 2020, 146, https://app.livestorm.co/new-york-adventure-club/the-secret-splendors-of-new-yorks-gilded-age-webinar-11920/live.

3. Stephen Birmingham, *Life at the Dakota* (New York: Random House, 1979), 14.

4. Birmingham, *Life at the Dakota*, 6.

5. Birmingham, *Life at the Dakota*, 19.

6. James D. McCabe Jr., *New York by Sunlight and Gaslight* (Hubbard, 1881), 86, https://www.google.com/books/edition/New_York_by_Sunlight_and_Gaslight/kyVEAQAAMAAJ.

7. James D. McCabe, *The Secrets of the Great City: A Work Descriptive of the Virtues and the Vices, the Mysteries, Miseries and Crimes of New York City* (Jones Brothers & Company, 1868), 38, https://www.google.com/books/edition/The_Secrets_of_the_Great_City/5wYyAQAAMAAJ.

8. Edwin G. Burrows and Mike Wallace, *Gotham: A History of New York City to 1898* (New York: Oxford University Press, 1999), 966.

8. The Pioneers: Marvelous Mansions and Ravishing Row Houses

1. "On the Riverside Drive," *Real Estate Record and Builders' Guide* 42, no. 1073 (October 6, 1888): 1188, https://rerecord.library.columbia.edu/zoom.php?image=https://www1.columbia.edu/sec/cu/lweb/digital/collections/cul/texts/ldpd_7031148_002/gallery/images/ldpd_7031148_002_00000380.jpg&vol=ldpd_7031148_002&page=ldpd_7031148_002_00000380.

2. *King's Handbook of New York City: An Outline History and Description of the American Metropolis* (Moses King, 1892), 217, https://www.google.com/books/edition/King_s_Handbook_of_New_York_City/cKkUAAAAYAAJ.

3. "On the Riverside Drive," 1188.

4. "A Residence in Riverside Park, New York City," *Scientific American*, March 1891, 38.

5. James D. McCabe Jr., *New York by Sunlight and Gaslight* (Hubbard, 1881), 203–4, https://www.google.com/books/edition/New_York_by_Sunlight_and_Gaslight/kyVEAQAAMAAJ.

6. Henry P. Willis, *Etiquette and the Usages of Society* (Dick & Fitzgerald, 1860), 27, https://www.google.com/books/edition/Etiquette_and_the_usages_of_society_cont/V1BgAAAAcAAJ.

7. Willis, *Etiquette and the Usages of Society*, 27.

8. Julius Chambers, *Seeing New York: A Brief Historical Guide and Souvenir of America's Greatest City* (American Sight-Seeing Boat & Transportation Co., 1906), 63, https://www.google.com/books/edition/Seeing_New_York/ikCxPLkdCFAC.

9. Thomas Cady, "New York's Riverside Park," *Munsey's Magazine* 20 (October 1898–March 1899): 82, https://babel.hathitrust.org/cgi/pt?id=uiug.30112046481013&view=1up&seq=92&q1=Matthews.

10. Cady, "New York's Riverside Park," 86.

11. "Boom in Real Property Strikes New York City," *New York Journal and Advertiser*, September 3, 1899, 14, https://www.loc.gov/resource/sn83030180/1899-09-03/ed-1/.

12. Christopher Gray, "Streetscapes/Frank Freeman, Architect: After a Century, a Fond Remembrance," *New York Times*, February 26, 1995, https://www.nytimes.com/1995/02/26/realestate/streetscapes-frank-freeman-architect-after-a-century-a-fond-remembrance.html.

13. See Chapter 1.

14. *Real Estate Record and Builders' Guide*, October 6, 1188.

15. Cady, "New York's Riverside Park," 86.

16. See Chapter 1.

17. Or second largest, depending on how "cathedral" is defined.

18. Christopher Gray, "The Last Great Charles Schwab Mansion," *New York Times*, July 8, 2010, https://www.nytimes.com/2010/07/11/realestate/11streets.html.

19. Christopher Gray, "A Twist on the Town House," *New York Times*, January 24, 2013, https://www.nytimes.com/2013/01/27/realestate/streetscapes-clarence-true-a-twist-on-the-town-house.html.

20. "Modern City Dwellings," *New-York Tribune*, February 3, 1901, 10, https://www.newspapers.com/image/467718763/.

21. Gray, "A Twist on the Town House."

22. In the spring of 2022, C. P. H. Gilbert's 25 Riverside Drive, on the southwest corner of 75th Street, was listed for sale at $65 million. According to realtor postings, the 12,000-square-foot,

seven-story Renaissance Revival mansion includes eight bedrooms, eight bathrooms, and two half-baths, a theater, seventy windows (among them, a set by Tiffany), and a rooftop conservatory made of copper. That's in addition to intricate period woodwork, original details, and a stunning array of exotic woods sourced in later years from around the world, including flooring from Parisian palaces. The home was built in 1897.

23. "West Side Is Itself a Great City," *New York Times*, March 10, 1895, 20–22, https://www.nytimes.com/1895/03/10/archives/west-side-is-itself-a-great-city-quarter-north-of-fiftyninth-street.html.

9. Movin' On Up: The Rise of the Apartment House

1. Lloyd Morris, *Incredible New York: High Life and Low Life from 1850 to 1950* (New York: Random House, 1951; rept. Syracuse, NY: Syracuse University Press, 1966), 110, https://www.google.com/books/edition/Incredible_New_York/ldnLaIrgJGEC.

2. Some previous fire regulations also imposed limits on building height, and these restrictions were incorporated into the 1901 Tenement House Act.

3. Justin Davis, Magnetic City: A Walking Companion to New York (2017), 176, https://www.google.com/books/edition/Magnetic_City/26K5DAAAQBAJ.

4. Stephen Birmingham, *Life at the Dakota* (New York: Random House, 1979), 17.

5. *King's Handbook of New York City: An Outline History and Description of the American Metropolis* (Moses King, 1892), 218, https://www.google.com/books/edition/King_s_Handbook_of_New_York_City/cKkUAAAAYAAJ.

6. *Kings Handbook*, 218.

7. *Kings Handbook*, 217.

8. Judson Davidson, "Sardine Life," *New York Magazine*, April 1, 2011, https://nymag.com/realestate/features/apartments/davidson-2011-4/.

9. See Chapter 14.

10. *Apartment Houses of the Metropolis*, Vol. 1 (New York: G. C. Hesselgren Publishing Co., 1908), 108, https://books.google.com/books?id=u5VAAQAAMAAJ.

11. *New-York Tribune*, August 29, 1909, 13, https://chroniclingamerica.loc.gov/lccn/sn83030214/1909-08-29/ed-1/seq-13/ocr/.

12. *New-York Tribune*, July 31, 1910, 45, https://www.newspapers.com/newspage/469240424/.

13. "For Rent on the Upper West Side in the 1930s," *Ephemeral New York* (blog), https://ephemeralnewyork.wordpress.com/2021/01/11/for-rent-on-the-upper-west-side-in-the-1930s/.

14. *King's Handbook*, 217–18.

15. Davis, *Magnetic City*, 178.

16. Birmingham, *Life at the Dakota*, 48.

17. *Federal Writers' Project: New York City Guide* (Best Books, 1939), 1:284, https://www.google.com/books/edition/New_York_City/KEwe-UMAYWEC.

18. Some motivation for the façade stripping may have been purely economic, rather than in response to legislation. As old façades began to crumble, tearing them down was less expensive than repairing them.

10. Downhill Racing: Moses to the Rescue

1. There was public support for homeless World War I vets, including those ensconced in this Hooverville, which was called Camp Thomas Paine. Companies sent food, and the city provided water. When the police announced plans to close the camp down, Mayor Jimmy Walker stayed the order of eviction.

2. The elevated West Side Highway was shut down in the 1970s after several sections collapsed; it was demolished in 1989. There were plans to replace it with "Westway," an underground highway to be topped by a huge real estate development. Part of the highway would tunnel under new landfill alongside the shoreline. After many years of community resistance and multiple environmental

impact studies—including, famously and finally, on the striped bass that lived under the old Hudson River piers—the city abandoned the project in 1985. The only remaining portion of the original West Side Highway is the elevated road from 59th to 72nd Streets, which links the highway to the Henry Hudson Parkway. Eventually, the new, grade-level six-lane West Side Highway was built, along West Street and, farther north, on Eleventh and Twelfth Avenues. In 1999, it was officially renamed the Joe DiMaggio Highway following the death of the legendary Yankees player, although most locals still refer to it by its original name.

3. Moses was neither the first to use landfill for Riverside Park nor the first to introduce playgrounds or recreational facilities, although he vastly expanded all of these. From 1910 to 1913, old gravel that previously had been used to pave Riverside Drive added fifteen acres of usable space to the park, some of which was allocated to two ball fields. Two playgrounds already existed.

4. Robert A. Caro, *The Power Broker* (New York: Vintage, 1975), 65.

5. Caro, *The Power Broker*, 66–67.

6. Caro, *The Power Broker*, 66–67.

7. Caro, *The Power Broker*, 343.

8. James S. Russell, "Masterpiece: Frederick Law Olmsted and Robert Moses's Priceless Riverside Park," *Wall Street Journal*, July 13, 2015.

9. L. H. Robbins, "Transforming the West Side: A Huge Project Marches On," *New York Times*, June 3, 1934, 155, https://timesmachine.nytimes.com/timesmachine/1934/06/03/95046347.html.

10. *Riverside Park Master Plan*, 65.

11. *Riverside Park Master Plan*, 123.

12. *Riverside Park Master Plan*, 91.

13. Deirdre Carmody, "Bringing Back the Grandeur of Riverside Park," *New York Times*, September 22, 1983, 33, https://timesmachine.nytimes.com/timesmachine/1983/09/22/issue.html.

14. Frank W. Crane, *New York Times*, August 27, 1939, 82, https://timesmachine.nytimes.com/timesmachine/1939/08/27/112716160.html.

15. Paul Goldberger, "Robert Moses, Master Builder, Is Dead at 92," *New York Times*, July 30, 1981, https://timesmachine.nytimes.com/timesmachine/1981/07/30/issue.html.

16. Cleveland Rogers, *Robert Moses: Builder for Democracy* (New York: Henry Holt, 1952), 89.

17. Nicolai Ouroussoff, "Complex, Contradictory Robert Moses," *New York Times*, February 2, 2007, https://www.nytimes.com/2007/02/02/arts/design/02mose.html.

11. Decline and Fall: Gritty City

1. These urban renewal efforts were part of Title 1 of the Housing Act of 1949, which allowed government to condemn land and seize buildings, evict their residents, demolish the buildings, then turn the land over to individuals for new construction agreeable to government. Although it required the government to assist in relocating tenants, some were forced to simply flee and fend for themselves instead.

2. Nicholas Pileggi, "Renaissance of the Upper West Side," *New York Magazine*, June 30, 1969, https://nymag.com/news/features/47182/.

3. Pileggi, "Renaissance of the Upper West Side."

4. *Riverside Park Master Plan*, 96.

5. The bridge's name was changed to Verrazzano-Narrows (that is, with two *z*'s) in 2018, to reflect the correct spelling of the name of the early European explorer of the Hudson River.

12. Getting Better: The 1980s until Today

1. In more recent years, the margin has more than narrowed: In some cases, Upper West Side real estate pricing has surpassed that of the Upper East Side. According to a Corcoran Group report, in the last quarter of 2020, on the Upper East Side the median apartment price was $927K and average per square foot price $1,389. The Upper West Side median apartment price was $1.4 million and

average per square foot price $2,104. An Upper East Side two-bedroom median sale price was $1.037 million; on the Upper West Side that number was $1.350 million.

2. *Riverside Park Master Plan*, 97.

3. *Riverside Drive and West End Avenue Report*, Summer 2011, Corcoran Group, 1, https://www.deannakory.com/pdf/1348255945.pdf.

4. Anastasia Galkowski, "City Has Allocated $348 Million to Repair Riverside Park's Infrastructure," Riverside Park Conservancy, May 6, 2021, https://riversideparknyc.org/city-has-allocated-348-million-to-repair-riverside-parks-infrastructure/.

13. The Seductive Seventies

1. The Historic Districts noted throughout also typically include streets beyond Riverside Drive.

2. Douglas Martin, "Eleanor Roosevelt Honored in Hometown Today," *New York Times*, October 5, 1996, https://www.nytimes.com/1996/10/05/nyregion/eleanor-roosevelt-honored-in-hometown-today.html.

3. Tom Miller, "Land Covenants and Seized Property," Landmark West, https://www.landmarkwest.org/72crosstown/1-riverside-drive/.

4. Tom Miller, "C. P. H. Gilbert's 1901 No. 1 Riverside Drive," *Daytonian in Manhattan*, January 3, 2013, http://daytoninmanhattan.blogspot.com/2013/01/cph-gilberts-1911-no-1-riverside-drive.html.

5. Radam was a gardener/botanist who believed that all diseases had a single origin and that his microbe killer could cure every one of them.

6. Norval White, Elliot Willensky, and Fran Leadon, *AIA Guide to New York City* (2010), 362, https://www.google.com/books/edition/AIA_Guide_to_New_York_City/togj61QSgk8C.

7. Robin Finn, "Gargoyles and Gaslight," *New York Times*, November 8, 2012, https://www.nytimes.com/2012/11/11/realestate/exclusive-3-riverside-drive-gargoyles-and-gaslight.html.

8. Finn, "Gargoyles and Gaslight."

9. See Chapter 8.

10. Christopher Gray, "The Last Great Charles Schwab Mansion," *New York Times*, June 8, 2010, https://www.nytimes.com/2010/07/11/realestate/11streets.html.

11. West End–Collegiate Historic District Designation Report, January 3, 1984, 193, http://s-media.nyc.gov/agencies/lpc/lp/1418.pdf.

12. Andrew Alpern, "Posh Portals of the Upper West Side," June 21, 2021, YouTube presentation, upperwestsidehistory.org, https://www.youtube.com/watch?v=fSl9CcVhU94.

13. It was also the abode of the actor Ben Gazzara and of Ellen "Nelly" Grant Sartoris, the only daughter of President Ulysses S. Grant, whose towering mausoleum was farther up the avenue.

14. The Elegant Eighties

1. An Orthodox Jewish school.

2. While six of the 80th to 81st Street homes are still extant, the True mansion on the northeast corner of 80th Street, 80 Riverside Drive, was replaced in 1927 by a red-brick apartment building, now called the Riverside Tower Hotel, the only hotel currently on Riverside Drive.

3. "Private House Sale: Merchant Buys Riverside Drive House, Held at $125,000," *New York Times*, August 31, 1922, https://timesmachine.nytimes.com/timesmachine/1922/08/31/99063222.html.

4. Sometimes called just Elizabethan Revival or Elizabethan.

5. Landmarks Preservation Commission, November 12, 1985, 1, 5, http://s-media.nyc.gov/agencies/lpc/lp/1568.pdf.

6. According to the Landmarks Preservation Commission, the "Moderne" is one variety of the modernistic styles generally grouped under the heading of Art Deco. Most references simply refer to the Normandy as an Art Deco building.

7. Landmarks Preservation Commission, Designation List 183, LP-1568, November 12, 1985, http://s-media.nyc.gov/agencies/lpc/lp/1568.pdf.

8. "The Soldiers and Sailors' Monument," *New York Times*, December 15, 1895, 4, https://www.newspapers.com/image/20452557/.

9. David W. Dunlap, "Building Blocks: Interior of Soldiers and Sailors' Monument Remains a Hidden Jewel," *New York Times*, May 20, 2015, https://www.nytimes.com/2015/05/21/nyregion/interior-of-soldiers-and-sailors-monument-remains-a-hidden-jewel.html.

10. Marjorie Cohen, "The Rice Mansion, a Reminder of Riverside Drive's Glory Days," *West Side Rag*, August 29, 2012, https://www.westsiderag.com/2012/08/29/more-than-100-years-later-the-rice-mansion-still-stands.

15. The Very Nice Nineties

1. "Riverside Park: Joan of Arc Memorial," New York City Department of Parks & Recreation, https://www.nycgovparks.org/parks/riverside-park/monuments/819.

16. The Happy Hundreds, Part 1: 100th–116th Streets

1. This count includes two locations above 129th Street—St. Walburga's Academy (between 140th and 141st Streets) and the Audubon Terrace Historic District (155th-156th Streets), as well as the Riverside–West 105th Street Historic District.

2. New Yorkers may best know Munson as the likely model for *Civic Fame* atop the Municipal Building. She modeled for leading sculptors such as Daniel Chester French, Alexander Stirling Calder, and Gertrude Vanderbilt Whitney. Sadly, the once famous muse attempted suicide at thirty-nine and spent the rest of her life in a mental hospital, until her death at the age of 105. She was buried in an unmarked grave until what would have been her 125th birthday, when her family installed a simple tombstone.

3. Andrew Dolkart, *Guide to New York City Landmarks*, New York City Landmarks Preservation Commission (New York: Wiley, 1992), 153.

4. Nicholas Roerich traveled widely through Asia and elsewhere and was knowledgeable about many religions, including Buddhism. Eastern spiritual values are reflected in much of his art. His wife, Helena Roerich, authored numerous books, including *The Foundations of Buddhism*.

5. Christopher Gray, "Streetscapes: The Master Apartments; A Restoration for the Home of a Russian Philosopher," *New York Times*, January 29, 1995, https://www.nytimes.com/1995/01/29/realestate/streetscapes-master-apartments-restoration-for-home-russian-philosopher.html.

6. Daniel J. Wakin, *The Man with the Sawed-Off Leg and Other Tales of a New York City Block* (New York: Arcade, 2018), xx.

7. Michael Kaplan, "This NYC Block Is Famed for Crime, Sex and Tragedy," *New York Post*, January 21, 2018, https://nypost.com/2018/01/21/this-nyc-block-is-famed-for-crime-sex-and-tragedy/.

8. "Four Fine New Dwellings. Illustrating Advanced Development on the Riverside Drive," *Real Estate Record and Builders' Guide*, October 4, 1902, 473, https://rerecord.library.columbia.edu/zoom.php?image=https://www1.columbia.edu/sec/cu/lweb/digital/collections/cul/texts/ldpd_7031148_030/gallery/images/ldpd_7031148_030_00000599jpg&vol=ldpd_7031148_030&page=ldpd_7031148_030_00000599.

9. "Four Fine New Dwellings," 473.

10. Tom Miller, "The 1902 Robt. B. Davis Mansion—330 Riverside Drive," *Daytonian in Manhattan*, October 2, 2013, http://daytoninmanhattan.blogspot.com/2013/10/the-1902-robt-davis-mansion-no-330.html.

11. "R. B. Davis Sues for Divorce," *New York Times*, June 13, 1911, 5, https://www.newspapers.com/image/20566243/.

12. Miller, "The 1902 Robt. B. Davis Mansion."

13. See Chapter 14.

14. Wakin, *The Man with the Sawed-Off Leg*, 53.

15. Although various documents show that Marlowe owned 337 Riverside Drive, more recent research by the historian Gilbert Tauber indicates that these reflect recording errors and that she actually owned 335 Riverside Drive.

16. "Women's Clubs Like This House," *Olney Enterprise* (Olney, TX), Friday, May 21, 1937, 13, https://www.newspapers.com/image/6451122/.

17. See Chapter 8.

18. "A Portrait House," *Real Estate Record and Builders' Guide*, August 21, 1909, 340, https://rerecord.library.columbia.edu/document.php?vol=ldpd_7031148_044&page=ldpd_7031148_044_00000382&no=1.

19. "A Portrait House," 340.

20. Some historians remain skeptical about whether the tunnel was real or simply part of urban legend. While twenty-first century references to its existence abound, the Landmarks Preservation Commission makes no mention of it, and the logistics of such an excavation seem daunting. However, a 2012 *New York Times* article included a photo identified as the tunnel. Constance Rosenblum, "Five Secrets Revealed," *New York Times*, February 19, 2012, https://www.nytimes.com/interactive/2012/02/19/realestate/20120219_cover_realestate.html.

21. "A Portrait House," 340.

22. "Morris Schinasi," Wikipedia, https://en.wikipedia.org/wiki/Morris_Schinasi.

23. At some point, the glass marquee was either replaced by or reinforced with metal and has since been painted over in white.

24. Andrew S. Dolkart, *Morningside Heights: A History of Its Architecture and Development* (New York: Columbia University Press, 1998), 309.

25. According to the October 24, 1909, *New York Times*, in 1909, the year of the Hudson-Fulton celebration, plans were announced to erect a "magnificent $3,000,000 water gate, the only one of its kind in the world" at Riverside Drive between 114th and 116th Street, as a memorial to Robert Fulton. It was to extend down the slope of the embankment and six hundred feet into the river. Along with this "landing stage," it was to comprise a large monument to Fulton flanked on one side by a reception building and on the other by a museum for nautical exhibits—all of it in white marble. It was never built.

26. Christopher Gray, "Streetscapes/The Colosseum and the Paterno, 116th Street and Riverside Drive; At Curves in the Road, 2 Unusually Shaped Buildings," *New York Times*, August 15, 1999, 213, https://timesmachine.nytimes.com/timesmachine/1999/08/15/989541.html.

27. Gray, "Streetscapes/The Colosseum and the Paterno."

28. Charles, on the other hand, opted to construct a $500,000, three-story marble "castle" farther uptown, just north of 181st Street and overlooking the Hudson. Built in 1908, demolished in the 1930s, and now the site of Castle Village, his home contained a mushroom vault, swimming pool, and Turkish bath, among other amenties.

29. Twenty electoral votes were questioned, meaning neither Tilden nor Rutherford Hayes had a majority. Congress appointed a review commission, Republicans had a one-seat advantage on the commission, and they decided that Hayes had won.

30. Karen Abbott, "The House That Polly Adler Built," *Smithsonian*, April 12, 2012, https://www.smithsonianmag.com/history/the-house-that-polly-adler-built-65080310/.

31. David J. Krajicek, "Where Death Shaped the Beats," *New York Times*, April 5, 2002, https://www.nytimes.com/2012/04/06/books/columbia-u-haunts-of-lucien-carr-and-the-beats.html.

32. Krajicek, "Death Shaped the Beats."

17. The Happy Hundreds, Part 2: 117th–129th Streets

1. In October 1885, Lawson N. Fuller complained that no attention was being paid to the ordinance requiring owners of goats to keep them off the highways and that they were roaming at will through

Riverside Drive. He reported counting ten there between 86th and 72nd Streets on a single day, five of them gnawing at the bark of trees.

2. *The World's Loose Leaf Album of Apartment Houses* (New York: World, 1910), https://www.google.com/books/edition/The_World_s_Loose_Leaf_Album_of_Apartmen/vD6smgEACAAJ.

3. Christopher Gray, "Streetscapes/Remembering an Architect Who Shaped the West Side," *New York Times*, June 11, 2006, https://www.nytimes.com/2006/06/11/realestate/remembering-an-architect-who-shaped-the-west-side.html.

4. Built with modern techniques, Riverside Church was completed in three years. St. John the Divine, constructed using techniques from the Middle Ages, remains unfinished.

5. Holland Cotter, "Urban Uplift: Sanctuaries for the Spirit," *New York Times*, December 24, 2009, https://www.nytimes.com/2009/12/25/arts/design/25churches.html.

6. Norval White, Elliot Willensky, and Fran Leadon, *AIA Guide to New York City* (2010), 505, https://www.google.com/books/edition/AIA_Guide_to_New_York_City/togj61QSgk8C.

7. See Chapter 8.

8. While there is a long-standing story that Riverside Drive was a failing real estate venture until it was chosen as the site of the president's memorial, clearly many other factors contributed to the area's impressive growth.

9. Richard T. Greener, an associate of Grant and the first African American Harvard graduate, supervised the campaign.

10. Stephen Jenkins, *The Greatest Street in the World: The Story of Broadway, Old and New, from the Bowling Green to Albany* (New York: G. P. Putnam's Sons, Knickerbocker Press, 1911), 302. A similar scene occurred during the 1976 Bicentennial Celebration. Thousands jammed Riverside Park and the Henry Hudson Parkway, the latter closed to traffic on the occasion, for Operation Sail '76. The event featured warships from twenty-two nations and more than 225 sailing ships flying thirty-one different flags, along with thousands of smaller craft, all along the Hudson.

11. "Amiable Child Monument," Riverside Park, https://www.nycgovparks.org/parks/riverside-park/monuments/1206.

12. The second private grave belongs to General William Jenkins Worth, a hero of the Mexican War of 1846–1848, who lies under the obelisk on a small pedestrian island at the corner of 25th Street and Broadway. Grant's Tomb, as previously noted, is not a grave but a mausoleum.

18. The Rest

1. Because of the Manhattan Fault, there is a gap in the Park between 129th Street and 135th Street. The Riverside Drive Viaduct runs above it.

2. At 155th Street, near where the Park ends, the Drive passes Trinity Cemetery, where such notables as Clement Clark Moore, John James Audubon, and former New York City mayor Edward I. Koch are buried. John Jacob Astor, who owned land on Riverside Drive but wouldn't live there, apparently had no objection to residing there post mortem. At 150th Street stands the Ralph Ellison Memorial, a bronze surround with a cutout of *The Invisible Man*, reflecting Ellison's 1952 novel of the same name. Located across from his former residence at the landmarked Beaumont Apartments at 730 Riverside Drive, and dedicated in 2003, it was designed by the African American sculptor Elizabeth Catlett and was her first public work in New York City. The building was also home to Marian Anderson, the first African American singer to perform at the White House and the first African American to sing with New York's Metropolitan Opera.

3. As part of the plan, an inland, ground-level highway was to replace the elevated one running along the river's edge. This has not happened.

4. This additional space is included in the total acreage for Riverside Park noted in Chapter 1.

5. The Hong Kong investors later sold the remaining unfinished areas to the Carlyle Group and the Extell Development Corporation.

INDEX

Stephanie Azzarone is a native New Yorker who has lived on Riverside Drive most of her adult life. A former journalist (freelancer for the *New York Times* and *New York* magazine, among others), she also ran an award-winning Manhattan public relations agency. Currently, she is studying for her tour guide certification to share her knowledge of Upper West Side life along the Hudson River with natives and tourists alike.

SELECT TITLES FROM EMPIRE STATE EDITIONS

Patrick Bunyan, *All Around the Town: Amazing Manhattan Facts and Curiosities, Second Edition*

Salvatore Basile, *Fifth Avenue Famous: The Extraordinary Story of Music at St. Patrick's Cathedral*. Foreword by Most Reverend Timothy M. Dolan, Archbishop of New York

William Seraile, *Angels of Mercy: White Women and the History of New York's Colored Orphan Asylum*

Andrew J. Sparberg, *From a Nickel to a Token: The Journey from Board of Transportation to MTA*

New York's Golden Age of Bridges. Paintings by Antonio Masi, Essays by Joan Marans Dim, Foreword by Harold Holzer

Daniel Campo, *The Accidental Playground: Brooklyn Waterfront Narratives of the Undesigned and Unplanned*

John Waldman, *Heartbeats in the Muck: The History, Sea Life, and Environment of New York Harbor, Revised Edition*

John Waldman (ed.), *Still the Same Hawk: Reflections on Nature and New York*

Gerard R. Wolfe, *The Synagogues of New York's Lower East Side: A Retrospective and Contemporary View, Second Edition*. Photographs by Jo Renée Fine and Norman Borden, Foreword by Joseph Berger

Joseph B. Raskin, *The Routes Not Taken: A Trip Through New York City's Unbuilt Subway System*

North Brother Island: The Last Unknown Place in New York City. Photographs by Christopher Payne, A History by Randall Mason, Essay by Robert Sullivan

Dorothy Day and the Catholic Worker: The Miracle of Our Continuance. Edited, with an Introduction and Additional Text by Kate Hennessy, Photographs by Vivian Cherry, Text by Dorothy Day

Joanne Witty and Henrik Krogius, *Brooklyn Bridge Park: A Dying Waterfront Transformed*

Sharon Egretta Sutton, *When Ivory Towers Were Black: A Story about Race in America's Cities and Universities*

Pamela Hanlon, *A Wordly Affair: New York, the United Nations, and the Story Behind Their Unlikely Bond*

David J. Goodwin, *Left Bank of the Hudson: Jersey City and the Artists of 111 1st Street*. Foreword by DW Gibson

Nandini Bagchee, *Counter Institution: Activist Estates of the Lower East Side*

Susan Celia Greenfield (ed.), *Sacred Shelter: Thirteen Journeys of Homelessness and Healing*

Elizabeth Macaulay-Lewis and Matthew M. McGowan (eds.), *Classical New York: Discovering Greece and Rome in Gotham*

Colin Davey with Thomas A. Lesser, *The American Museum of Natural History and How It Got That Way*. Forewords by Neil deGrasse Tyson and Kermit Roosevelt III

Wendy Jean Katz, *Humbug: The Politics of Art Criticism in New York City's Penny Press*

Lolita Buckner Inniss, *The Princeton Fugitive Slave: The Trials of James Collins Johnson*

Mike Jaccarino, *America's Last Great Newspaper War: The Death of Print in a Two-Tabloid Town*

Angel Garcia, *The Kingdom Began in Puerto Rico: Neil Connolly's Priesthood in the South Bronx*

Jim Mackin, *Notable New Yorkers of Manhattan's Upper West Side: Bloomingdale–Morningside Heights*

Matthew Spady, *The Neighborhood Manhattan Forgot: Audubon Park and the Families Who Shaped It*

Robert O. Binnewies, *Palisades: 100,000 Acres in 100 Years*

Marilyn S. Greenwald and Yun Li, *Eunice Hunton Carter: A Lifelong Fight for Social Justice*

Jeffrey A. Kroessler, *Sunnyside Gardens: Planning and Preservation in a Historic Garden Suburb*

Elizabeth Macaulay-Lewis, *Antiquity in Gotham: The Ancient Architecture of New York City*

Ron Howell, *King Al: How Sharpton Took the Throne*

Phil Rosenzweig, *Reginald Rose and the Journey of "12 Angry Men"*

Jean Arrington with Cynthia S. LaValle, *From Factories to Palaces: Architect Charles B. J. Snyder and the New York City Public Schools*

Boukary Sawadogo, *Africans in Harlem: An Untold New York Story*

Alvin Eng, *Our Laundry, Our Town: My Chinese American Life from Flushing to the Downtown Stage and Beyond*

Peter Quinn, *Cross Bronx: A Writing Life*

Ron Goldberg, *Boy with the Bullhorn: A Memoir and History of ACT UP New York*

For a complete list, visit www.fordhampress.com/empire-state-editions.